out & about
with kids
seattle

fourth edition

out & about
with kids
seattle

the ultimate family guide for fun *and* learning

fourth edition

Ann Bergman

SASQUATCH BOOKS
SEATTLE

Printed in the United States of America
Published by Sasquatch Books
Distributed by PGW/Perseus
15 14 13 12 11 10   9 8 7 6 5 4 3

Cover design: Rosebud Eustace
Interior design: Lesley Feldman
Interior maps: Lisa Brower/GreenEye Design
Interior icons: Jennifer Pearce
Interior composition: Sarah Plein

Library of Congress Cataloging-in-Publication Data
Bergman, Ann.
 Out & about with kids Seattle : the ultimate family guide for fun and learning /
Ann Bergman. -- 4th ed.
   p.
 ISBN-13: 978-1-57061-596-2
 ISBN-10: 1-57061-596-9
 1. Seattle (Wash.)--Guidebooks. 2. Family recreation--Washington (State)--Seattle--
Guidebooks. I. Title. II. Title: Out and about with kids Seattle.
 F899.S43B487 2009
 917.97'77204--dc22
                    2009008420

Sasquatch Books
119 South Main Street, Suite 400
Seattle, WA 98104
(206) 467-4300
www.sasquatchbooks.com
custserv@sasquatchbooks.com

Contents

How to Use This Book

Our information was current at press time, but things change. Please confirm hours, prices, and location before setting out for your destination.

"Parent Tips" boxes offer advice on how to make your outing more enjoyable and less stressful. If you are looking for ideas on what to do and where to go, browse through our Quick Index at the back of the book.

The following icons appear throughout the book:

 Classes and/or workshops for kids

 Birthday parties

 Educational field trips

 Wheelchair/stroller accessible

 Recommended playground

 Restaurant nearby

Introduction

Since this book was first published in 1993 much has changed in Seattle. I've raised five children here and edited *Seattle's Child* magazine for 23 years, and it is clear to me that the opportunities for family fun and learning just keep getting better.

Despite some movement by families to the suburbs, the parents who have chosen to raise their children in the city have shaped Seattle into a more family-friendly place, and examples of these changes are easy to spot: in the increased number of restaurants that not only welcome but cater to parents eating out with the kids, the expanded offerings by local museums and theaters to educate and entertain young audiences, and the marvelously creative playgrounds that have sprung up in most of our city park, thanks to the hard work of parent volunteers. Even many of the drinking holes in this town—the coffeehouses—have added play areas for the tots!

This completely revised fourth edition includes what is new, updates all content from previous editions, and we've added two maps, to help you get where you want to go easier.

Venturing out with kids should be one of the highlights of parenting but figuring out where to go, hours, cost, and all the other logistics can discourage even the most adventurous parent. I hope after reading these pages you'll be inspired to explore the Emerald City with your kids—and when you do, *Out and About with Kids, 4th Edition*, will be your trusted guide.

Ann Bergman

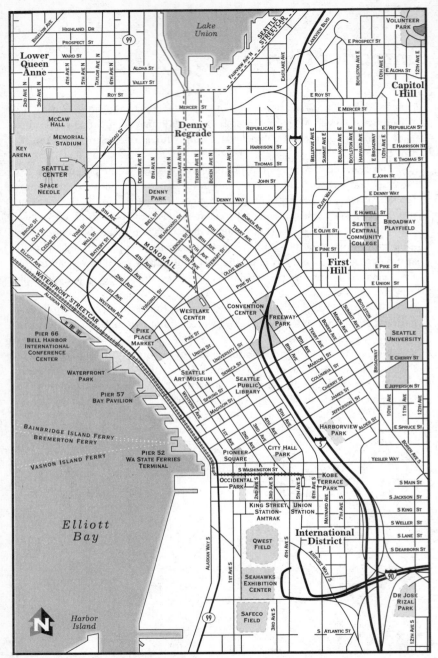

Downtown Seattle

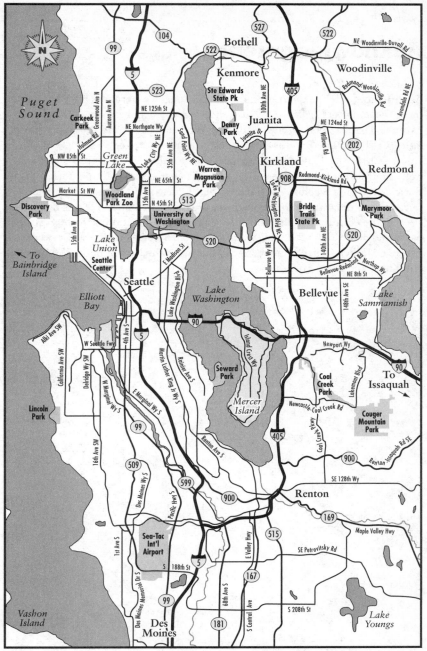

Seattle Metro Area

Acknowledgments

As with any guidebook, our diligent and thorough researchers are what have made *Out and About Seattle with Kids* a well-respected and valuable resource for parents. Thanks to the following parents who contributed to this and earlier editions: Erika Lee Bigelow. Stephanie Dunnewind, Toddy Dyer, Jennifer Duvall, Chris Stay (calendar editor at *Seattle's Child*), and Virginia Smyth, as well as our team of child researchers for our fourth edition, Annie Rorick, Lily Rorick, and Aoife Bigelow. Their patient willingness to go on just one more outing and their unfailingly honest feedback are the heart and soul of this book.

On the editorial/production side, I am deeply grateful for the high standards and dedication of the able team at Sasquatch Books, including Gary Luke, Terence Maikels, Kurt Stephan, Sarah Plein, Liza Brice-Dahmen, Francesca Hill Kubo, and Karin Mullen.

Chapter 1

Exploring the City

From the **Olympic Sculpture Park** to the north
and the **International District** to the south,
with the **Pike Place Market** and **waterfront** in
between, downtown Seattle is a place you can
make part of your everyday family life or enjoy
exploring as "tourists" in your own town. North,
south, and east lie **neighborhoods** full of fun and
educational opportunities.

Pike Place Public Market

The Pike Place Public Market, located at Pike Street and First Avenue in downtown Seattle, doesn't attract more than 9 million shoppers a year for its farm-fresh goods alone. What does draw people—both residents and tourists—are its lively atmosphere; beautiful displays of produce, flowers, and other food products; crafts; great restaurants; and funky small shops.

Officially opened in 1907, the Market has grown to encompass a wide variety of merchants and wares, plus ethnic groceries and bakeries, restaurants, and novelty shops. Though its existence has been threatened twice, once by developers in the early 1970s and again by investors who wanted to make it more commercial in the 1980s, it has survived and been labeled a National Historic District, character intact.

Hours: The Market is open daily, year-round, except for Thanksgiving, Christmas, and New Year's Day. Hours vary by merchant; during peak farm season (May–Oct.), many farmers have their stalls set up and ready by 8 A.M. Some restaurants stay open until late in the evening. Sundays are voluntary opening days for merchants—so if you plan to visit a specific shop then, call ahead of time to check its hours. You can also confirm hours at the Market's website: *www.pike placemarket.org.*

Essentials: Parking can be frustrating in the Market area, especially on sunny summer days. Whatever you do, don't get stuck driving on Pike Place (the road that goes through the Market). You might find a parking space, but it will come at a price since traffic along this street moves along much slower than the pedestrians walking on either side.

Parking at the Market's parking garage one street west of the Market (1531 Western Ave., 206-621-0469) is a good option. It's connected to the Market's Main Arcade by an elevator and skybridge walkway, offers special rates at certain times of the day, and free parking for shopping trips under an hour. Also, some merchants validate parking when you make purchases in their store. If you need to get to the waterfront from the Market, you can take the elevator from the parking garage mentioned above, or take the elevator or stairs located at the southern end of the Market, to Western Avenue (see the Pike Place Market Hillclimb below).

Public transportation by bus is a much easier and less expensive way to get to the Market and if you aren't sweating the traffic and finding a parking place, you'll have more fun and so will the kids. From all neighborhoods in

Seattle as well as the suburbs there are bus routes that lead to downtown with the Market an easy walk from bus stops on or near Pike and Pine, between First and Fifth avenues.

Restrooms in the Market are located at the southern end of the Main Arcade down the stairs just west of the Market Piggy Bank sculpture and on the first floor of the Down Under area near Pike Place Chinese Cuisine. As with any public restroom, don't send a child in alone. *The Pike Place News*, a complimentary newspaper, is available at many locations throughout the Market. It includes news and a map of the nine-acre Market area.

The Market Information Booth, on First Avenue S. and Pike Street, offers shopping and restaurant brochures, maps, and tour information. It is open daily, 10 A.M.–6 P.M. Make sure to ask for a *Kids' Market Walk* guide, which suggests items for kids to watch for and gives them space to note their observations. Also at the booth is Ticket/Ticket, open Tues.–Sun., noon–6 P.M., with half-price day-of-show tickets to local theater, music, and comedy productions.

Parent Tips

Trying to negotiate a stroller through the Market is virtually impossible because of the crowds. Use a front- or backpack instead.

There are two kinds of stalls at the Market: highstalls and daystalls. Highstalls are produce stands that hold angled displays of fruits and vegetables from all over the world. Daystalls are low tables coated in metal, where farmers and craftspeople sell their wares.

Notice the musical notes painted on the floor. Musicians with a permit can perform anywhere there is a painted note. There are 14 throughout the Market. The number painted inside the musical note tells musicians how many people can perform there at one time.

If your kids need to run off some energy, take them to Victor Steinbrueck Park, a small grassy area at the north end of the Market. There are plenty of benches, two totem poles, and spectacular views of the Olympic Mountains and Elliott Bay. It's a popular place for an outdoor picnic (and often, the homeless, so be prepared for panhandling).

Market Heritage Tours

(206) 774-5249

Hours: Tours start Wed.–Fri., at 11 A.M. Reservations are required 24 hours in advance for weekday tours. Saturday tours begin at 9 A.M., are free, and require no reservations.

Tickets: $10/adults, $7/seniors (55 and over) and children (under 18)

The Pike Place Market Preservation and Development Authority (PDA, 206-682-7453) offers tours to the public that blend history with current information, anecdotes, and shopping tips. PDA also offers tours to Seattle schoolchildren through a program called How Does the Market Grow (teachers can call 206-774-5257 for information). Weekday PDA tours meet at the Market Information Booth at 1st Avenue and Pike Street. Saturday tours are conducted by Friends of the Market board members and meet at Rachel the piggy bank, where Pike Street ends at the Market.

The following highlights of the Market are meant to be happened upon, rather than sought out. Only by strolling and exploring the many nooks and crannies will your family gain a sense of the Market's offerings and its significance to the community.

Note that it is possible to literally eat your way through the Market—and it's tempting to do just that! You will happen upon numerous small restaurants and stalls selling food items, which can easily be carried and munched on as you make your way through the Market.

Main Arcade

Along the west side of Pike Pl., and the south side of Pike St.

The Main Arcade is easy to find: just listen for the hollering fishmongers and the wet slap of fish being tossed among them. It's an amusing spectacle that always attracts a crowd. A sign at the Pike Place Fish Co. warns, "Caution: Low Flying Fish."

There's much more to be seen, however, including colorful rows of fruits and vegetables, seasonal fresh-cut flowers, handmade children's clothing and toys, homemade jams and honeys, handcrafted silver jewelry, pottery, paintings, photographs, unidentifiable junk, and lots of action. Many farmers offer samples of their latest products and produce, as well as recipes and information about the locations of their U-pick farms.

Don't miss Rachel, the fat, bronze piggy bank that kids love to sit on, pet, and stuff with spare change (the $6,000–$9,000 a year collected goes to social service programs at the Market). The clock and pig are located where Pike Street meets Pike Place.

This bustling scene, plus a variety of musicians, balloon sculptors, and other entertainers, is exciting for kids. At the south end of this section don't miss Daily Dozen Doughnuts, where you can watch the doughnut machine plunk out tiny doughnuts, served hot in paper sacks, either plain or rolled in cinnamon sugar.

If you can find enough space to stand still and look down at the floor, you will see the names of various patrons who gave donations to help replace the Market's old wooden floor in the mid-1980s. There are 46,500 tiles in all. (One bears the names of Ronald and Nancy Reagan; another is designated as The Very First Tile.)

Down Under

This section of the Market sits under the Main Arcade and is home to a fantastic variety of interesting shops. A few dollars of souvenir money will extend the attention span and expand the shopping enthusiasm of the kids. The following are just a few of the many interesting places to visit in this area.

....

The Bead Zone
(206) 903-6196

Brimming with semi-precious gemstones and beads of all kinds: glass, crystal, coral, turquoise, seed, and sterling silver.

....

The Candy Store
(206) 625-0420

A good place to satisfy your sweet tooth—there's even cotton candy.

....

Charlotte's Web
(206) 292-9849

There are lots of collectibles here, including Boyd's Bears, Raggedy Ann and Andy, and characters from *The Wizard of Oz* and *Winnie the Pooh*.

Danny's Wonder Freeze
(206) 382-0932

Kids will enjoy the amusement park—style fast food, including hot dogs and milk shakes.

Golden Age Collectables
(206) 622-9799

This store is full of comic books, modern and old, for children and adults (be forewarned that some of the material is not appropriate for kids). Also, there are baseball and other sports cards, movie posters, signed baseballs, movie star autographs, role-playing games, and *Star Wars* stuff.

Grandma's Attic
(206) 682-9281

A one-of-a-kind collection of dollhouse miniatures and furniture along with dolls, bears, and lighthouses.

The Great Wind-Up
(206) 621-9370

The employees here do more than ring up the sales—they keep about a dozen toys flipping, barking, walking, and hopping. The store claims to have the largest collection of wind-up and animated toys in the Northwest, a number of which can be tested on a counter exclusively for this purpose. The only problem is that the counter is high, even for an adult, so young kids will have to be lifted up to play (a clever ploy to make sure that patrons supervise their kids).

Holy Cow Records
(206) 405-4200

Introduce your kids to the first medium for recorded sound: vinyl, platters, 45s, and 78s. Also shop for new and used videos, CDs, and DVDs.

Market Coins
(206) 624-9681

Lots of old baseball cards, stamps, and coins will attract the serious and amateur collectors in the family.

Market Magic Shop
(206) 624-4271

This shop sells a wide variety of supplies for magicians of every level. You'll find everything from gags to juggling supplies, rubber chickens to ventriloquist dummies, puzzles, books, and videos. The helpful staff is more than willing to recommend a trick suited to abilities of the budding magician.

Old Seattle Paper Works and Giant Shoe Museum
(206) 623-2870

The store sells old posters, magazines, and newspapers. Nearby you'll find an old-fashioned peep-show type of museum where you pay a small fee to have a curtain lift to reveal, yes, big shoes.

Raven's Nest Treasures
(206) 343-0890

This curio shop offers arts, crafts, and jewelry from local artists.

Tabula Rasa
(206) 682-2935

The antique and handmade miniature books here will enchant kids who are into tiny objects.

Women's Hall of Fame
(206) 622-8427

Want an easy lesson on women's history? The Hall of Fame offers history lessons about prominent women in the arts, sciences, literature, civil rights movement, athletics, travel, and civil services. You'll find books, posters, rare postcards, videos, Wonder Woman and Rosie the Riveter items, coffee mugs, bumper stickers, clothing, and other gifts.

Post Alley Market

Post Alley runs along the east side of Pike Place, and the Post Alley Market complex includes the Corner Building, the Sanitary Market, the Triangle Building, the Stewart House, and the Soames Dunn Building. This is the area to grab a hungry youngster a snack; kid (and grown-up!) favorites include mac 'n'cheese from Beecher's, noodles from Malaysia Station, baguette sandwiches from Le Panier, Humbow from Me Sum Pastry, and hot dogs from Yellow Taxi.

Beecher's Handmade Cheese
(206) 956-1964

Watch cheese being made right before your eyes at this flagship store for a company that is fast gaining a national reputation for fine cheeses. Try the curds, scrumptious macaroni and cheese, or a yummy grilled cheese sandwich, or sample one of the delicious pure, all-natural cheeses.

The Crumpet Shop
(206) 682-1598

This shop features a selection of teas, crumpets, scones, preserves, and other treats. With dozens of crumpet toppings from which to choose, everyone in the family should be sated.

La Vaca
(206) 467-9262

There's always a long line at this take-out lunch spot, which makes yummy fresh burritos from scratch and without lard.

Le Panier
(206) 441-3669

This very French bakery delights with classic baked goods like croissants and eclairs.

Malaysia Station
(206) 624-8388

The take-out counter here serves up delicious noodle and vegetable dishes, as well as tasty barbecued pork and chicken.

Paper Moon
(206) 443-0675

Along with a great selection of cards, this shop also carries a variety of Market posters.

Pike Place Market Creamery
(206) 622-5029

Even if you don't need a pint of cream or yogurt, stop by this shop for its interesting cow-themed knick knacks, from cow cups to Udderly Smooth body lotion.

Piroshky-Piroshky
(206) 441-6068

The pastries here are stuffed with 15 different fillings, from apple to smoked salmon. Get them while they're hot.

Rainier Hardware
(206) 448-9415

Maybe you're not looking for a hammer or nails—but how about a key chain? If there's a kid in your family that collects them, you'll find a great selection here.

Shy Giant Frozen Yogurt and Ice Cream
(206) 622-1988

The Shy Giant was one of the West Coast's first frozen yogurt shops.

Starbucks
(206) 448-8762

Sure, there are Starbucks coffee shops located on just about every corner of Seattle—so what's special about this one? The Pike Place Market store was the original location, opened long before the chain spread out across Seattle and the country.

Taxi Dogs
(206) 443-1919

Way down at the end of the Market, just before you get to Virginia, sits a tiny take-out spot offering all kinds of yummy hot dogs—from the plain but fabulous beef dog to salmon dogs and everything in between.

Three Girls Bakery
(206) 622-1045

One of the oldest businesses in the Market, this place bakes its own breads and other goodies and makes some of the biggest and best sandwiches in town. Don't bother trying to get a counter seat with the kids—it's much too popular, especially at lunchtime. Soups are also delicious.

Pike Place Hillclimb

This series of steps off of Western Avenue connects the Market to the water-front, with several shops and restaurants along the way. Don't miss the Bug Safari (206-285-2847), an "insect zoo" with a large collection of live insects on display. See Chapter 2 for more details on Bug Safari.

....

The Waterfront

On the downtown Seattle waterfront you'll find the good, the bad, and the ugly. Stand on Pier 62 facing Elliott Bay and feast your eyes on the sparkling waters and the glorious Olympic Mountains beyond. Remind your kids that more than one hundred years ago Native Americans used this very spot for landing their boats. Notice the bustling seagoing traffic and the picturesque ferries.

Now turn around to behold the ugly—the Alaskan Way Viaduct, a dinosaur of a freeway that crudely interrupts downtown's graceful slope to the water and serves as a hideous and noisy testimony to the price of urban non-planning. Damaged in the 2001 Nisqually earthquake, the viaduct is overdue for replacement, but in the short term at least, this piece of visual blight will remain.

There are also endless shops filled with mounds of souvenirs dotting the waterfront. But don't be discouraged. Despite this area's helter-skelter development, or perhaps because of it, there is plenty here for the kids.

What follows is a description of things to see and do on the waterfront from the south end at Pier 48, at the base of Washington Street, to the north end at Pier 70, at the base of Broad Street. There is much to see by just strolling along. Or you can skip the tourist walk and just visit one of the three main attractions—the Seattle Aquarium at Pier 59, Odyssey: The Maritime Discovery Center at Pier 66, and the Olympic Sculpture Park at Pier 70. Each of these places makes a wonderful family outing that you will likely want to repeat many times.

Boat Tours

There is so much water around Seattle that getting out on the water is an essential part of exploring the city with kids. While you might consider the tours below for tourists, in fact they are a great way to see your hometown from a different vantage point. You can choose from an excursion on salt water Puget Sound or fresh water Lake Washington, or tour the canal that connects the two bodies of water.

Argosy Cruises
Departs from Piers 54, 55, and 57 and South Lake Union
(206) 623-1445; (800) 642-7816
www.argosycruises.com

Hours: Daily, one-hour narrated cruises, year-round except Christmas and Thanksgiving; longer cruises Apr.–Sept.; call for departure times.

Tickets: Costs vary depending on the tour and the season; children under 4 are free. Group rates available.

You don't need to wait for out-of-town guests to embark on a boat tour of the city. Kids will delight in going under, rather than over, familiar bridges and picking out landmarks they have grown accustomed to viewing from a different angle. The narratives are lively and informative—even native Seattleites will probably learn something new about their hometown.

The 2.5-hour Cruise on the Locks tour is the most interesting of the four excursions offered by Argosy Cruises, because it includes a trip through the Hiram M. Chittenden Locks from salt to fresh water. Tours depart daily April through September. The two-hour Lake Washington Cruise goes from the houseboat district of Lake Union out to the large homes that line the lake, daily April through September.

A one-hour tour is offered daily year-round along the Seattle waterfront around Elliott Bay, including the shipyards and Duwamish Waterway. This tour offers a fascinating look at the downtown waterfront, a central part of Seattle's identity that is easily overlooked when traveling by land.

There are also brunch, lunch, and dinner cruises plus themed cruises. Every Christmas season for over 60 years, Argosy has presented Christmas Ship cruises that include holiday performances by choirs on-board and thousands who gather on the shores to have bonfires and watch the beautiful ships. Check the Argosy website for schedule/cost.

Emerald City Charters (Let's Go Sailing)

Pier 54

(206) 624-3931; (800) 831-3274

www.sailingseattle.com

Hours: May 1—Oct. 15; call for times.

Tickets: $25–$40/adults, $18–$30/children under age 12

Take a 1.5-hour harbor sailing excursion or a 2.5-hour sunset sail on a 70-foot performance yacht. Passengers can help sail or just sit and enjoy the trip. The boat carries up to 49 passengers. Bring your own snacks.

Fremont Ferry

(206) 713-8446, (206) 284-2828

www.seattleferryservice.com

Hours: Schedule varies seasonally, check website

Tickets: Sunday Ice Cream Cruise: $11/adults, $7/ages 5–13, $2/children under 5. Ice cream $2–$4. Friday Brown Bag Cruise and Saturday Lake Cruise: $15/adults, $7/ages 5–13, $2/children under 5.

A cruise with Captain Larry Kezner on the m/v *Fremont Avenue*, a 50-foot steel-hulled, vintage-style ferry, is an easy, fun and affordable way to get out on the water with the family (and your leashed dog!). The 45-minute Sunday Ice Cream Cruise departs every hour on Sundays from 11 A.M.—5 P.M. during spring and summer. Root beer and chocolate floats, coffee, and soft drinks are available on-board ($2–$4). Friday Brown Bag and Saturday Lake Cruises run through the summer from 11:45 A.M. to 2:15 P.M. These 60-minute cruises into Lake Union and Portage Bay also offer ice cream floats on-board.

Cruises depart from South Lake Union Park. The m/v *Fremont Avenue* is moored just to the west of the old navy armory building. To add to the fun, take the South Lake Union Streetcar from downtown Seattle to get to South Lake Union Park. Check the website for exact schedule—wedding and other party charters will sometimes take the ferry out of commission for public tours.

Ride the Ducks of Seattle
Fifth Ave. N. and Broad St.
(206) 441-3825; (800) 817-1116
www.ridetheducksofseattle.com

Hours: Hourly year-round; also on the half hour during summer

Tickets: $23/adults, $13/children 12 and under

These odd-looking "ducks" (amphibious vehicles), not surprisingly spend time on both land and water—including a drive down to Pioneer Square, past the Pike Place Market, and along the waterfront. They depart from a lot at the corner of 5th Avenue N. and Broad Street, just east of the Seattle Center. A rapid-fire narrative, à la Disneyland Jungle Cruises, keeps the group entertained and the entry and departure from land to water at Lake Union is a big thrill.

Tillicum Village Tour
Departs Pier 55
(206) 933-8600
www.tillicumvillage.com

Hours: Year-round; departure times vary

Tickets: $65/adults, $25/ages 5–12, free/ages 4 and under

Just eight miles from Seattle in Puget Sound lies Blake Island, a Washington state park with nearly 500 acres of natural forest and beaches that is accessible only by boat. It is also home to Tillicum Village, where guests can enjoy a baked salmon dinner, a Native American stage production, and arts and crafts demonstrations. Some adults are put off by the touristy style of the tour, and the food is not the best, but it is a fun and memorable Northwest treat.

Pier 48

At the Washington Street Public Boat Landing, take the time to look over the fine totem pole that sits inside the park and to read the historical plaques on the guard railings.

Pier 50–Pier 53

Pier 50 marks the beginning of the Colman Dock, the terminal for ferries heading to Bremerton on the Kitsap Peninsula, Bainbridge Island, and Vashon Island (passengers only). Walking onto the Seattle-to-Bainbridge ferry is a great outing with a kid, and a fine way to show off Seattle to out-of-town visitors. The ride is about 35 minutes. You can just stay on and ride right back to Seattle, or get off at Bainbridge and head to the town of Winslow, within walking distance from the ferry dock. In Winslow, you'll find a variety of restaurants (Streamliner Diner is recommended), shops, and a farmers market every Saturday from May through October. For a longer ride, take the Bremerton ferry at the adjacent dock (60 minutes). While on the ferry, you can enjoy a meal or snack—purchased on-board—or bring your own food. Just north of the terminal, on Pier 53, sits Fire Station No. 5, home of two magnificent fireboats, the *Alki* and the *Chief Seattle*. On a summer day you might be lucky enough to see the fireboats out in the bay spraying their hoses up toward the sky in a majestic waterworks display.

Parent Tips

Watch kids extra carefully when walking the Seattle waterfront: the guardrails next to the water are not childproof.

You may view the endless tourist shops as pure torment, but many school-age kids are thrilled to putter around looking at cutesy souvenir items. Just be sure to give each child a spending limit before you enter the first store.

Pier 54–Pier 57

At Pier 54, the tourist shops begin in earnest. If you are determined not to shop, either walk briskly or jump on a tour boat. Otherwise, summon up your patience and take the kids for some fun browsing.

....

Ye Olde Curiosity Shop
Pier 54

Ye Olde Curiosity Shop, Too
Pier 55
(206) 682-5844

Hours: Daily. Summer hours 9 A.M.–9 P.M.; fall/winter hours Mon.–Thurs. 10 A.M.–6 P.M., Fri.–Sun. 9 A.M.–9 P.M.

Since 1899, this one-of-a-kind landmark has drawn waterfront visitors inside to alternately ooh, aah, and cringe. Don't be misled by all the souvenir items towards the front; instead, head to the back of the store to see the weird attractions that make this a place for the curious indeed. Look for fully dressed fleas, shrunken heads, Sylvester the mummy, a bean that will hold 10 ivory elephants, and the Lord's Prayer written on a grain of rice.

Pier 57–Pier 59

The Bay Pavilion on Pier 57 is home to several shops, the Seattle Sourdough Baking Company (which sells delicious breads), and a hidden delight: a grand old carousel.

Seattle Waterfront Arcade and Carousel

(206) 903-1081

www.seattlewaterfrontarcade.com

Hours: Opens daily 11 A.M., closing time varies

Tickets: $1.50/carousel ride

This is a large collection of arcade games that prides itself on offering the latest video game equipment. Cotton candy, popcorn, and more arcade goodies are offered. Birthday party packages are available that include merry-go-round rides. The indoor vintage carousel is located next door.

Waterfront Park

Pier 59

This park has ample space to run (no grass though) and plenty of places to sit. With an unparalleled view of the water and mountains, it is a fine place to rest and revive before visiting the Seattle Aquarium, located just to the north. Note the plaque on the railing above the park commemorating the landing of the *Portland* in 1897. It was loaded with about two tons of gold from the Klondike and lit the fuse for the gold rush that was to blast Seattle out of its early economic slump.

Access to the Pike Place Market via the stairs (the Pike Place Market Hillclimb) is across the street from the north end of the aquarium. There's also an elevator in the parking garage near the stairs that will take you to the market.

Seattle Aquarium
1483 Alaskan Way (Pier 59, Waterfront Park)
(206) 386-4300
www.seattleaquarium.org

Hours: Daily, 9:30 A.M.–5 P.M., with special holiday hours—check website. Closing time is the time of last admission; exhibits close one hour later.

Admission: $15/adults (ages 13 and up), $10/youth (ages 4–12), free/3 and under

Given Seattle's location on the edge of Puget Sound, it should come as no surprise that the city hosts one of the best aquariums in the country. All ages can touch as well as view up close the wonders of the underwater world. The aquarium frequently offers one-day or multi-day classes and tours, including San Juan Orca whale watching and Skagit River floats to view the eagles, beach walks, and trips to the Cedar River salmon runs, so be sure to check the website for current offerings. (See Chapter 2 for more details.)

Pier 62–Pier 63

This is the former site of the One Reel's popular Summer Nights on the Pier concert series, that has now moved to South Lake Union Park (and been renamed Summer Concerts at South Lake Union). The two piers owned by the City of Seattle Parks and Recreation Department and designated "open space" offer a quiet place to enjoy the view. According to the parks department "the Piers are aged and deteriorating and therefore can no longer bear heavy weight." Don't miss the wire mesh artwork fencing around the pier's perimeter. It includes a series of questions, painted in red on a dense chain-link perimeter handrail fence, that fade and reappear depending on the viewer's position and the conditions of light, sky, and water. Questions include: Who Salutes Longest? Who Prays Loudest? Who is Free to Choose? Who Laughs Last? Who Makes History? and Who is Bought and Sold?

Just adjacent is the Bell Street Pier Cruise Terminal and public marina. In the summer, you'll frequently see cruise ships and other large vessels docked here. If you're lucky enough to own your own boat, you can moor it at the marina, which offers short-term moorage (call 206-615-3952).

Pier 66

The Bell Street Pier houses an international conference center, several restaurants, and Odyssey: The Maritime Discovery Center. Restaurants include the Bell Street Deli (206-441-6907), Anthony's Fish Bar (206-448-6688, an excellent place to grab a quick meal), the casual Anthony's Bell Street Diner (206-448-6680), and the upscale Anthony's Pier 66 (206-448-6688).

There is also a fun, kid-friendly fountain and sculpture at Pier 66, and chances are good you will find an enormous cruise ship anchored at the dock. This is a great place to enjoy fish-and-chips or fish tacos and enjoy the maritime scene.

....

Odyssey: The Maritime Discovery Center
2205 Alaskan Way
(206) 374-4000
www.ody.org

Hours: Tues.–Thurs., 10 A.M.–3 P.M.; Fri., 10A.M.–4 P.M.; Sat.–Sun. 11 A.M.–5 P.M.

Admission: $7/adults, $5/seniors and students ages 5–18, $2/ages 2–4, free/ under 2; annual membership: $60/family

Opened in 1998, the maritime center is a popular attraction, featuring three outstanding interactive exhibit areas to educate visitors about the sea and its economic importance to Seattle and Puget Sound: Ocean Trade, Sustaining the Sea, and Sharing the Sound. There has been some difficulty with funding the museum, so call before you go to make sure hours are the same. See the "Museums" section in Chapter 3 for more details.

Pier 69–Pier 70

At the northern end of the waterfront you'll find Pier 69, home of the Victoria Clipper boat service to Victoria (See "Out of Town Excursions," Chapter 10), as well as Pier 70, a renovated 1910 building that was a terminal for ocean liners and now hosts more shops and restaurants. Just beyond Pier 70 are two treasures not to be missed: Myrtle Edwards Park and Olympic Sculpture Park.

Myrtle Edwards Park

This is a skinny stretch of land extending north from Pier 70 and the north terminal of the Waterfront Streetcar. It has a winding concrete path for bikes and strollers and plenty of benches to sit and soak up salt air and enjoy one of the grandest views in a city famous for fabulous vistas.

Olympic Sculpture Park

2901 Western Ave.
(206) 654-3100
www.seattleartmuseum.org/OSP

Hours: Daily, from ½ hour prior to sunrise to ½ hour after sunset

Admission: Free

Part playground, part park, and part museum, the Olympic Sculpture Park, sitting just beyond Pier 70, opened in 2008 and has become a favorite place for families who want to let kids romp while enjoying a remarkable sculpture collection and a knockout view of Elliott Bay. All kids, regardless of age, seem to enjoy the size and beauty of the works of art. You can also stand on a bridge and watch trains go by or walk down to Myrtle Edwards Park, a thin strip of a park that runs along the water. There is a cafe, gift shop, and restrooms.

Pioneer Square

The history of Pioneer Square is one of the more interesting tales of Seattle, one that will likely prompt even the most distracted youngster to listen. From the city's incorporation in 1869 to the late 1880s, it was a thriving business district, where most of Seattle's 40,000 residents lived and worked. But on June 6, 1889, a furniture maker in the area left a pot of glue on a hot stove unattended, resulting in a huge fire that burned the young city to ashes in mere hours.

The real capper to the story is that you and the family can still visit the Seattle of the late 1800s—at least what remains of it! Because of the Great Fire and a poorly planned sewage system, the community decided to rebuild the city atop the old one and, in effect, raised the street level by one story. The old city is still accessible by guided tour and can be seen through some of the sidewalk grates in the area.

Today, Pioneer Square is an eclectic mix of landmarks, loft apartments, galleries, interesting shops, and restaurants. It extends north from the Seahawks' stadium on Cherry Street, and from Alaskan Way east to Second Avenue, encompassing some of the most interesting architecture of stone and brick in the city. You may still see some evidence of the 2001 Nisqually earthquake, which damaged some of the area's old brick buildings. Don't forget to look up when walking around Pioneer Square, as the art extends far above eye level.

If you want to explore the galleries with your child, avoid First Thursdays, the monthly event when new exhibits open and galleries don't close until late

Parent Tips

Pioneer Square has plenty of parking meters and parking lots, but they can fill up if there's an event at Qwest Field, nearby home of the Seattle Seahawks NFL football team, or several blocks further south, Safeco Field, home of the Seattle Mariners baseball team. Probably the easiest place to park is under the Alaskan Way Viaduct, but there are also parking lots scattered throughout the area. Some merchants participate in a parking validation program (go to *www.pioneersquare.org/token* for a list of participants).

evening, attracting throngs of Black Turtleneck People. Going during the week is a better bet. Just be sure to keep the following recommendations in mind.

The first, of course, is to use common sense. If your child does not respond to the words "Don't touch," he is not ready for the gallery experience, unless you want to start an expensive collection of damaged art. Best to teach your child to regard the entire gallery as a piece of art. That means no hands on the walls and no climbing around on ledges or stairs. Second, if you have more than one child in the 2- to 8-year-old range, arrange to take only one.

Third, don't take your child to more galleries than his creative intellect can swallow. Choose a weekday or weekend day, when the galleries aren't apt to be too crowded, and go through two or three. There are a lot of shops in between galleries that have fun, brightly decorated windows to peer into, and several areas to share a snack and discuss what you've seen. Finally, realize that most of the gallery owners in Pioneer Square agree that "well-behaved" children are welcome guests and that part of a gallery's mission is educational. Check the local paper for reviews of current exhibits after the first of each month.

Occidental Park

Situated in the center of historic Pioneer Square on Occidental Avenue between S. Main and S. Washington, this cobblestoned area is the site of summer concerts and the Seattle Fire Festival in June. Central to its decor are a pergola, several benches, and totem carvings, including "Tsonqua" (a welcoming spirit) and the tall, thick "Sun and Raven" pole.

....

Grand Central Arcade
214 First Ave. S.

This two-story complex lies just west of Occidental Park. The complex features a sitting area with a fireplace and scattered tables. Inside are a few shops and The Grand Central Bakery and Deli (206-622-3644), a great place to get a sandwich, soup, or a delicious loaf of bread. You can watch the bakers through large glass windows. During the summer months, enjoy your food outside on a nearby bench.

Klondike Gold Rush Visitor Center
319 Second Ave. S.
(206) 220-4240
www.nps.gov/klse

Hours: Daily, 9 A.M.–5 P.M.

Admission: Free

This little museum, set up by the National Park Service, sits on the northwest corner of Jackson Street and 2nd Avenue S. It documents the Klondike gold rush of the late 1800s through a number of different media. (See the "Museums" section of Chapter 3.)

Seattle Fire Department Headquarters
S. Main St. and Second Ave. S.
(206) 386-1400

The station is not set up for drop-in guests, but half-hour tours can be arranged in advance. If you're just passing by, check out the sculptures of firefighters that decorate the exterior corner of the building.

Waterfall Park
S. Main St. and Second Ave. S.

Heading east from Occidental Park, you wouldn't guess this small place across from the fire station is a park because of the large surrounding fence. Though it is privately maintained, it is open to the public and provides a nice, peaceful setting for a snack (as long as you like the sound of falling water). It marks the site of the original offices of United Parcel Service, started here in 1907. With several water fountains, the park's main feature is (yep!) a waterfall. Use it as a bargaining tool, if you want some time for your own shopping: "Just let me go into this one last shop, then we'll go see the . . ."

Pioneer Place and First Avenue

You'll probably walk past Pioneer Place without noticing it. But the triangular area where Yesler Way, First Avenue, and James Street intersect is where the word "pioneer" really comes into play. Adorned with a 1905 pergola and a very tall totem pole, it marks the site of Seattle's first settlement. Heading south, First Avenue is lined with shops and a few restaurants. A few shops here might be of interest to someone in the family.

....

Agate Design
120 First Ave. S.
(206) 621-3063

Agate Design has impressive geodes on display along with many other stones for the rock hound in your life.

....

Elliott Bay Book Company
101 S. Main St.
(206) 624-6600
www.elliottbaybook.com

Elliott Bay Book Company is a favorite bookstore of local literary buffs. It has one of the best children's books sections in the city. Downstairs, the Elliott Bay Café sells delectable scones, muffins, salads, and sandwiches.

....

Magic Mouse Toys
603 First Ave. S.
(206) 682-8097

Across the street from Pioneer Place sits an exceptional two-story toy store with a wide assortment of art supplies, games, collectibles, and toys. One small room is devoted entirely to puzzles. You'll also find a nice selection of children's books. The staff is knowledgeable and amicable; kids are welcome and encouraged to do what comes naturally: play!

Underground Tour

608 First Ave. S.

(206) 682-4646; (888) 608-6337

www.undergroundtour.com

Hours: Daily, year-round

Tickets: $15/adults, $12/seniors and students ages 13–17, $7/ages 7–12. Not recommended for kids under age 7.

This 90-minute tour takes you beneath Pioneer Square to see what's left of 1889 Seattle. Pioneer Square was literally rebuilt over the old city after the Great Fire. The tours are offered year-round and include many interesting historical facts (as well as several corny jokes). Reservations are suggested, as tours fill quickly; advance reservations are required for groups. Arrive at least 30 minutes early. The tour is not wheelchair or stroller accessible; wear comfortable walking shoes. Be warned that some kids don't find this tour at all interesting; it requires a penchant for history, a vivid imagination, and an appreciation of subterranean scents.

Other Pioneer Square Places of Interest

Qwest Field and Events Center

800 Occidental Ave. S. (at King St.)

(206) 381-7555

www.qwestfield.com

Hours: Tours daily, year-round, at 12:30 P.M. and 2:30 P.M. No tours on game and event days and major holidays. Group tours available; call for information.

Tickets: $7/adults, $5/youth ages 4–12, free/ages 3 and under

Completed in July 2002, Qwest Field replaced the Kingdome as home to Seattle's professional football team. If you can't afford a ticket to a football game, you can still see the stadium by taking a tour. Tours cover areas not usually open to the public, including the press box, a luxury suite, and the playing field. There's a lot of walking on these 1.5-hour tours, so be sure to wear comfortable shoes. Tours depart from the Seahawks Pro Shop, located on the west side of Seahawks Stadium along Occidental Avenue. Completely wheelchair accessible.

Rialto Movie Art
81 S. Washington St., lower level
(206) 622-5099

An extraordinary collection of movie posters, TV show collectibles, PEZ dispensers, and original period dolls. Hours are unpredictable, so call before you go. It is located downstairs in the basement of an old building, worth the effort if anyone in your family is an old movie buff.

Safeco Field
1250 First Ave. S.
(206) 346-4000; (206) 346-4241 (tour information)
www.seattlemariners.com

Hours: Tours on Tues.–Sun., year-round. Apr. 1–Oct. 31, daily, 10:30 A.M., 12:30 P.M., and 2:30 P.M. on no-game days; 10:30 A.M. and 12:30 P.M. when games are 6 P.M. or later. Nov. 1–Mar. 31, 12:30 P.M. and 2:30 P.M. Group tours and birthday tours available; call for information.

Tickets: $8/adults, $6/ages 3–12, free/ages 2 and under

The Seattle Mariners major league baseball team calls Safeco Field home. Highlights of the one-hour tour include visits to the press box, luxury suites, field, dugout, and visitors' clubhouse. Tours require approximately one mile of walking, but are wheelchair (and stroller) accessible.

Depart from the team store on the First Avenue S. side of Safeco Field. Tickets are available there daily, at other team store locations in downtown Seattle and Bellevue Square, and through Ticketmaster.

Smith Tower Observation Deck
Second Ave. S. and Yesler Way
(206) 622-4004

Hours: Apr.–Oct., Mon.–Fri. 10 A.M.–sunset; Sat.–Sun. 10 A.M.–sunset. Nov.–Mar., Sat.–Sun. 10 A.M.– 3:30 P.M.

Admission: $7.50/adults, $6/students (with ID), $5/ages 6–12, free/ages 5 and under. Group and classroom rates available.

At the Smith Tower, you can enjoy the thrill of stepping into an elevator that is manually operated by a uniformed elevator operator. The brass-and-copper caged elevators are original to the building. The elevator operator will give you a brief rundown of the Smith Tower's history on the way up, but your kids will likely be more captivated by his actions than his words. This is a true, old-fashioned elevator, run not by pushing buttons but by maneuvering a brass lever. The shaft and pulley are visible from inside, a thrilling sight for aspiring engineers. When you get out on the observation deck on the 35th floor, look to the right of the elevator and you will see the Otis elevator motor that just pulled you up.

The observation deck wraps around all four sides of the tower, offering views of Mt. Rainier, the Olympic and Cascade Mountains, and all the sights of Pioneer Square.

The Smith Tower was built between 1911 and 1914; at that time it was the tallest building west of the Mississippi. The entire building was constructed with various stones and metals in an attempt to make the building fire resistant.

Parent Tips

North of the Smith Tower on Yesler Way is the Pioneer Square Station downtown transit tunnel, with underground bus service south to the International District Station, and north to the Westlake Center. You can ride buses between Jackson and Battery Streets and the waterfront and Sixth Avenue free all day.

International District/Chinatown

The International District lies between Fifth Avenue S. and 12th Avenue S., S. Dearborn Street and W. Washington Street. Shops, businesses, and restaurants representing all Asian cultures—Chinese, Japanese, Korean, Vietnamese, Filipino, Thai, among others—anchor this spirited and fascinating section of town.

Though the International District's boundaries are somewhat defined, there is no dragon gate to say you've arrived, no tourist strip that contains all the must-see shops and sights, and no 24-hour bustling crowd. Instead, it is a scattered, unspoiled treasure of Seattle. Make sure to point out the details on the street lamps to your children, and plan to hold up the younger ones so that they can look at the more interesting store windows, especially along the north side of S. King Street, where they'll come face-to-glass with some large fish, roasted delicacies, and other colorful spectacles. Note also some of the colorful portals and balconies along Seventh Avenue S.

Parent Tips

We don't recommend going on a leisurely walking tour after dark, because the area is fairly desolate and can be intimidating. However, this shouldn't stop you from taking the kids to one of its many great restaurants for dinner. During the day, when many elderly Chinese women are out doing their shopping, this is clearly a safe and vibrant neighborhood.

Parking can be tight, but the district is easily accessible by bus.

Chinatown Discovery Tours
(206) 623-5124
www.seattlechinatowntour.com

Hours: Tours scheduled by appointment.

Tickets: $14.95–$43.95/adults, $10.95–$25.95/children. Group rates for 10 or more adults or schoolchildren.

The Chinatown Discovery Tours were started by and are still run by Vi Mar, a prominent, entertaining, and highly informative Seattle native, to educate people and to promote understanding, acceptance, and support of the city's Asian community. She offers several different tour packages, including the 1.5-hour Touch of Chinatown; the two-hour Nibble Your Way through Chinatown; the three-hour Chinatown by Day, featuring a six-course dim sum lunch; and the 3.5-hour Chinatown by Night, with an eight-course banquet. Tours are also offered for schools and youth groups. The tour meets at different locations, depending on the tour and the group.

With over 128 nieces and nephews and three children of her own, Vi is no stranger to children, and she spends the first part of the tour in the office getting the kids' minds in motion—asking pointed questions and engaging them with stories of her own experiences as a Chinese woman born and raised in the area.

Though the walking part of the tour is short, Vi will tailor the tour to cover whatever interests the group, so be sure to state your areas of interest before the tour.

Danny Woo International District Community Garden
Kobe Terrace Park
S. Main St. and Maynard Ave. S.

In 1976 Seattle's Japanese sister city, Kobe, gave the International District a four-ton, 200-year-old stone lantern, with the stated hope that it would "shed light on the friendship between the peoples of Kobe and Seattle forever." The concrete lantern, which sits upon a bed of rocks, is not going to make your kids jump up and down with excitement, but the walk through the park and the Danny Woo Community Garden below is entertaining enough. The garden features winding cobblestone and gravel paths, as well as small produce plots.

Hing Hay Park
S. King St. and Maynard Ave. S.

This small park in the center of the International District is a community gathering place. It's marked by the ornate red-and-orange Grand Pavilion, designed and constructed in Taipei and donated by the Taiwanese government. Hing Hay means "good fortune" in Chinese and maybe if your family has a seat on one of the many benches in this red-bricked park, some luck will rub off on you.

On the north side of the park, check out the colorful wall mural, which tells the history of Asians in Seattle, from their early efforts in building the railroads to their modern-day involvement in the community. Kids will notice the primary figure in the mural is a dragon.

International Children's Park
S. Lane St. and Seventh Ave. S.

If you are exploring the area with young children, take them to this little park for a break—a nice green spot in a sea of concrete and asphalt. The park features a winding slide, a bridge, some big climbing rocks, and a dragon sculpture kids can sit on (with a little help). There's also grass and several benches. If you've been exploring on foot and heading south, this is a good turnaround spot; there's not much of interest beyond here.

Tsue Chong Noodle Co.
801 S. Weller St.
(206) 623-0801

This company, which has been operated by four generations of the Louie family since 1917, makes fortune cookies and 19 kinds of Chinese noodles. Call for information on tours of the factory.

Uwajimaya Village
600 Fifth Ave. S.
(206) 624-6248

Hours: Mon.–Sat., 9 A.M.–10 P.M., Sun., 9 A.M.–9 P.M.

Even if you see nothing else in the International District, you'll get a good flavor of the community by visiting Uwajimaya Village, which opened in 2000. This urban development project includes the flagship grocery and gift store that bears its name, a food court, a variety of other stores, and above it all, apartments. The food court and grocery/gift store are of most interest. Parking is free with purchase.

Take the kids down food aisles to show them the culinary delights of Japan, China, Korea, and the Philippines, or to the gift area to see the colorful assortment of dolls, stationery, and textiles. These interesting items are sure to arouse their curiosity.

A trip to Uwajimaya is never complete without examining some of the less familiar fruits and vegetables; visiting the live geoduck, crab, and clam tanks; and browsing through the book area. It's a good idea to plan your visit to correspond with lunchtime—and then head to the food court after you've completed your shopping. A wide array of small restaurants encircles the food court. Try Korean, Chinese, or other Asian cuisine.

Before you leave, take another walk around and notice the packaging and labels on soda, candies, and toys (three things bound to appeal to kids); then treat everyone to a box of rice candy as you depart—they won't believe that they can eat the transparent wrapping!

Wing Luke Asian Museum
719 S. King St.
(206) 623-5124

Hours: Tues.–Sun., 10 A.M.–5 P.M.; first Thurs. and third Sat., 10 A.M.–6 P.M.

Admission: $8/adults, $6/seniors and students, $5/ages 5–12, free/children under 5, free/all ages on the first Thurs. of the month. See the "Museums" section of Chapter 3 for more information.

Neighborhoods

Fremont

During the last few years, Fremont has fought to keep its distinctive funky flavor, as low-rise (and not always welcome) new office buildings have been constructed along the Ship Canal. To some die-hard Fremont fans, the modern buildings just don't fit in. But for the most part, the Fremont funkiness is still alive. The neighborhood makes the claim that when in Fremont, you are in the "Center of the Universe."

Drive north over the Fremont Bridge—itself an attraction as it opens to allow boat traffic through—and look for a parking spot. "Park in Fremont," a helpful brochure available at many Fremont locations, details more than two dozen parking areas—some free, some pay, some for customers only.

As you begin your Fremont tour, also look for a free "Walking Guide to Fremont" available at various kiosks and search for Fremont's fun public art. The basic area you want to explore includes N. 34th Street, N. 35th Street, and N. 36th Street from about Evanston Avenue N. to Aurora, plus Fremont Place.

If your kids can handle a walk of several blocks or if you have a stroller, head for the path which is part of the Burke Gilman Trail, along the banks of the Ship Canal. There are several places to sit and watch the boats go by, including rowers from the nearby boathouse. At the western end of the grassy area along the canal there is an overlook with a bench down a short flight of stairs.

Seasonal events include the infamous Solstice Parade and the Fremont Fair in June; Oktoberfest, usually on a weekend in September; and Trolloween on Halloween. Year-round Fremont Sunday Markets are a fun, low-key event for families. There are plentiful food booths, street entertainers, and craft and clothing stalls, as well as a farmers market. (Open 10 A.M.–4 P.M. Nov.–Mar., until 5 P.M., Apr.-Oct., *www.fremontmarket.com.*)

Art and Movies

At the north end of the Fremont Bridge sits the sculpture *Waiting for the Interurban*, perhaps Seattle's most famous piece of public art. Five commuters stand in wait—and are almost always decorated and dressed for some occasion.

The Fremont Troll, a huge statue devouring a real Volkswagen Bug, is tucked under the Aurora Bridge at Aurora and N. 36th Street. Kids love to climb all over this monster. A 53-foot-long rocket, attached to a storefront at Evanston Avenue N., and N. 35th Street, marks the "official" Center of the Universe. Several spots around the neighborhood have markers with information on Fremont's history, art, and landmarks.

....

Edge of Glass Gallery
513 N. 36th St.
(206) 632-7807
www.edgeofglass.com

Newly remodeled and expanded, this gallery/studio frequently features artists creating their work on-site. The public is invited to watch this creative process. Check the website for featured events.

....

Fremont Outdoor Cinema
Phinney Ave. N., between N. 34th and N. 35th Sts
(206) 634-2150
www.fremontoutdoormovies.com

Hours: Opens at 7:30 P.M., movie starts at dusk

Tickets: $5/donation suggested

The popular Fremont Outdoor Cinema draws crowds with lawn chairs on warm summer evenings. Bring your own compact seating or blankets. Call or go to the website to check out scheduled movies.

Shops

....

Essenza
615 N. 35th St.
(206) 547-4895

At Essenza you'll find mostly exquisite fragrances and lotions, but a corner of the shop is devoted to charming baby clothing and accessories.

....

Fremont Place Book Co.
621 N. 35th St.
(206) 547-5970

This is a good general bookstore with a strong selection of kids' books.

University of Washington and the U District

If it's a nice day, a visit to the University of Washington campus and nearby U District is a fine outing with kids. An obvious starting point is the Burke Museum of Natural History and Culture (see the "Museums" section of Chapter 3). Take time after your museum visit to stroll through the University of Washington campus. Red Square is a bricked expanse that offers running space, beautiful architecture, and a spectacular view of Mt. Rainier and the campus' Drumheller Fountain. You can reach Red Square from the Burke Museum by walking down Memorial Way. Red Square is right next to the Henry Art Gallery (see the "Museums" section of Chapter 3). Suzzallo Library, the graduate library, is the architectural highlight of the campus, and if your kids are well behaved, take a quick tour to check out its architecture and sheer immensity. Northeast of Red Square is the grassy Quad, which is stunning in the early spring when the cherry trees are blossoming. If you had an aerial view, you would see that the trees are planted in the shape of a W. Make sure you point out the gargoyles decorating the old buildings.

On the other side of the Montlake Bridge are the Museum of History and Industry and the Washington Arboretum (see the "Museums" section of Chapter 3, and Chapter 6, respectively, for details). On-campus dining options include the HUB (the student union building) cafeteria, located east of Red Square, past Suzzallo and Allen Libraries.

For more UW information, see *www.washington.edu*. The following are two highlights of the campus, the UW Observatory and the Waterfront Activity Center.

UW Observatory
17th Ave. N.E. and N.E. 45th St.
(206) 543-0126

Hours: Open only first and third Weds.; Mar., Oct., and Nov. 7–9 P.M.; Apr.–Sept. 9–11 P.M. Closed late Nov.–Feb.

Admission: Free

Stay on campus until dark or come back for a visit to the UW Observatory. On clear nights, visitors can look at the sky through a six-inch refractor telescope; on cloudy nights, a slide show on astronomy is presented. Guides are on-site to answer questions and help operate the telescope. All ages are welcome. Children should be accompanied by an adult. Groups of 10 of more require reservations.

Waterfront Activity Center
(206) 543-9433
depts.washington.edu/ima/IMA_wac.php

Hours: May 1–Aug. 31, Mon.–Fri., 10 A.M.–9 P.M., Sat.–Sun., 9 A.M.–9 P.M.

Rates: $7.50/hour

Down at the southern end of campus, south of Husky Stadium at the east end of the parking lot, you can rent canoes and rowboats May through August. There must be one person 18 or over with valid ID to rent a boat; there's a maximum of 3 persons, including children, allowed per canoe and 4 persons per rowboat. It is a short crossing through the Montlake Canal to reach the Arboretum on the opposite side, where you can have a wonderful time exploring Foster Island and the edges of the Arboretum, including bringing along a picnic and stopping to eat it on the banks of the lake.

Nearby the Waterfront Activity Center is a climbing rock that kids will enjoy trying to scale (the lower part anyway). A large grassy area nearby is perfect for a picnic, and a trail runs along the Ship Canal. This area is a popular viewing place on Boating Day, which features a boat parade and crew races on the first Saturday in May.

The Ave.

After your campus visit, head over to "the Ave.," as University Way N.E. is known. A major effort has been mounted to clean up this area—at one point it was being overwhelmed by street people. Along the Ave. there are many shops targeted to college kids that will also appeal to school-age kids tired of the Gap and Pottery Barn look. The University Book Store (4326 University Way N.E., 206-634-3400) has perhaps the best selection of children's books in the city, including books for middle-school and high-school readers. The staff in the children's department is very helpful at recommending titles.

The University District Farmers Market, held at the University Heights Community Center playground (N.E. 50th and University Way N.E.), is open Saturday mornings from spring to fall, and often has special activities such as cooking demonstrations.

The Ave. also hosts the University District Street Fair (206-527-2567) in May. This granddaddy of Northwest street fairs features 500 booths, music, a children's festival area, an ethnic dance stage, and plenty of good people-watching and food.

West Seattle

Getting out to West Seattle can be half the fun if you take a boat to get there. The Elliott Bay Water Taxi service operates seven days a week, from the end of April to the end of October, between Pier 55 at the foot of Spring Street on the downtown waterfront and Seacrest dock in West Seattle. Crossing time is approximately 12 minutes. Cost is $6 for ages 6 and up, children under 6 are free. Once you arrive there is a free shuttle van that will take you to Alki Point and the West Seattle Junction or Admiral Way. The schedule may change due to water conditions or season (or funding, which has been tenuous), so call (206) 205-3866 or check the website (*transit.metrokc.gov/tops/oto/water_taxi.html*) before you go.

There are at least two streets where you can have fun strolling and exploring in West Seattle: Alki Avenue and California Street. Start down near the water along Alki Avenue, where a good bike trail runs from Alki to Lincoln Park (see the "Biking" section in Chapter 6).

Alki Avenue/California Avenue

Businesses along Alki Avenue have a definite "beach" feel—a little funky but fun. It's a good place to find a bite to eat. Across the street from the beach are numerous boardwalk eateries, including Spud Fish and Chips (2666 Alki Ave. S.W., 206-938-0606), which offers some of the best fish-and-chips in the area. If the kids don't like fish or clams or oysters, they can still carbo-load on the delicious fries, which are peeled, cut, and fried fresh each day.

Pegasus Pizza (2758 Alki Ave. S.W., 206-932-4849) serves up fabulous pizza—try the Greek version—in an attractive setting with plenty of windows facing the fine views. Dine inside or use the take-out window and picnic on the beach. Pegasus is open daily, for dinner only. Alki Café (2726 Alki Ave. S.W., 206-935-0616) offers baked goods, seafood, and pasta, and is open for breakfast, lunch, and dinner.

Alki Point Lighthouse (3201 Alki Ave. S.W., 206-841-3519, *www.light housefriends.com/light.asp?ID=112*) is open 1:30—4 P.M. on weekends from Memorial Day to Labor Day.

Before you depart West Seattle, head to the main business district, which runs along California Street. Several blocks long, this lively area is filled with restaurants, cafes, and shops. There are a number of consignment and thrift stores that sell items for kids and adults. Retail spots of interest include the toy store, Curious Kidstuff (4740 California Ave. S.W., 206-937-8788). Also check out Again and a Gain (4832 California Ave. S.W., 206-933-2060), a children's clothing consignment shop. The Electric Train Shop (4511 California Ave. S.W., 206-938-2400) is for train enthusiasts. Capers (4521 California Ave. S.W., 206-932-0371) combines a cafe with tasty food and a retail store that features baby items, furniture, and home decorating accents.

For snacks stop in two Seattle institutions: Husky Deli (4721 California Ave. S.W., 206-937-2810) for some great ice cream, or let the kids satisfy their sweet tooth at Borracchini's Bakery (4737 California St. S.W., 206-935-8944).

If you are ready to take a break, check what's playing at the Admiral Theatre (2343 California Ave. S.W., 206-938-3456), a renovated movie house with a cruise ship interior that plays second-run films at discount prices.

As you're walking around, you'll notice that most stores have wide awnings that offer shade in the summer and rain protection in the winter—making the street a pleasant place to stroll throughout the year. You're also sure to notice the murals—11 in all, on various buildings along California, depicting historic moments in West Seattle's history. (You can find descriptions of them at *www. westseattle.com/site/murals.*)

Chapter 2

Animals Up Close

Seattle and the surrounding region present many opportunities to learn about and enjoy animals—from the exotic to the domestic. **Woodland Park Zoo** is one of the best zoos in the United States for both the animal inhabitants and the people who visit. The **Seattle Aquarium** has always enjoyed a reputation for excellent teaching about marine life, and newly remodeled, the building now matches the high-caliber exhibits. City kids can also visit **farm animals** at several parks in the area and there's a little gem of a zoo—**Cougar Mountain Zoo**—right in Issaquah. Forest animals native to the Northwest are on view from trams at **Northwest Trek Wildlife Park** in Eatonville and after major improvement, **Point Defiance Zoo and Aquarium** in Tacoma is well worth the drive from Seattle. Finally, don't overlook two more collections of out-of-the-ordinary animals—the **Washington Serpentarium** outside Monroe and **Bug Safari**, a storefront "insect zoo" near the Pike Place Market.

Zoos & Aquariums

Woodland Park Zoo
5500 Phinney Ave. N., Seattle
(206) 548-2500
www.zoo.org

Hours: Open daily, year-round, including all holidays except Christmas. Opens
9:30 A.M. year-round; closes 4 P.M., Oct. 1–Apr. 30, closes 6 P.M., May 1–Sept. 30.

Admission: Oct. 1–Apr. 30: $11/ages 13–64, $8/ages 3–12, free/ages 2 and under.
May 1–Sept. 30: $15/ages 13–64, $10/ages 3–12, free/ages 2 and under. Annual
memberships to the zoo are available, as well as joint Woodland Park Zoo and
Seattle Aquarium annual memberships—a good option if you have an animal
lover in the house.

Essentials: Parking is available in lots next to the north and south entrances for
$4.50. Outside food is allowed (no alcoholic beverages or cooking/BBQ). You
can also buy food at the Rain Forest Food Pavilion (near Jaguar Cove), which has
indoor and outdoor seating areas. At the Boardwalk Sausage Company (near the
Raptor Center), you'll find only outdoor seating. Snack huts are available at several locations around the zoo. Rent single strollers ($5), double strollers ($7),
wagons ($7), and wheelchairs ($5) at Visitors Assistance in the south gate plaza.
Single strollers are also available in Smarte Cart dispensers at the west and
north gates for $3.

Located 10 minutes north of downtown Seattle, the award-winning Woodland
Park Zoo is home to a wide array of animals, most living in beautifully designed
"natural" habitats. Spread over 62 rambling acres, you can visit all the major
exhibits on a 3- to 4-hour tourist-type outing or purchase an annual family pass
and make shorter, more frequent visits that allow you to delve into the lesser-
known exhibits and take the time to get acquainted with your favorite animals.

No matter how often you visit, your time at the zoo will be enhanced if you
take advantage of the many excellent educational programs offered daily. Check

out the schedule on the zoo website before you go or find it posted at the zoo entrances. Regularly scheduled programs that are especially popular with kids include hand feeding the giraffes on a raised platform in the African Savannah ($5 person, 2 and under free), the elephant talk at 2 P.M. where the elephants often steal the show by cavorting in the pond, a talk on raptor birds (you get to sit down on bleachers and rest weary legs), and petting the farm animals in the Contact Area near the Family Farm area.

A few other sights that never fail to delight include: hippos playing in the water in the African Savannah exhibit (look closely to spot their mostly submerged bodies), the up-close view of the Komodo dragon lizard, the gorilla exhibit where the gorillas watch the humans as intently as the humans watch the

Parent Tips

The animals are most active and the zoo grounds least crowded when the zoo opens at 9:30 A.M. or late in the day around closing time.

Don't miss the seasonal "Butterflies and Blooms" exhibit that runs from late May through Sept. 30. Admission is $1 extra, free for children 2 and younger.

Feeding time is always extra fun: Hippos get plants to munch on at 9:30 A.M. On Fridays between 11 A.M. and noon you can watch ocelots and piranhas chow down. Gorillas receive forage foods between 9:30 and 10:30 A.M. with another snack time at 1:30 P.M. (Check exact times on website before your visit.)

Kids can feed seed sticks ($1) to the colorful parrots in the Willawong Station, where over 200 free-flying birds fly.

If it is rainy or extra cold, check out the Rainy Day Tour on the zoo website.

Woodland Park Zoo has exceptional seasonal events, including Zoo Tunes concerts in the summer, Bunny Bounce Egg Hunts in the spring, the Pumpkin Prowl in October, and holiday breakfasts in December. Check website for details.

If you want to nurse your baby in a beautiful and private place, go to the nursing area in the Zoomazium. With high ceilings and glass that lets you see out but nobody see in, it provides a serene break for you and babe. If only all public places paid such close attention to creating pleasant places to breastfeed.

gorillas, and the incredible underwater view of river otters and brown bears swimming (not in the same pool!), in the Northern Terrain exhibit.

The Tropical Rain Forest exhibit also makes a vivid impression as visitors ascend from the floor of the forest to high up in the canopy and on the Trail of Vines; orangutans hang out among the trees and waterfalls while siamangs make themselves known with extremely loud shrieks.

The Night exhibit is pitch black, but most children love it once their eyes adjust and they can play the game of trying to spot the bats, raccoons, and best of all, the mesmerizing slow loris carrying on their "daytime" routines in the dark. The Night exhibit is connected to the Day exhibit—a much more exciting place than its name suggests—with close-up views of reptiles and amphibians including the anaconda, poison dart frog, crocodile, and side-necked turtle. Both the Day and Night exhibits are good for a rainy or cold day.

Don't overlook the Zoomazium, a beautiful new indoor play space for human animals (toddler through 8 years) with play structures in the form of a 20-foot tree with a long slide inside, a mountain area with surfaces that can be climbed and descended, and a swinging rope bridge. There's also a parent zone adjacent to the toddler zone, where you can sit and enjoy the show.

One of the reasons the zoo is so popular with local residents is that new exhibits are added frequently. Recent additions include the African wild dogs, the flamingos, Jaguar Cove, and in summer of 2009, the completely rebuilt Humbolt penguin exhibit.

Finally, the beautifully restored 1918 carousel, with 48 hand-carved wooden horses, beckons from the far corner of the zoo's North Meadow ($2/person; open year-round). It is a fitting way to end a day at the zoo.

Nearby fun: Red Mill Burgers, Top Ten Toys, Woodland Park, Green Lake Playground

....

Seattle Aquarium
1483 Alaskan Way, Seattle (Pier 59, Waterfront Park)
(206) 386-4300
www.seattleaquarium.org

Hours: Daily, 9:30 A.M.–5 P.M., with special holiday hours—check website. Closing time is the time of last admission; exhibits close one hour later.

Admission: $15/adults (ages 13 and up), $10/youth (ages 4–12), free/3 and under. If you like to visit frequently, an annual family membership is a good deal. There are joint aquarium and Woodland Park Zoo annual memberships available also. If you want to combine an Argosy Cruises Harbor Cruise with an aquarium visit, ask about the combination package.

Essentials: Wheelchairs available, but no stroller rentals. Metered parking is available across the street from the aquarium. Also check out the Public Market Parking Garage (1531 Western Ave.); there is access to the garage from Alaskan Way. Members of the aquarium get a $1 discount at this garage, but must have their parking ticket validated by an aquarium cashier. It is easy to catch a city bus to downtown Seattle and from downtown, walk down the Pike Street Hill-climb via the Pike Place Market. The new Café at the aquarium is located on the second floor overlooking the Puget Sound Great Hall and the Window on Washington Waters exhibit. It serves sustainable seafood as well as burgers, pizza by the slice, handcrafted sandwiches, salads, and soups. An adjoining outdoor balcony is a good place to relax on nice days and watch the bustling vessel activity on Elliott Bay. There are also numerous fish-and-chip places to eat along the waterfront.

Located on Pier 59 of the downtown waterfront, the Seattle Aquarium completed a two-year remodel in June of 2007. The most spectacular new exhibit, Window on Washington Waters, is a 120,000-gallon tank showcasing native Washington marine life. With a 20-foot by 40-foot angled acrylic window that weighs more than 55,000 pounds and is 12.5 inches thick, it is the stunning focal point of the new three-story Puget Sound Great Hall. Divers take to the water in this exhibit three times a day to feed the fish and give a talk. They are wearing specialized masks that enable them to talk back and forth with the viewers. (Check the website for the exact times of diver shows.)

The other new exhibit located just beyond the Great Hall is a 40- by 8-foot tank with dramatic waves. It makes a real impression on the kids while providing lessons on the cause and impact of the constant wave action of the sea.

In the next big room you'll find all kinds of amazing sights: There's the Ocean Oddities—look for the potbelly seahorses, pinecone fish, cowfish, and the eerie flashlight fish, and the Myth, Magic, and Mystery exhibit displaying the peculiar Australian leafy sea dragons and elegant seahorses from all around the world. You can't miss Puget Sound's famous giant Pacific octopus displayed in all her weird glory, the moon jellies in their donut tank, and two large exhibit pools that have "touch zones" with naturalists stationed nearby, ready to offer tidbits of information and answer questions. After leaving this area don't overlook the underwater view of diving birds—tufted puffins and common murres—diving to find their food.

More than halfway through the aquarium, you'll come upon the underwater dome featuring a 400,000-gallon tank filled with fish. This is a good place to take a break. You can sit on benches in this "inside-out" aquarium and observe life under the sea. If you schedule your visit for about 1:30 P.M., you'll witness the aquarium's divers feeding the dome residents. You'll probably also see the divers cleaning: they wipe 85 to 100 windows a day!

The most "action-packed" part of the aquarium, the marine mammal exhibit, features an indoor/outdoor view of the always-entertaining sea otters, harbor seals and fur seals. The Seattle Aquarium has the distinction of being the first facility in the world to host a successful live birth of a sea otter. Thanks to the underwater mammal viewing area, visitors can view these mammals above or below the surface of the water.

Your visit to the aquarium will be more interesting if you take advantage of the daily programs. The octopus talk and diver shows are two of the most popular with kids. Check the aquarium website homepage for details. First Family Sunday offers special family activities, including a free craft project for kids.

Nearby fun: Anthony's Fish Bar, Argosy Harbor Tours, Pike Place Market, Odyssey Maritime Discovery Center, Ye Olde Curiosity Shop, Olympic Sculpture Park, Ferry Rides, West Seattle Water Taxi

Parent Tips

Visitors' maps are free and offer an overview of the featured exhibits. Keep your receipt in order to leave and reenter the aquarium on the same day

Young babies are typically mesmerized by the sight of colorful tropical fish, so the aquarium is a great "first" outing for parents eager to show their youngster the wonders of the sea. The aquarium is easily accessible to strollers but bringing your youngest visitors in a backpack will give them the best view and avoid you having to lift them up and down.

Lootas, Little Wave Eater is a charming children's book by well-known children's author Clare Hodgson Meeker that tells the adventure story of how Lootas the otter came to live at the aquarium. Reading it before your visit will add to the excitement of seeing Lootas.

Cougar Mountain Zoological Park

19525 S.E. 54th St., Issaquah
(425) 391-5508; (425) 392-6278 (education)
E-mail: cougarmzoo@aol.com
www.cougarmountainzoo.org

Hours: Jan.–Nov., Wed.–Sun., 9 A.M.–5 P.M. except major holidays.; Dec. 1–Dec. 23., daily, 10 A.M.–4:30 P.M.

Admission: $10.50/adults, $9.50/seniors over 62, $8/children ages 2–12, free/ages under 2

Essentials: To reach the zoo coming from Seattle, take Exit 15 from I-90 and go south on Highway 900 (Renton–Issaquah Road). Turn right onto Newport Way, and then turn left up the hill (south) onto S.E. 54th Street at the Zoo Landmark Sign. Cougar Mountain is located approximately one-quarter mile up S.E. 54th Street. Parking is free. The zoo features a small snack bar and tables.

Established in 1972 by Cougar Mountain Academy, a private school, this 14-acre teaching zoo sits 15 miles east of Seattle, five minutes off I-90 in Issaquah. It specializes in threatened and endangered animals and birds, and has 10 "animal worlds": cougars, reindeer, emus, macaws, lemurs, alpacas, wallabies,

Parent Tips

Paths are gravel, so negotiating with a stroller can be tricky; bring a backpack for babies. The zoo is small enough that most preschoolers can easily walk it.

In December, the Reindeer Festival at Cougar Mountain Zoological Park gives kids a chance to visit Santa's Reindeer Farm, permanently located at the zoo. The farm comes equipped with all the appropriate accoutrements: Santa's two-story house; the elves' workshop; barns, pastures, and play areas for the reindeer team; Santa's sleigh collection; and a runway for takeoffs and landings. Selective zoo exhibits are open during the Reindeer Festival.

cheetahs, tigers, and cranes. Visitors can walk through the zoo at their own pace or take a guided tour; experienced volunteer docents will answer questions.

The small scale of the zoo and numerous bronze animal statues, along with the opportunity to hand feed many of the animals, make it an especially good place to visit with young children. With their outstanding education program, it is also a popular place for school field trips. Daily lectures by zoo docents add much to the pleasure of a visit to Cougar Mountain Zoo; check the website for details.

....

Point Defiance Zoo and Aquarium
5400 N. Pear St., Tacoma
(253) 591-5335
www.pdza.org

Hours: Daily, Jan. 1–late Apr., 9:30 A.M.–4 P.M.; Late Apr.–late May, 9:30 A.M.–5 P.M.; Late May–Sept. 1, 9:30 A.M.–6 P.M.; Sept. 2 –Sept. 28, 9:30 A.M.–5 P.M.; Sept. 29–Dec. 31, 9:30 A.M.–4 P.M. Closed July 18, Thanksgiving Day, and Christmas Day.

Admission: $11/adults, $10/seniors and disabled adults, $9/children ages 5–12, $5/children ages 3–4, free/children 2 and under; discounts for Pierce County residents. Annual memberships available.

Essentials: From Seattle take Exit 132 off of I-5 and follow signs to Highway 16. Turn left at the Sixth Avenue exit from Highway 16; turn right onto Pearl Street and follow the signs to Point Defiance Park, home of the zoo and aquarium. Parking is free and located adjacent to the zoo. Stroller rentals are available for $6 on a first-come, first-served basis (double strollers $8). You'll want to spend several hours at the zoo, so it's a good idea to bring a picnic, or be prepared to have a snack or meal at one of the snack bars located throughout the park grounds.

Point Defiance Zoo and Aquarium specializes in animals from around the Pacific Rim. Several years ago, Tacoma voters approved a $35 million bond issue to make major improvements to the zoo and by 2005 over 70 percent of the zoo and aquarium had been rebuilt, including the Kids' Zone, the Asian Forest Sanctuary, and an outdoor theater with live-animal shows. In 2008 they were in the process of raising an additional $7 million to bring new animals to the zoo, including the clouded leopard and the red wolf. It sits on 29 acres inside the spectacular Point Defiance Park on the shores of Puget Sound in Tacoma and is a "hidden jewel" for Seattle families, who might not appreciate yet just how much this zoo and aquarium have grown up.

For families with young kids, the most popular improvement is the Kids' Zone. Intended for ages 3–8, this is a place where kids can climb on a giant spiderweb, play in a lily pad water fountain (open May–Sept., bring an extra set of clothes), and crawl through a darkened scorpion tunnel, among other things. The Animal Avenue, another section of the Kids' Zone, opened in 2008. Here you'll find kid's-eye views of some of the most engaging animals—meerkats and lemurs (the lemurs play on a miniature version of the kids' play structure)—plus the not-so-cute mole rats and more than a dozen other animals extra suited to kid viewing. In the Contact Junction area, kids can feed the goats, groom a lamb, or pet a guinea pig.

Rocky Shores is another popular exhibit with kids. Beluga whale, Pacific walrus, sea otters, and tufted puffins live in this award-winning habitat where you can view animals above and below the water. The North Pacific Aquarium was renovated in 2008. Here you'll find Northwest native salmon, rockfish, jellies, bay pipefish, and the giant Pacific octopus.

Just inside the zoo entrance at Milgard Plaza sits the re-created 1917 C. W. Parker carousel with Washington State–themed horses on the outer ring and endangered species on the inner ring, hand-carved by the Washington Antique Carousel Society. It operates from noon to 3 P.M. daily during the summer and on weekends all winter, with special holiday hours during Zoolights.

As always, taking advantage of the numerous animal presentations will add to the fun and learning experience of your visit. The Shark Feeding and the Wild Wonders Outdoor Theater Animal Presentation in the new outdoor theater are especially popular with families. Check the website for daily schedules or look for it posted at the front entrance.

While you are visiting Point Defiance Zoo and Aquarium, leave some time to explore the home of the zoo, Point Defiance Park. It is one of the most beautiful city parks in the Pacific Northwest.

Farm Animals & Salmon

Farrel-McWhirter Park

19545 Redmond Rd., Redmond

(425) 556-2300

Hours: Daily, 8 A.M.–dusk

Admission: Free

Directions: Follow Highway 520 east until it ends and turns into Avondale Road. Follow Avondale for one mile and turn right onto Novelty Hill Road. After one-quarter mile, turn onto Redmond Road. Drive one-half mile to the park, which is on the left.

Salmon Spawning

If you grow up in Seattle you'll learn about salmon. We study, celebrate, marvel at, and eat them. Some kids are put off by the violent struggle, but most kids enjoy watching first-hand a part of the epic journey that takes place in our region every year from early September to mid-November as salmon swim from the ocean through the locks, through Lake Washington, and up the rivers to spawn.

Two big local events honor and celebrate salmon. Salmon Homecoming (*www.salmonhomecoming.com*) is a popular annual event hosted by the Seattle Aquarium and the Salmon Homecoming Alliance. The weekend-long celebration on the Seattle waterfront includes cultural presentations, such as Northwest traditional gatherings, Pow Wows, and Cedar Canoe events, along with sponsored environmental fairs, educational outreach activities, salmon bakes, and even salmon runs (people, not fish). The Issaquah Salmon Days (*www.salmondays.org*) in early October is a two-day festival at the Issaquah Hatchery in downtown Issaquah that draws more than 150,000 people. It celebrates the annual return of the salmon to the streams and the Issaquah hatchery with exhibits, a grand parade, delicious foods, live entertainment, and many fun activities specifically geared to kids.

In the 1930s, the McWhirter family built the farm for a summer home. Elise Farrel-McWhirter, a horse trainer, willed the property to the city of Redmond, and upon her death in 1971, the land became a public park.

Driving through second-growth forest in this 68-acre park, you'd never guess that hidden behind the trees is a farm with ponies, pigs, goats, and rabbits. Expect to make at least two rounds past the pens of friendly animals.

If you can drag the kids away from the animals, this park on the eastern edge of Redmond also encompasses a large, open field, an orchard, and two miles of trails. Charlotte's Trail, an asphalt trail that is wheelchair accessible, runs the length of the park. There is also a 1.5-mile equestrian loop. Even the restroom, located in a converted silo, is worthy of a visit—it has a fun lookout on top.

The following are several good salmon-viewing areas to watch our Northwest salmon spawning:

Ballard Locks, 3105 N.W. 54th St., Seattle. You don't have to leave the city to watch salmon on their return upstream. During the height of the spawning season, at the Ballard Locks that connect saltwater Puget Sound to freshwater Lake Washington, you can look through underwater windows and see hundreds of salmon struggling up the fish ladders into the lake.

Issaquah Salmon Hatchery, 125 E. Sunset Way, Issaquah, (425) 392-1118), puts 1 million juvenile salmon in Issaquah Creek each spring. Issaquah celebrates the salmon's return each fall with a Salmon Days Festival in October. The hatchery has a docent program that answers public questions about the fish.

Cedar River, (206) 386-1584; *dnr.metrokc.gov/wlr/pi/cedar-river-naturalists.htm*. Each fall, you can join volunteer naturalists at sites along the Cedar River to see spawning salmon. Volunteers tell visitors about the natural and human history of the river, and the life cycle and habitat needs of the fish, including Puget Sound chinook salmon, a threatened species. You also learn what we can do to ensure the return of these special creatures. Volunteers are stationed from 11 A.M.–4 P.M. on weekend days in the fall at four sites: Renton Library, Riverview Park, Cavanaugh Pond, and Landsburg Park. These sites have limited parking; please carpool!

The Redmond Parks Department hosts a variety of excellent programs for children of all ages at Farrel-McWhirter, including farm activities, preschool classes, and breakfasts with the animals, pony-riding classes, and summer day camps. They also have a great birthday party package for the child that loves farm animals.

Forest Park Animal Farm

802 Mukilteo Blvd., Everett

(425) 257-8300

Hours: Early June–late Aug., daily, 10 A.M.–4 P.M.

Admission: Free

Directions: From Seattle take I-5 north. Take the Broadway exit (Exit 192) from the left lane of I-5. Stay left at the fork in the ramp and merge onto Broadway. Take the 41st Street ramp toward Mukilteo and Evergreen Way. Go straight on 41st Street, which turns into E. Mukilteo. The park is on your left.

This farm is home to a variety of animals such as rabbits, pigs, goals, ducks, ponies, calves, and llamas. Free pony rides are often offered on weekends in June and daily in July and August (weight limit 70 pounds and subject to volunteer staff availability). Children can get a handful of feed for a quarter. Popular farm programs include Breakfast with the Animals and Barnyard Birthdays. Farm-related day camps are also offered during the summer. The park also has a great playground with a new water feature and an indoor swimming pool.

Kelsey Creek Community Park/Farm

13204 S.E. Eighth Pl., Bellevue

(425) 452-7688

Hours: Year-round, dawn–dusk; public viewing of animals daily, 9:30 A.M.–3:30 P.M.

Admission: Free; group tours for preschools, schools, and parties are $2.50/person.

Parent Tips

Spring brings the arrival of many baby animals at Kelsey Creek. If you want to give your child a chance to watch a birthing scene or see some new babies, call in early spring to find out the EDTs (expected delivery times) of the pregnant animals.

Pay close attention to the directions—it is easy to get lost driving there.

Directions: From I-405, take the S.E. 8th Street exit and head east. Pass under the train trestle and go straight across the Lake Hills Connector Road. The road will wind through a residential area; go straight through the first stop sign. Where the street comes to a T (at the second stop sign), turn left, and the park will be on the right.

Essentials: As you enter the park there are signs directing you to parking. After you park, there are stroller-friendly walkways up to the barn, but it is close enough for a toddler to manage the walk. There are no restroom facilities at the barn, but they are nearby at the playground.

The lovely, big red barn sitting in this hidden-away park near Bellevue houses the usual assortment of farm animals—horses, goats, sheep, rabbits, and a pig. Children can wander through the barn at their own pace, enjoying up-close views of their favorite farm animals. Down along a pretty creek is a nice playground for the toddlers and preschoolers with a nearby restroom. The 150-acre park also offers paved and gravel trails, plenty of open lawns, and a covered picnic area, so take lunch and enjoys the setting. Also on park grounds is one of Bellevue's oldest structures, the Frazier cabin. It was built at another location in 1888 and moved to the park in 1974. Craft and animal-care classes are offered year-round. There are special events, including sheep shearing in mid-March and the Farm Fair in early November and Living History Programs for families.

Off the Beaten Path

Northwest Trek Wildlife Park
11610 Trek Dr. E., Eatonville
(360) 832-6117
www.nwtrek.org

Hours: Open daily year-round, at 10 A.M. (except holiday closures). Closing time varies between 3 and 6 P.M., depending on season. Call or check website for exact closing times and holiday closures. Apr.–Oct., tram departs every hour beginning at 10 A.M.; last tram is on the closing hour. Nov.–Mar., trams depart at 10:30 A.M., noon, 1:30 P.M., and 3 P.M.

Admission: $15/adults (ages 13–64), $13.50/seniors, $10/children ages 5–12, $7/children ages 3–4, free/children under age 3; discounts for Pierce County residents.

Essentials: Take Exit 142B (Puyallup) from I-5 and travel south on Highway 161 for 17 miles.
Parking is free. There are plenty of tables for picnicking, a sheltered picnic pavilion, and the Fir Bough Café, which offers a variety of food, including burgers, salads, and doughnuts. Strollers and wagons are available for rental for $5.

This park owes its existence to the generosity of Dr. and Mrs. David T. Hellyer, who in 1971 donated more than 700 acres of beautiful land to the Metropolitan Park District of Tacoma to create a protected place where over 200 native Northwest animals could roam freely.

You know you're not in a typical zoo when the naturalist tour guide has to nudge bison out of the road so she can drive a tram past. Or when she warns that even if she sees a moose, she's not stopping the tram to look because it's rutting season and the male moose are very aggressive.

Tram tours take visitors through the park, much of which is a free-roaming habitat for large North American animals, including bighorn sheep, elk, bison, caribou, mountain goats, and deer. This trip can be either wonderful—such as when the animals are so close you can take pictures of their nose hairs—or disappointing, when the animals are hanging out away from the road. But the drive itself is pretty, passing through forest, meadows, and wetlands, and kids usually enjoy the hide-and-seek aspect of the tour and the excitement of riding the tram. The guides also provide plenty of interesting information about the behavior of these magnificent animals, which will hold the attention of most school-age kids.

In addition to the tram tour, a more traditional zoo area offers close-up views of raccoons, beavers, badgers, river otters, skunks, wildcats, grizzly and black bears, and wolves. (The beavers and otters can also be viewed underwater.) Strollers and wheelchairs can easily navigate the wide, paved paths. Strollers and wagons are not needed if you plan to just ride the tram but come in handy if you want to walk the paved 0.75-mile loop trail and visit the small zoo. There are also more than five unpaved miles of hiking trails through wooded areas, so you might want to bring a backpack for youngsters. Guides to native plant life are available at the train entrance and the office.

At the Cheney Discovery Center, kids can touch frogs and snakes, pet animals' fur, have their picture taken with a (stuffed) bear, and try out the many learning boxes, which offer activities such as listening to a tape of animal sounds and trying to identify them.

Try to allow at least three hours to take in all the activities at Northwest Trek: the one-hour tram tour, hands-on activities at the Discovery Center, a visit to the walk-through zoo, browsing in the gift shop, and lunch in the cafe.

Trek holds special activities year-round, including hayrides, breakfasts, animal-care camps, elk-bugling tours (Sept.–Oct.), and Hoot 'N Howl (for Halloween).

....

Washington Serpentarium

22715-B Hwy 2, Gold Bar
(360) 668-8204
www.reptileman.com

Hours: 365 days a year, 10 A.M.–6 P.M.

Admission: $6/adults, $5/children

It is a nondescript building in an unlikely location—one mile east of Monroe on Highway 2—but the Washington Serpentarium holds one of the most comprehensive collections of reptiles on the West Coast. Lovingly displayed in cages ideal for

Parent Tips

The Reptile Man is a fantastic entertainer for birthday parties. Once he arrives in a van full of lizards and snakes and unpacks his giant iguana, the kids will be enthralled.

If your child is interested in owning a snake, turtle, lizard, or frog, look at the Reptile Man's website under "Reptiles as Pets." It includes lots of valuable information for parents, such as why NOT to get an iguana (they grow six feet long, have many health problems, and bite hard).

viewing, this is the dream zoo for the youngster in your house who has developed a passion for snakes, lizards, and other reptiles. Among the many creatures you'll see are black mambas, anacondas, a blue-tongued skink, a Chinese water dragon, a king cobra, and a horned viper, plus the world's largest spiders and centipedes and even a two-headed turtle. There are also several snakes that kids can hold (all venomous snakes are surgically devenomized!).

The passion and vision behind this remarkable place comes from a Northwest legend, Scott Peterson—the Reptile Man. He has made over 800 school and corporate appearances in the Northwest, and entertained at hundreds of birthday parties, spreading his immense knowledge and love of these often-maligned creatures.

Bug Safari
1501 Western Ave., Suite 304
Pike Street Hill Climb, between Pike Place Market and Seattle Aquarium
(206) 285-BUGS (2847)
www.seattlebugsafari.com

Hours: Mon., 11 A.M.–7 P.M.; Tues.–Sat., 10 A.M.–7 P.M.; Sun., 11 A.M.–6 P.M. Closed for frequent school field trips—call ahead to confirm it is open.

Admission: $8/adults, $6/children ages 3–12, free/ages 2 and under

Both the inhabitants and the location of the Bug Safari are unlikely. Tucked into the Pike Street Hill climb below the Pike Place Market, this storefront "insect zoo"—with gift shop, lab, and a display area full of little tanks on shelves—had to be certified by the Department of Agriculture. An insect

Parent Tips
This is a great place to take a school field trip—Brian Rolf does an excellent job entertaining and educating the kids. Be sure to plan a school visit far in advance, as it's getting very popular.

admirer since childhood, proprietor Brian Rolf has assembled an incredible collection of insects, along with informative exhibits to teach and show about the bug world.

Look carefully and you'll see the Goliath bird-eating tarantula, green diving beetles, lash-tailed vinegaroon scorpion, hissing cockroach, and many other crawly things you likely won't recognize. Everything is safely behind glass, so curious budding entomologists can study closely these wonders of nature without fear of something crawling up their shirtsleeves. The Bug Safari also includes equipment to start a bug collection.

Chapter 3

Culture for Kids

Don't let the word "culture" scare you. **Art, music,** and **drama** capture the attention of all kids, as long as they are age-appropriate and presented as a fun time, not something that will be "good for them." Also, parents need not fear that they will feel like foreigners in a strange land at a **cultural event**. All the arts organizations included in this book offer events, classes, and workshops geared towards novices. Finally, cost should not keep you away—our community abounds with **free** or **low-cost arts opportunities** for families. So go forth and enjoy exploring the rich world of the arts with your child!

Museums

Bellevue Art Museum
510 Bellevue Way, Bellevue
(425) 519-0770
www.bellevueart.org

Hours: Tues.–Sun., 10 A.M.–4:30 P.M. except Fri. (open until 9 P.M.) and opens at 11 A.M. Sun.

Admission: $7/adults, $5/students, free/children under 6

After closing in 2003 due to financial difficulties, BAM reopened in 2005 with a focus on traditional craft mediums of wood, glass, and metal. Docent-led tours on Tuesday through Friday for groups of 10 or more include kids as young as 5 in their talks. Saturdays there is a free art project. The Bellevue Arts and Crafts Fair (previously known as the Pacific Northwest Arts and Crafts Fair), a three-day event at Bellevue Square across the street, is one of Bellevue's most popular art happenings.

Burke Museum of Natural History and Culture
University of Washington, N.E. 45th St. and 17th Ave. N.E., Seattle
(206) 543-7907; (206) 543-5590 (24-hour recorded information)
www.washington.edu/burkemuseum

Hours: Daily, year-round, except closed New Year's Day, July 4, Thanksgiving Day, Christmas. 10 A.M.–5 P.M.; first Thurs. of the month, 10 A.M.–8 P.M.

Admission: $8/adults, $5/students, free/under 4. Free for everyone first Thurs. of the month. Higher admission may be charged for some exhibits.

Essentials: Parking is available on campus. The $12 parking fee is prorated, so you'll be issued a partial refund upon exiting if your visit is under 4 hours. Parking before noon on Saturday is $6 and prorated for visits less than one hour. Parking is free after noon on Saturday and all day Sunday. If you plan a visit during a Saturday in the fall, make sure there isn't a UW home football game. On those days, you have a lot of competition for parking, both on and around campus. You'll also find parking in public lots along University Way. Several Metro bus routes stop near campus. The museum cafe offers delicious goodies, such as scones, cookies, and muffins, as well as a few sandwich selections.

Kids will quickly shorten the name of the Burke Museum of Natural History and Culture to "the dinosaur museum." That's because, when the museum was renovated in late 1997, curators pulled out some of the more exciting aspects of Washington's history—dinosaurs, volcanoes, wooly mammoths—and tried to make them more accessible and understandable for children.

The first floor is devoted to a permanent exhibit, Life and Times of Washington State. Life and Times is broken up into sections, each with a kiosk where kids can punch a time card that explains the various epochs. The kiosks also have video screens with educational "newscasts."

You'll find the mostly real remains of a 40-foot-long allosaurus threatening a stegosaurus, which, despite the pointed plates down its back, looks like it might lose the battle. An elasmosaur, a sleek marine reptile bearing a fair resemblance to the Loch Ness Monster, hangs overhead. Children can measure themselves against the thigh bone of a 140-million-year-old sauropod, check out a clutch of real dinosaur eggs, and view the skull of a triceratops. (Dinosaur remains have never actually been found in Washington.)

Children can also walk through a volcano for an inside glimpse into the state's not-so-peaceful mountains or crawl inside a replica of the impression made by the decayed body of a 15-million-year-old two-horned dinosaur trapped in lava.

The Ice Age portion of Life and Times features more skeletons, including an enormous mastodon and a vicious-looking saber-toothed tiger. The exhibit's final section highlights some of the natural resources that present-day Washington offers. A 9-foot-long transparent wall shows 1,000 insects.

The other permanent exhibit, Pacific Voices, doesn't have as much kid appeal as Life and Times, since most artifacts are inside no-touch display cases. Still the bright masks, outrigger canoe models, and puppets will hold a child's attention for a while, as will the video productions. A few pullout drawers allow children to discover such things as costumes, masks, and puppets to play with.

The Burke also hosts many excellent traveling exhibits and outstanding events throughout the year, many specifically directed to families. Check the website often to keep up on offerings.

The museum store is full of items for kids, including books, puppets, dinosaurs, toys, and games.

....

Center for Wooden Boats
1010 Valley St., Seattle
(206) 382-2628
www.cwb.org

Hours: Daily year-round; late Mar.–late May, 10 A.M.–6 P.M.; late May–Sept.1, 10 A.M.–8 P.M.; Sept.–early Nov., 10 A.M.–6 P.M.; early Nov.–late Mar., Tues.–Sun., 10 A.M.–5 P.M.

Admission: Free, but donations gladly accepted. Boat rentals range from $10–$40 per hour.

It is difficult to be a resident of the "Boating Capital of the World" without catching a little of the own-a-boat fever. This hands-on floating maritime museum, at the south end of Lake Union, is about the easiest way imaginable to give the kiddos a boat ride with no strings attached—free boat rides are offered every Sunday 2–3 P.M.

The center features a collection of approximately 100 wooden rowing, sailing, and paddleboats. Many of them are moored along docks, where you can stroll and enjoy the floating collection. (Parents can stop by the Oar House or the Boat House and borrow life vests for little ones.)

The staff at the center builds and restores small watercraft using a variety of tools from the past and the present, so there is always some building or restoration activity going on in the shop. You might even get an impromptu lesson on varnishing, knot tying, or woodworking during your visit. Periodically, the center holds toy-boat building workshops, as well as sailing lessons and serious boat building. There are also summer classes for kids, as well as after-school projects.

Inside the Boat House, you'll find old photos, canoes, and shells hanging from the ceiling, and an old binnacle (the housing for a large compass). There are also several model boats, as well as a shelf of children's books and a comfortable couch.

You can rent boats for $10–$40 per hour. Life jackets are supplied for everyone. Most boats require no previous experience, but if you want to rent a sailboat, you'll have to have your skills checked out by staff ahead of time. The annual Wooden Boat Festival is a fun diversion over Fourth of July weekend. Activities include small-boat races, toy-boat building, face painting, music, food, contests, and maritime crafts. Admission is free.

....

The Children's Museum
305 Harrison St.
Seattle Center House, lower level, Seattle
(206) 441-1768
www.thechildrensmuseum.org

Hours: Mon.–Fri., 10 A.M.–5 P.M.; Sat.–Sun., 10 A.M.–6 P.M. Closed Thanksgiving Day, Christmas Day, and New Year's Day.

Admission: $7.50/adults and children, $6.50/ages 55 and over, free/under age 1. Annual membership, $65/family.

Essentials: Paid parking is available around Seattle Center. Ample food is available upstairs at the food court.

Shrink the world down to a child's size and you have the experience offered by the Children's Museum. With room after room of hands-on activities, this place will keep your kids amused (and painlessly educated about physics, foreign cultures, health, and history) for hours. The museum features permanent exhibits, is host to special exhibits, and offers activities in its studio space. For preschoolers and young school-age children, there is no better place to spend a few hours—especially when it's dreary and rainy outside. But be forewarned, you're not the only one with that thought!

The permanent exhibits include Mountain Forest, a simulated mountain with rocks kids can look under, a cave, a hollow log, animal costumes, a camping tent, and a rock slide. There is even a small climbing wall they can try to inch across. Cog City teaches cause and effect, as kids pull levers and use pulleys to send balls moving through pipes and mazes. The Go Figure exhibit explores math and literacy. The Neighborhood is pretty basic but one of the kids' favorite areas as it includes a supermarket for grocery shopping, a Metro bus and a fire truck to drive, a restaurant with tables to serve, and a doctor's office equipped with instruments to check vital signs. Bijou Theatre has an actual stage where kids can control the lighting and sound effects to tell two stories or make up their own. The youngest visitors will enjoy Discovery Bay, a special toddler area (for ages 2 and younger) with a sea theme.

Don't forget to stop by Imagination Station, the museum's drop-in art studio, where kids can work with professional artists to create a variety of masterpieces. The hands-on workshops and activities at Imagination Station are excellent, featuring quick and interesting creative activities.

The museum can get crowded, especially on weekends and school holidays. If you have a choice, visit during the week. Amenities at the museum include a stroller parking area up front, kid-height water fountains and sinks, and an excellent gift shop filled with quality educational toys.

The museum has an extensive program of educational activities including daily programs at 10:30 A.M. for ages 1—5 years and at 3 P.M. for ages 6—10 years (check website to confirm times). Programs are organized around daily themes and spotlight one area of child development, such as language or emotional development. Parents participate with their children and there is no extra cost. Regular events include storytelling by the Seattle Storytellers Guild, an Inventor's Club on Saturdays, and Cultural Sundays.

....

Experience Music Project/Science Fiction Museum and Hall of Fame
Fifth Ave. S., between Thomas and Harrison Sts,; Seattle Center, Seattle
EMP (206) 367-5483; (877) 367-5483
SFM (206) 724-3428
www.empsfm.org

Hours: Open daily, Memorial Day—Labor Day,10 A.M.—7 P.M.; Labor Day—Memorial Day, 10 A.M.—5 P.M.

Admission: $15/adults, $12/seniors and youth 5—17, free/under 5. All-access night provides free admission to both museums between 5—8 P.M. on the first Thurs. of every month.

Essentials: While visiting the EMP/SFM, you can have a meal at the Revolution Bar and Grill, which has a decent kids' menu. The website has extensive suggestions about parking and public transportation.

If anybody in your family is into rock and roll, you'll want to visit the Experience Music Project, an interactive museum dedicated to rock and roll and designed by acclaimed architect Frank O. Gehry. EMP is filled with artifacts, including the world's largest collection of Jimi Hendrix memorabilia, which may not be as meaningful to kids as it is to their parents. EMP's main exhibit area tells the story of a century of American popular music, from jazz and blues to hip-hop. Highlights include the Guitar Gallery, which charts the history of this instrument and displays dozens of guitars.

For kids, the most popular part of the museum is likely to be the Sound Lab, a studio where everyone can make their own music with computer-guided instruments such as guitars, keyboards, and drums. On Stage gives visitors an opportunity to perform in front of a virtual concert audience.

EMP/SFM makes a big effort to include activities of interest to families, including Family Days, featuring a visiting band and special family activities. Educational programs include Experience: The Band, a collaboration between EMP and Berklee College of Music, for middle and high schoolers, lessons and workshops for ages 13 through adult, Rock 'N Science summer day camp for grades K–4, and much more. The museum also features traveling exhibits and a variety of special programs for kids, including an arts camp during the summer, instrument lessons, and Little Wings, a music program for toddlers and preschoolers. There's also a cool section of the website called "Spin Kids" with information about current exhibits and every month a new activity.

The other occupant of the Frank Gehry–designed building, is the Science Fiction Museum, "devoted to thought-provoking ideas and experiences of science fiction." You need to be a fan of science fiction to appreciate this showcase of founder Paul Allen's collection of science fiction memorabilia, although seeing Captain Kirk's command chair from USS *Enterprise* will likely impress anybody.

Frye Art Museum
704 Terry Ave., Seattle
(206) 622-9250
www.fryemuseum.org

Hours: Tues., Wed., Fri., and Sat., 10 A.M.–5 P.M.; Thurs. 10 A.M.–8 P.M.; Sun., noon–5 P.M. Closed Mon.

Admission: Free

Essentials: Free parking is available in a lot across the street at Terry Avenue and Cherry Street. The museum's wide rooms are easily navigated by a stroller. The museum store includes a small children's section with books and art supplies. The Gallery Café serves soups, salads, sandwiches, and desserts.

The Frye Art Museum is a good place for kids' first exposure to art, because it's small but worthwhile, all on one floor, and if they hate it you haven't shelled out anything since admission and parking are free. The museum, which features three permanent galleries, and three changing exhibition galleries, opened to the public in 1952 after Charles Frye left his fortune and collection in trust to create a free public art museum.

The recently remodeled museum includes one of the country's most extensive collections of 19th-century German art, as well as works by early 19th- and 20th-century American artists and French impressionists. The American paintings include pieces by such artists as Mary Cassatt, John Singer Sargent, and Andrew Wyeth. Like most art museums, the tone is quiet and reverent, so it's probably best for either kids who will be in strollers or children who know not to run around and yell.

The Frye's Education Gallery showcases artwork from the museum's many educational activities, including student work. The museum offers art education workshops for children year-round in basic drawing, painting, and ceramics. Guided public tours are offered on Sundays at 12:30 and 3 P.M. Group tours are by reservation.

Henry Art Gallery

University of Washington, 15th Ave. N.E. at N.E. 41st St., Seattle
(206) 543-2280
www.henryart.org

Hours: Tues., Wed., Fri.–Sun., 11 A.M.–5 P.M.; Thurs. 11 A.M.–8 P.M. Closed Mon.

Admission: $10/adults, free/high school and college students with ID and children under age 13. Free for all ages every Thurs., 5–8 P.M.

Essentials: Parking is available in the underground Central Parking Garage at N.E. 41st Street. On Sundays, parking is usually available for no fee. The Henry has a cafe, which serves snacks and beverages. Food can be eaten out in the Sculpture Court on nice days.

The Henry was the first public art museum in Washington state, donated in 1927 by Horace C. Henry, a local tycoon. Included in this donation was his personal collection of early 20th-century works.

The Henry opens new exhibits of modern and contemporary art about every six to 12 weeks, showcasing a variety of artists and artistic mediums. A 1997 expansion quadrupled the museum's size, offering a light, airy new space for its permanent collection and educational programs. The Henry has one of the most successful and well-designed educational programs in the city, offering lectures, curriculum support for educators, workshops, classes, and tours.

The museum has a store, which includes a children's section with games, books, and art-related toys. Special age-appropriate docent-led school and group tours are offered Tuesday through Sunday, but reservations must be made at least four weeks in advance.

KidsQuest Children's Museum
Factoria Square Mall, Bellevue
(425) 637-8100
www.kidsquestmuseum.org

Hours: Tues.–Sat., 10 A.M.–5 P.M., except Fri., closes 8 P.M. Sun., noon–5 P.M.

Admission: $7/ages 1–100 years; free/under 1 year. Free all ages on Fri., 5–8 P.M.

KidsQuest Children's Museum opened in 2005 inside Factoria Mall and it is a very popular place for parents with young kids—especially on a rainy day. The centerpiece exhibit is The Backyard, where kids can build blanket forts, climb, and slide. Another popular permanent exhibit is Waterways, where kids can race boats, splash in step pools, paint, make music, and more—all with water. The Garage gives kids a place to play with tools, build inventions, and play instruments in the garage band. There's also a Thomas the Train table. The museum also offers a summer program for ages 4–11 with week-long themes.

Klondike Gold Rush National Historical Park
NW corner of Jackson St. and Second Ave. S.
(206) 553-7220
www.nps.gov/klse

Hours: Daily, 9 A.M.–5 P.M. Closed Thanksgiving, Christmas, and New Year's Day.

Admission: Free

You and your kids have probably passed by this little museum in Pioneer Square dozens of times and never thought about going in. However, everyone can relate to wanting to strike it rich, and because of this age-old desire, Seattle was able to prosper in its early years. So this museum tells a pretty good story, which makes it fun for all ages. The National Park Service, which set up this historical "park," has done a thorough job in using a variety of media, including maps, photos, slides, and films, to document the gold rush and its enormous effect on Seattle. Your kids will enjoy seeing the shovels, picks, and other tools used by the prospectors, and watching the rangers demonstrate how to pan for gold.

During the summer months, daily gold-panning demonstrations, ranger programs, and a walking tour of the Pioneer Square Historical District are offered. A visit through this interesting "park" is a quick and easy stop, and once you do it, you and your kids will know at least two things: Learning history can be painless, and finding gold is easier dreamed than done.

Museum of Flight
9404 E. Marginal Way S., Seattle
(206) 764-5720
www.museumofflight.org

Hours: Daily, 10 A.M.–5 P.M.; first Thurs. of the month, until 9 P.M.

Admission: $14/adults, $7.50/youth ages 5–17, free/children ages 4 and under. Free for all ages the first Thurs. of the month, 5–9 P.M.

Essentials: Take Exit 158 from I-5 and follow the signs along E. Marginal Way for about one-quarter mile. The museum is next to the Boeing Field. Parking is abundant and free. Metro bus Route 174 takes you there from Sea-Tac Airport or downtown Seattle. Strollers are not available for rent, although if you bring your own you can easily negotiate one throughout the exhibits. Wings Café offers a deli menu with sandwiches, soup, and hot dogs.

In most cities, an airplane museum will have a couple of old planes, a bunch of models, and maybe some historical displays. But in Seattle, the birthplace of Boeing, the real planes outnumber the models. It's one of the nation's premier flight museums—a not-to-be-missed attraction, especially if you've got a child with more than a passing interest in things that fly.

Dozens of airplanes, ranging from simple gliders to fighter jets, hang from the ceiling of the vast steel-and-glass Great Gallery. Others are modeled on the floor for a closer look. The large, airy museum is very kid-friendly, with plenty to do as well as observe. Older enthusiasts can learn about the history of flight from the earliest aircraft to the space stations of the future. Younger folks will be impressed with all the gadgets and machinery.

When kids get tired of gazing at the different aircraft, they can try out one of the simulators, which include the pilot-controlled, full-motion X-Pilot, which allows unlimited loops and rolls, and the Hubble Space Telescope docking units. Visitors can also sit in the actual cockpits of a couple of planes: an F/A-18 Hornet fighter and an SR-71 Blackbird.

The Flight Zone is a special interactive youth area, which include hands-on activities that demonstrate such aerodynamic concepts as flight instrumentation and propulsion. There is also a collection of small planes that kids can sit in and pretend to fly—there are even levers that move the wings. Kids should also enjoy the Apollo exhibit, with space suits and a mock-up of a Lunar Roving Vehicle on display. Bring a camera to snap a picture of your child posing as an astronaut.

On the top level of the three-floor museum, visitors can pretend to be air traffic controllers in the Tower. Older children will appreciate the science and technology; younger kids will have a ball listening to telephones and pushing buttons. In the museum's control tower, which looks out over Boeing Field, speakers relay the actual "tower chatter" between pilots and the real control tower. Binoculars and more buttons and gauges add to the fun.

The Red Barn, the birthplace of the Boeing Co. and its original manufacturing facility, features historical displays and models; videos play old film footage of the flying machines.

In June 2004, the museum opened a major new area, the Personal Courage Wing. Inside this three-story addition are aircraft and memorabilia from World Wars I and II. Interactive experiences, theatrical sets, dioramas, displays, and flight simulators are used to immerse the visitor in this period of history.

Outside the museum, you'll find more airplanes, including the original Air Force One, which you can tour. Parents should enjoy walking on the plane that carried former Presidents Eisenhower and Kennedy on historic missions. Also outside is the museum's newest acquisition: a British Airways Concorde. You can tour this history-making aircraft, free with your museum admission. Kids also won't want to miss the gift shop, which has a large selection of models, books, clothes, and aircraft-related toys.

The Museum of Flight has an extensive education department, including the Challenger Learning Center, where participants work together on a simulated space mission. Many of the programs are geared to school groups, but there are also sleepover opportunities, summer camps, and weekend programs. Fees are charged for most programs.

Complimentary guided tours of the museum are offered every day throughout the day, and free films are also offered at the museum daily.

The museum also hosts frequent special events and exhibits. If your budding aviator is fascinated with the Blue Angels, for instance, don't miss the opportunity to see these planes up-close during the Seafair Festival in August: The Blue Angels park at the museum. Other aircraft frequently visit the museum. Check the calendar on the museum's website for the latest details on upcoming events and special activities.

....

Museum of History and Industry
2700 24th Ave. E., Seattle
(206) 324-1126
www.seattlehistory.org

Hours: Daily, 10 A.M.–5 P.M.; first Thurs. of the month, until 8 P.M.

Admission: $7/adults, $5/seniors and youth ages 5–17, free/ages 4 and under. Free to all ages the first Thurs. of the month.

Essentials: Free parking is available on the grounds. MOHAI's layout is open and spacious with ample room to maneuver wheelchairs and strollers. The downstairs restroom (auditorium lobby) has a changing table. Except for snack machines, food is not available in the immediate area, but you can bring a lunch to enjoy outside the museum. The museum sets out tables during the summer. MOHAI is scheduled to move sometime after 2008, but location and dates have not yet been determined.

A family attraction since 1952, the Museum of History and Industry—MOHAI— is a kid-friendly museum. It has places to play and make history-related crafts, and exhibits that feature hands-on activities.

Boomtown: Seattle Before the Great Fire re-creates a section of an 1880s First Avenue, with a barber shop, general store, and other shops visitors can peek into to see actual machines, tools, and products used by settlers. Kids can dress up in period clothes and visit a restaurant on Yesler's Wharf.

In Salmon Stakes, children can climb aboard a boat to haul in salmon and walk through an early-20th-century cannery and into a bunkhouse. The Great Seattle Fire educates children about the fire that ravaged the city in 1889. It also shows some of the antiquated equipment used to battle the flames. Metropolis 150 gives the whole family a look back at Seattle's first 150 years, while Gorilla in Our Midst: Bobo brings vistors face-to-face with one of Seattle's biggest 20th-century celebrities and one of Woodland Park Zoo's most famous residents.

Other galleries showcase changing exhibits from the Smithsonian, Library of Congress, and other institutions. In addition, MOHAI offers special events for families throughout the year that complement and enhance the temporary exhibits.

The gift shop at the entrance to the museum has many interesting items for sale including T-shirts, classic toys, books, and videos.

Storytimes for ages 4–7 (and a parent) are offered at 10 A.M. every Thursday when a MOHAI educator will share a fascinating story connected to local history, including Native culture and pioneer journeys. The MOHAI educator also shares fun finds for kids throughout the museum and the kids create a craft they can take home. Outside the museum, kids will enjoy the deck gun (a relic from the battle-ship USS *Colorado* that's been a favorite of Seattle kids since the early 1960s), and running around the 1890 Seattle fire bell. Both sit next to the lower parking lot.

If you continue to the east end of the parking lot, you'll find the start of the Foster Island Nature Trail, leading into the Washington Arboretum. This is a delightful walk with kids, but be prepared during rainy season for wet trails. There are numerous places for a young child to fall in the water on this walk, so it is not safe for a non-swimming child; ;keep your eyes on young children at all times.

From July to September, the museum hosts weekly History Walking Tours, and special family events are held throughout the year (including holiday events in December).

....

Nordic Heritage Museum
3014 N.W. 67th St., Seattle
(206) 789-5707
www.nordicmuseum.com

Hours: Tues.–Sat., 10 A.M.–4 P.M.; Sun., noon–4 P.M. Closed Thanksgiving Day, Christmas Eve, Christmas, and New Year's Day.

Admission: $6/adults, $5/seniors, $4/children in grades K–12, free/children under 5

Located in the once strongly Scandinavian Ballard neighborhood, the Nordic Heritage Museum shows how immigrants from Denmark, Finland, Iceland, Norway, and Sweden shaped the Pacific Northwest. Take a journey back in time and follow the path of a Scandinavian immigrant from the old country to Ellis Island to the American frontier in the interactive exhibit Dream of America. Children can explore the realistic logging and fishing rooms and check out the Scandinavian customs and traditions highlighted in the museum's five galleries. The museum also hosts special exhibits that highlight various aspects of Scandinavian life, arts, crafts, and design. Monthly children's programs offer hands-on activities such as weaving, celebrations, and even a dress-alike birthday party for Pippi Longstocking.

The museum hosts special events for families, including Tivoli-Viking Days, which transforms the museum's grounds into a Viking marketplace in July; Yulefest, a Nordic event in November; First of Advent, with a gingerbread house workshop; and Children's Christmas in Scandinavia. All events include music, food, and children's activities.

. . . .

Northwest African American Museum
2300 S. Massachusetts St., Seattle
(206) 518-6000
www.naamnw.org

Hours: Wed., 11 A.M.–4:30 P.M., Thurs., 11 A.M.–7 P.M., Fri., 11 A.M.–4:30 P.M., Sat., 11 A.M.–4 P.M., Sun., noon–4 P.M. Closed Mon. and Tues.

Admission: $6/adults, $4/students, free/ages 5 and under

The journey to open a museum that told the story of African Americans in the Pacific Northwest was a long and arduous one, but finally in 2008, Seattle gained this long overdue place where the achievements and struggles of African Americans in our community will be explored with changing exhibits. The Northwest African American Museum is a place "where youth, adults and families can honor the past and articulate the future."

Odyssey: The Maritime Discovery Center

2205 Alaskan Way, Pier 66, Seattle

(206) 374-4000

www.ody.org

Hours: Tues.–Thurs., 10 A.M.–3 P.M.; Fri., 10 A.M.–4 P.M.; Sat.–Sun., 11 A.M.–5 P.M.

Admission: $7/adults, $5/seniors and ages 5–18, $2/children ages 2–4, free/ under 2

Essentials: Parking available at meters across the street. There are also several paid parking lots nearby.

From Portage Bay to Puget Sound, Seattle is an area where boats and the water are in view at almost every turn. The harbor was a vital part of the city from its earliest days, and many residents depended on the shipping and fishing industries for their livelihood. Odyssey pays homage to that history, and brings it into the 21st century. Odyssey is the nation's only contemporary, interactive maritime museum—a high-tech, high-touch museum that enhances awareness and stimulates thinking about human connections to the seas and waterways. Through its changing exhibits and programs, Odyssey provides children and adults with a chance to gain insight into the environmental, economic, and social issues of the contemporary maritime world. Visitors learn about transportation, trade, fisheries, maritime industries and labor, safety and security, resource management, and waterborne recreation.

Odyssey encourages visitors to "bounce around" the museum, engaging in hands-on activities while interacting with one another. The museum has three galleries with many interactive exhibits. In the Sharing the Sound Gallery, visitors can navigate a ship, find out how various vessels are built, learn about ship navigation, and go for a simulated kayak ride. Kids can explore and play on an authentic, small-scale fishing vessel in the Sustaining Sea Gallery, as well as learn what a typical day at sea is like. In the Ocean Trade Gallery, visitors learn how an apple gets from Wenatchee to Bangkok, gain understanding about the physics behind propulsion by pedaling a full-sized ship propeller, and operate a crane to load containers from truck and train onto a ship. There are also two replicas made of Lego bricks: a 12-foot model of the largest container ship in the world and a model of an Issaquah Class ferry. Lego fans will enjoy the play tables and Lego bricks available to visitors, thanks to a donation from the company that makes Lego.

When you have finished your visit to Odyssey, you and your kids will have a new appreciation for the role that shipping, trade, and fishing play in the lives of Puget Sound–area residents—not to mention that the kids won't want to leave.

....

Olympic Sculpture Park

2901 Western Ave.
(206) 654-3100
www.seattleartmuseum.org/OSP

Hours: Open every day, from ½ hour prior to sunrise to ½ hour after sunset

Admission: Free

Part playground, part park, and part museum, the Olympic Sculpture Park opened in 2008 and has become a favorite place for families who want to let kids romp while enjoying an amazing sculpture collection and a knockout view of Elliott Bay. All kids, regardless of age, seem to enjoy the size and beauty of the works of art. You can also stand on a bridge and watch trains go by or walk down to Myrtle Edwards Park, a thin strip of a park that runs along the water. There is a cafe, gift shop, and restrooms.

....

Pacific Science Center

200 Second Ave. N., Seattle Center, Seattle
(206) 443-2001; (206) 443-IMAX (IMAX theater); (206) 443-2850 (laser show)
www.pacsci.org

Hours: Daily, 10 A.M.–6 P.M.

Admission: Exhibits and IMAX $15/adults, $12/children ages 6–12; $10/children ages 3–5; free/2 years and under. Special Engagement IMAX only $10.75/adults, $8.75/children ages 3–12. Laser shows $8/Fri. and Sat.; $5/Thurs. Annual membership, $80–$100/family. Some special exhibits may require extra admission fees.

Essentials: Paid parking is available in nearby lots, or in the James Albert Claypool Memorial Garage at the corner of Second Avenue N. and Denny Way, where there is a covered walkway into the south entrance of the Science Center. If your group gets hungry, you can fill up at the Fountains Café or leave the Science Center and head over to the food court in the nearby Center House. Just be sure to get a hand stamp before you leave, so you can return again after eating.

The Pacific Science Center is a fantastic place to take kids because the fun (and educational) exhibits appeal to all ages, including adults. With the center's interactive displays, there is no question science is cool. Young children will enjoy pushing buttons on interactive exhibits and meeting small animals; teens will be thrilled to watch themselves deliver a weather report on TV; and in the midst of a rainy Seattle winter, there's nothing like a visit to the tropical butterfly exhibit. With more than 200 hands-on exhibits, it really is a science playground. Allow at least a full afternoon.

Perennially popular with younger kids is the robotic dinosaur exhibit—although very young children may be frightened by the authentic-looking creatures of the Mesozoic era. Creatures on a smaller scale are featured in Insect Village, which is immediately adjacent to the tropical butterfly exhibit.

Kids who are fascinated by the beach and ocean can see how Puget Sound's tides and current work in a 100-square-foot scale model of the Sound. Nearby is a kind of mini-zoo, featuring snakes, other reptiles, amphibians, and a colony of east African naked mole rats.

Kids of all ages seem to gravitate toward Body Works, where they can test their reaction time and balance, climb on a bicycle to see how much energy they can produce, and learn a lot about nutrition. In the Technology exhibits area, you can have a virtual reality soccer experience, create art and music with computers, and challenge a robot to a game of tic-tac-toe.

After all the energetic exploration, you and the kids may be ready to relax by watching an IMAX movie at one of the two PSC theaters. Each theater shows two or three different films over the course of the day, so it's not unusual to have a choice of several films. If your heart is set on seeing a specific film, call ahead and check film times—and make sure the film you want to see isn't sold out. You can buy tickets ahead of time online. Of the two theaters, the Boeing IMAX Theater is newer. Films are shown on a screen six stories high and 80 feet wide. This is where you can see 3-D films using a headset that brings the images on screen to life. The older Eames IMAX Theater has a screen that's 35 feet high and 60 feet wide.

Laser Fantasy is another theater inside the Science Center that is well worth experiencing. (It is also one of the few places in town that provides good evening entertainment for teenagers.) Viewers can lie back in comfy chairs or stretch out on the carpeted floor to watch a laser light show accompanied by music. The shows, only available in the evenings, feature brilliant colored lasers choreographed to popular music.

The gift shop is outstanding, offering one of the best places in town to find creative, educational toys and children's books. Save time for browsing. With all the cool stuff inside, don't miss the fun displays outdoors in the area between the center's buildings. All ages will enjoy the interactive water fountains where visitors can spray water cannons to make metal sculptures spin, and thrill-seekers will be challenged to ride the High Rail Bicycle 15 feet above the ground—on a rail one inch wide!

Popular annual events include the Model Railroad show in November, and the Bubble Festival in August. Also watch for special visiting exhibits. There is also an outstanding and very popular day camp program during summer months as well as spring breaks, and occasional sleepovers at the Science Center are available for groups and open to the public on certain dates.

Rosalie Whyel Museum of Doll Art
1116 108th Ave. N.E., Bellevue
(425) 455-1116
www.dollart.com

Hours: Mon.–Sat., 10 A.M.–5 P.M.; Sun., 1–5 P.M.

Admission: $7/adults, $6/seniors, $5/children ages 5–17, free/children under 5

This peach-and-cream Victorian-style mansion is home to more than 1,200 dolls, as well as teddy bears, toys, dollhouses, miniatures, and other childhood memorabilia. The 13,000-square-foot museum, which cost collector Rosalie Whyel $3.5 million to build, opened in 1992 to celebrate the history, technology, and artistry of doll making. The collection appeals to all ages, from preschool to seniors, and includes everything from antique dolls dating back to 1650 to Barbie. The collection even includes two ancient Egyptian tomb dolls. All the displays are housed within glass cases, safe from little hands. Save time to visit the gift shop, which sells dolls, toys, and gift items.

Seattle Art Museum
1300 First Ave., Seattle
(206) 543-3100 (recorded information); (206) 654-3121 (box office)
www.seattleartmuseum.org

Hours: Tues.–Sun., 10 A.M.–5 P.M.; Thurs.–Fri., 10 A.M.–9 P.M. Closed Mon., as well as Thanksgiving, Christmas, and New Year's Day.

Admission: $13/adults, $7/students 13–17, free/children ages 12 and under when accompanied by an adult. Free for all ages on first Thurs. of month.

Essentials: The parking garage is underneath the museum and offers special rates for museum goers. Several Metro bus routes stop right outside the museum. The museum is fully accessible to strollers and wheelchairs. A tasty cafe is located off the main stairwell, or just walk one block north to the Pike Place Market to eat.

The best time to visit the Seattle Art Museum (SAM) with young children may be during one of the Family Days, when hands-on activities help children learn about the museum's current featured exhibit. (Check the website for dates.) However, SAM's marvelous exhibits and education program makes the museum a comfortable and fun place for families anytime.

SAM has had many loyal and generous patrons through the years, perhaps most notably its founder and primary benefactor, Dr. Richard E. Fuller. His collections of Japanese and Chinese art and other works formed a small but important holding for the Seattle Art Museum, which he and his family financed and opened in 1933 in Volunteer Park. Today that building is the home of the Seattle Asian Art Museum.

SAM opened its downtown location in late 1991 and then did an extensive renovation and expansion (almost doubling its space) into a spectacular Robert Venturi–designed building in 2007. Children will enjoy the famous 48-foot-tall *Hammering Man*, weighing in at over 20,000 pounds, located just outside the south entrance. From the moment you enter the new main entrance on First Avenue, it is obvious this is no ordinary museum. *Cai-Qiang's Inopportune: Stage One* greets you with seven white actual cars somersaulting across the ceiling, fiber-optic lights shooting from them.

If you want to greatly increase your chances of a successful visit, try following your child's lead as you explore the museum. You'll have the added bonus of noticing some art pieces you might not have looked at closely if you were taking your own tour. There are more than 2,400 pieces of art on display in about 268,000 square feet so don't expect to cover it all or museum fatigue will destroy all good intentions. Pick and choose a few sections that draw your child's attention and leave when everybody's interest and energy level is still running high so they'll want to come back for more.

....

Seattle Asian Art Museum
1400 E. Prospect St., Volunteer Park, Seattle
(206) 654-3100
www.seattleartmuseum.org

Hours: Summer: Tues.–Sun., 10 A.M.–5 P.M.; Winter (Sept.–June): Wed.–Sun., 10 A.M.–5 P.M., Thurs., 10 A.M.–9 P.M. Closed Mon. year-round; also closed Tues. during winter months. Closed Christmas Day and New Year's Day.

Admission: $3/suggested donation, free/children ages 12 and under. Free for all ages first Thurs. and Sat. of month. Annual membership, $65/family.

Essentials: Parking is free and right next to the museum. If used within a week, your ticket is good for one free visit to the Seattle Art Museum.

Large statues of Buddha, delicate Japanese wall hangings, and intricate jade carvings are highlights of the Seattle Asian Art Museum, housed in the Seattle Art Museum's former home in Volunteer Park. Most of the art is in display cases, though an educational resources room offers hands-on activities such as kids' books, clothes to try on, and an educational video. Older children will find the art an interesting introduction to Asian religions and philosophies.

Be sure to pick up a "Self-Guided Tour" brochure when you arrive. You'll find educational information and activities for children. The museum also hosts regular concerts as part of its Performance in the Parks series, which runs year-round and has a different theme each month.

The best day to visit is the first Saturday of the month, when admission is free and the museum sometimes stages free family activities and programs, including a series of films. The museum store has a small children's section with games and toys.

Parent Tips

While you are at the Seattle Asian Art Museum, take time to visit the wonderful conservatory located nearby. It's an especially good place to visit during the winter months, when colorful, blooming tropical plants will momentarily transport you from Seattle's rainy gloom. There is also a good playground at the northeast corner of Volunteer Park and a few blocks east of the park on Galer and 17th Avenue E., the popular Volunteer Park Café serves fabulous cookies and pastries, as well as delicious lunches and dinners.

Wing Luke Asian Museum

719 S. King St., Seattle
(206) 623-5124
www.wingluke.org

Hours: Tues.–Sun., noon–5 P.M., first and third Thurs., 10 A.M.–8 P.M.

Admission: $8/adults, $6/students, $5/children ages 5–12; free/under 5 years. Also free for all ages Thurs. Annual membership, $50–$99/family and friends.

Essentials: Paid parking is available on the street or in nearby lots. One of Metro's underground stations is located at Fifth and Jackson, where you can catch buses to and from Pioneer Square, University Street, Westlake Mall, and Convention Place, free of charge. The Waterfront Streetcar also comes nearby. The museum is located in the International District, home to several of the cities best Asian restaurants, so finding a snack or a meal will not be difficult.

The Wing Luke Asian Museum showcases the many contributions of Seattle's Asian communities. In 2008, after a decade of planning, it moved into a permanent location in an elegant building with over twice the previous room for exhibits. Several exhibits moved from the former location, including the *Densho Project*, where visitors use computer workstations to review a digital archive of oral history interviews, historical photographs, and related documents about the experiences of Japanese Americans before, during, and after World War II.

An annual exhibit on Asian New Year celebrations usually opens in January and runs until early spring. Tours and craft sessions often complement the featured exhibits.

Music

The following organizations offer many opportunities for young people to listen to and learn about music. Most orchestras and choirs in our community offer special programs intended to build interest in music from a very early age.

The many youth symphonies and choirs also offer public performances. These concerts provide a great opportunity for kids to join a symphony or choir or attend a low-cost concert and watch young people perform.

Bellevue Eastside Youth Symphonies

(425) 467-5604
www.byso.org

Children and youth up to age 21 play and perform with four graded orchestras, depending on their ability level. There's also a harp ensemble. BYSO complements and builds upon school and private music instruction. There are a number of public performances throughout the year, including a holiday concert and some free performances. Concerts take place at a number of Eastside venues.

Bellevue Philharmonic Orchestra

Theatre at Meydenbauer Center, 11100 N.E. Sixth St., Bellevue
(425) 455-4171; (206) 325-6500 (tickets)
www.bellevuephil.org

Season: Oct.–May, plus Fourth of July Outdoor Concert

Admission: Varies with performance

In addition to a Masterworks, Steinway and Pops series, the Philharmonic offers numerous performances for youngsters. The Little Maestro Series is a dynamic introduction to classical music for children ages birth to six. Kids move and sing to the music in these five interactive concerts October to March. In addition there is a Young Artists' Debut Concert, featuring young, local gifted musicians. The orchestra also does considerable outreach in the schools through its Sound Adventures in the School program, which brings live music into local classrooms.

Columbia Choirs of Metropolitan Seattle
(425) 486-1987
www.columbiachoirs.com

The Columbia Choirs is a community-based, non-sectarian choir training singers from age 3 through adult. Rehearsals take place in Redmond, Auburn, and Renton, with approximately 400 singers from 15 school districts rehearsing once or twice a week. Columbia Choirs sponsors singing festivals that provide an excellent opportunity to have your child learn about choir music and explore their interest in joining a choir.

Island Choral Experience
(206) 232-8007
www.islandchoralexperience.com

Island Choral Experience includes the Island Children's Choir, with the voices of 90 boys and girls in grades 4–6; and Island Sounds, a 75-voice choir of girls in grades 7–12. Both Mercer Island groups offer two performances: a concert in December featuring holiday music, and another concert in June, with a different theme each year. The concerts are well staged with costumes and sets and often feature a medley of songs and dance. Popular and classical music are performed. Mercer Island High School is the most frequent venue for these two groups. All performances are appropriate for the whole family.

Music Center of the Northwest
901 N. 96th St., Seattle
(206) 526-8443
www.mcnw.org

Music Center for the Northwest, which calls itself Seattle's community music school, offers concerts and recitals throughout the year. Many are good opportunities to introduce children to classical and other styles of music. The Music Center also offers a wide range of music lessons for children and adults at reasonable cost.

Northwest Girlchoir
6208 60th Ave. N.E., Seattle
(206) 985-3969; (206) 985-3973 (tickets)
www.northwestgirlchoir.org

The Northwest Girlchoir, composed of girls in grades 3–12, has been performing for family audiences for more than 20 years. Five auditioned choir levels serve ages 8–18, two non-auditioned programs serve ages 4–7. The choir offers several outstanding formal concerts each year, at venues that have included Town Hall and Meany Theatre. In 2008 two Eastside Choirs that do not require auditions were added, for ages 4–K and grades 1–2.

Olympic Music Festival
(206) 527-8839
www.nwco.org

Hours: Late June–early Sept., Sat. and Sun., 2 P.M.

Admission: Lawn seating, $16person, free/children ages 5 and under. Barn seating, $25/adults, $20/s tudents, $16/ages 6–17 (under age 6 not admitted to the barn)

If your idea of bliss is sitting outside on a beautiful summer day, surrounded by rural beauty while live classical music wafts through the air, you'll want to put the Olympic Music Festival on your summer schedule. The festival takes place in a turn-of-the-20th-century barn on a picturesque 40-acre farm on the Olympic Peninsula. The farm is located 11 miles west of the Hood Canal Bridge, one-half mile south of Highway 104, on Center Road.

While concert-goers can opt to buy tickets to sit inside the barn, the real attraction for families is to sit on the lawn outside the barn. You can't see the musicians, but you can hear them just fine, and the informal setting is perfect for children who don't enjoy sitting still for long periods.

The festival is held on Saturday and Sunday afternoons beginning the last weekend in June and running through the first weekend in September. Concerts start at 2 P.M. with the barn opening at 1 P.M. There are small discounts if tickets are purchased in advance.

Pacifica Children's Chorus
(206) 527-9095
www.pacificachoirs.org

Founded in 1993, the Pacifica Choirs have grown to include four performing levels. Young singers are offered a choral experience based on the approach fostered by Hungarian composer Zoltan Kodály. Participation in the choir is open to grades K through 12; auditioning is required.

The choir presents a blend of music, dance, prose, and drama at their two or three public concerts a year, and performs all types of music (folk, classical, jazz, and contemporary), while primarily focusing on folk.

Rainier Chamber Winds
(206) 780-1021; (800) 956-WIND
www.rainierchamberwinds.org

The only professional wind ensemble in the Northwest, the Rainier Chamber Winds offers special concerts for children, featuring original commissioned compositions that tell stories with narration, much in the tradition of *Peter and the Wolf*. During the free concerts, children sit close to the musicians and learn about the instruments, the stories, and the music.

Renton Youth Symphony Orchestras

Carco Theater, 1717 Maple Valley Hwy., Renton

(425) 430-6700

www.ci.renton.wa.us/commserv/rec/ryso.htm

The orchestra, composed of students in grades 9–12, performs for the public two times a year—in May and December. A prerequisite to participating in the program is that students must participate in a school program.

Seattle Chamber Music Society

Summer Festival: Lakeside School, 14050 First Ave. N.E., Seattle; Overlake School, 20301 N.E. 108th St., Redmond

Winter Festival: Benaroya Hall, 200 University St., Seattle

(206) 283-8808

Admission: $16–$35; $8, family concert

The Seattle Chamber Music Summer Festival is an extraordinary opportunity to hear fine music for free, if you are willing to sit outside on the lovely lawns. Bring blankets and picnics. Children under age 6 are not allowed in the concert hall, but they are probably better off outside anyway. Concerts last about two hours, so be sure to bring sweaters if you sit outside.

This popular month-long series, started by UW cello professor Toby Saks, is well known for its top-notch performances by local and international talent and for the charming ambience of the Lakeside and Overlake School grounds. Music-loving families can enjoy the concert without paying to sit inside, thanks to a stereo system that pipes music out of the hall onto the pastoral campus grounds. Weather permitting, anyone can bring a blanket and picnic and enjoy the music for free, while children play and dance.

The Seattle Chamber Music Society also offers a family concert during the year as part of both the Summer Festival and Winter Festival. Family concerts are generally intended for ages 6–10, along with parents and grandparents. Concerts last about 45 minutes; the cost is $8/ticket.

The Seattle Chamber Music Society has an excellent outreach program for middle and high school students, including invitations to open rehearsals.

Seattle Girls' Choir

(206) 526-1900
info@seattlegirlschoir.org
www.seattlegirlschoir.org

The highly acclaimed Seattle Girls' Choir has six choirs, from junior preparatory to advanced, for girls ages 6–18. Prime Voci, the Seattle Girls' Advanced
Choir, is internationally renowned. Participation is fun and includes the opportunity to attend choir summer camp at beautiful Ft. Flagler. Auditions are low-
key and no previous musical experience is necessary. The choir performs
frequently in the Seattle area, including with the Argosy Christmas Ships in
December, a spring festival concert in May, and a summer concert.

Seattle Symphony

Benaroya Hall, Second Ave. and Union St., Seattle
(206) 215-4747 (tickets); (206) 215-4700 (administration)
www.seattlesymphony.org

Season: Sept.–July

The Seattle Symphony offers an impressive array of concerts for adults. Equally
impressive are the programs for children and teens. You can get series tickets
for all the programs, and that's a good way to go, since single-ticket sales for
these special concerts can be very limited.

The Tiny Tots program, a series of five 40-minute concerts, is for children
birth to age 5. Concerts are offered at child-friendly times on Fridays and Saturdays. The concerts offer participatory and listening activities and feature
musical performers, including Let Your Music Shine, the Rainier Chamber
Winds, and Seattle Symphony musicians.

Discover Music is a long-standing popular series designed to introduce
kids ages 5–12 to the world of classical music. Concerts are at 11 A.M. on Saturday
mornings, with pre-concert activities beginning at 10 A.M. Performers are
expert at captivating young audiences with entertainment that is cleverly laced
with lessons in music basics. Families can also come one hour early and participate in a variety of hands-on activities, such as making instruments and learning new tunes.

Hands-on "Discover Music Enhancement Classes" to build on the experience of the Discover Music series are also offered, and include a craft project used in a musical play, dance, and percussion activity. Classes are offered Oct.–May, 2 P.M.–3 P.M. on Sunday. Cost is $3/class, call (206) 336-6600 to register.

The Seattle Symphony also offers occasional free community concerts, designated especially for families. Its Symphony on Wheels outreach program is designed to bring music into the community.

Seattle Opera
McCaw Hall, Seattle Center
(206) 389-7600; (206) 389-7676 (tickets)
www.seattleopera.org

The Seattle Opera offers discount student tickets and Family Day Matinees, when students accompanied by an adult pay $15. Family Days also feature special activities oriented to young people in the lobby, as well as complimentary admission to both the pre-show "Overtures" and post-show Q&A session.

Seattle Youth Symphony Orchestra
11065 Fifth Ave. N.E., Ste. A, Seattle
(206) 362-2300
www.syso.org

Season: Nov.–May

The Seattle Youth Symphony Orchestra, the largest such organization in the country, serves more than 1,100 young musicians through four full programs, three summer programs, and partnerships with local schools. Through generous financial aid programs, all interested students may participate. Each orchestra performs three concerts a year. Performances are held at several venues in Seattle including Meany Theatre on the UW campus and Benaroya Hall in downtown Seattle. Young performers invariably give first-rate concerts and provide fine role models to inspire the young musicians in your family. The company runs summer programs—Marrowstone, a residential program at Western Washington University in Bellingham, and Marrowstone in the City, held in Seattle.

Soundbridge Seattle Symphony Music Discovery Center

Benaroya Hall, Second Ave. and Union St., Seattle
(206) 336-6600
www.seattlesymphony.org/soundbridge

Hours: Tues.–Sun., 10 A.M.–4 P.M.

Admission: $7/adults, $5/ages 5–18, free/under 5

If your kids have an inkling of interest in music—and every child does—you won't want to miss Soundbridge, the Seattle Symphony's center devoted to musical education for all ages. This wonderful facility has a series of exhibits sure to enthrall as well as to educate. At the Listening Bar, visitors can listen to more than 500 symphonic works; the Science of Sound Wall explains how hearing works, the relationship between music and science, and how the physical properties of sound relate to music making. There's an oscilloscope that displays actual sound waves. In another area, visitors can explore—through seeing, touching, and hearing—the various instruments that make up a symphony orchestra. At the Meet the Musicians station, kids can hear symphony musicians talking about their relationship to music. Interactive kiosks throughout Soundbridge connect visitors with an array of information about instruments, pieces of music, and the music world.

Soundbridge also provides another facet of the outstanding education program offered by the Seattle Symphony. Workshops for families, classes for young kids from infants on up, programs for teachers, and musical birthday parties are also offered.

University of Washington School of Music

(206) 543-1201
www.music.washington.edu/events

Admission: Prices vary; some concerts are free

The University of Washington School of Music presents musical entertainment throughout the year, performed by students, faculty, and guest artists. Concerts are held at Meany Theatre and other sites on campus. Programs include vocal, instrumental, and group and solo performances, including pieces by contemporary artists as well as the masters.

UW World Series
Meany Theatre, University of Washington
(206) 543-4880 (tickets); (206) 543-4882 (administrative office)
www.uwworldseries.org

Season: Oct.–May

Admission: Prices vary by performance

More than a music series, the UW World Series is a performing-arts series that includes dance, acrobatics, and musicians representing cultures from throughout the world. Some performances will be of more interest to families than others. There are some daytime performances especially for children.

Theaters

Auburn Ave. Theater
10 Auburn Ave., Auburn
(253) 833-5678
www.ci.auburn.wa.us/arts/auburn_avenue_theater

For over 30 years, the Auburn Theater has brought to the town of Auburn Broadway musicals, children's theater, and concerts. After the Douglas family, producers of the dinner theater that performed in this location for 20 years, leased the theater to the city of Auburn, it was revived as a place where all ages can enjoy quality entertainment. Check the website for the many events suitable for families.

Parent Tips

Ticket/Ticket (401 Broadway Ave. E., Seattle, and at the Pike Place Market Information Booth, 206-324-2744) sells half-price day-of-show tickets for theater, dance, music, and comedy productions. Tickets must be purchased at the booths with cash only.

....

Bainbridge Performing Arts

The Playhouse, 200 Madison Ave. N., Bainbridge Island
(206) 842-8569 (box office); (206) 842-8578 (business office)
www.bainbridgeperformingarts.org

For almost 50 years, Bainbridge Performing Arts has been an integral part of the Bainbridge Island community, presenting a wide variety of theater productions, including dramas, musicals, and children's favorites. In its home at The Playhouse (a short walk from the Winslow ferry), BPA hosts a theater school, The Edge Improv, a chamber music series, concerts, and performances by the Bainbridge Orchestra.

....

Bellevue Civic Theatre

Meydenbauer Center, 11100 N.E. Sixth St., Bellevue
(425) 235-5087
www.bellevuecivic.org

This community theater specializes in comedies and musicals. Most are not appropriate for very young children, but would be enjoyed by teens. A recent season included the musical revue *Forever Plaid* and the Pulitzer Prize winner *Crimes of the Heart*. Watch for special family-oriented plays around the holidays.

....

Civic Light Opera

Shoreline Conference Center, N.E. 185th Ave. and First St. N.E, Seattle
(206) 363-2809
www.seattlemusicaltheatre.com

Season: Sept.–May

Admission: $25–$35/person

Don't be misled by the world "opera" in the title of this organization. Instead of traditional operas in foreign languages, the Civic Light Opera does four Broadway-style musical productions each season.

5th Avenue Theatre
1308 Fifth Ave., Seattle
(206) 625-1900, (888) 5TH-4TIX
www.5thavenuetheatre.org

Season: Aug.–May

Admission: $20–$80; discounts available on preview nights

If you're looking for a Broadway musical experience, this is the place to come. The 5th Avenue season usually includes a number of popular family-friendly musicals.

The 5th Avenue also offers theater classes for youth, outreach in the schools, and the 5th Avenue High School Musical Theatre Awards, an exciting "Tony Awards" annual event in June honoring achievements of high school drama students that is fun and motivating for the aspiring drama student to watch.

Langston Hughes Cultural Arts Center
104 17th Ave. S., Seattle
(206) 684-4757
www.seattle.gov/parks/centers.langston.htm

This cultural performing-arts center is operated by the Seattle Department of Parks and Recreation. It offers a variety of cultural and educational events, including theater productions aimed at a family audience that reflect the cultural diversity of the surrounding neighborhoods, the Central District and the International District. A summer youth theater program culminates in a public performance.

Northwest Puppet Center

9123 15th Ave. N.E., Seattle

(206) 523-2579

www.nwpuppet.org

Season: Sept.–May

Admission: Call or check website for prices.

A Seattle child's theater education is not complete until they see a puppet performance at the Northwest Puppet Center. Seattle's only permanent puppet theater offers seven exceptionally well-produced productions for the entire family each year. Puppet companies from around the world are featured, as are performances by the award-winning resident company, the Carter Family Marionettes. The center, which is housed in a former church in a residential neighborhood, strives to present different styles of puppetry. The center has a small picnic area and playground that can be enjoyed before and after the show.

Piped Piper

Everett Performing Arts Center, 2710 Wetmore Ave., Everett

(425) 257-8600

www.villagetheatre.org

Season: Oct.–May

Admission: $12–$14/person

Piped Piper is the company-in-residence of the Everett Performing Arts Center, and is affiliated with the Village Theatre, which offers performances in both Everett and Issaquah. It has an extensive program of performances for schools in the Snohomish County area as well as public performances, including music, theater, and even vaudeville.

Renton Civic Theatre
507 S. Third St., Renton
(425) 226-5529
www.rentoncivictheater.org

Season: Aug.–June

Admission: $22/adults, $18/ seniors and students 18 and under

Renton Civic Theatre, a professional theater located in downtown Renton, offers a full season of musicals, dramas, and comedies, most of which are suitable for families. Recent productions included *The Fantastiks*, *The Best Christmas Pageant Ever*, and *Spider's Web*, an Agatha Christie mystery. Productions are most suitable for older children.

Seattle Children's Theatre
Charlotte Martin Theatre and Eve Alvord Theatre, Seattle Center, Seattle
(206) 443-0807; (206) 441-3322 (tickets)
www.sct.org

Season: Oct.–May

Admission: $7–$40/adults, $13–$30/children 17 and under. Flex passes available.

Rated one of the top children's theater companies in the United States, Seattle Children's Theatre offers some of the very best in family entertainment. Most seasons offer several world premieres, with some productions targeted at younger (ages 1–4) and older (ages 11–18) children. Performances include a question-and-answer period with the actors after the show—always a big hit.

In addition to its theater productions, the SCT Drama School offers year-round theater arts classes, workshops, day camps, and a summer program for students ages 3–21. It also has a Deaf Youth Drama Program, one of only a few in the country.

Seattle Public Theater at the Bathhouse
7312 W. Green Lake Dr. N., Seattle
(206) 524-1300
www.seattlepublictheater.org

Season: Sept.–Aug.

Admission: Prices vary

Seattle Public Theater is the resident theater company at the Bathhouse Theatre, a charming little space sitting on the north shore of Green Lake. This talented group offers five or six main-stage shows each year, along with an outstanding summer youth program and year-round classes for kids. Attendance of their production of *The Best Christmas Pageant Ever*, based on a popular children's book by Barbara Robinson, has become a holiday tradition for many Seattle families. Shows that are the outcome of the youth program are free to attend. These youth shows often include at least one Shakespeare performance every summer and are an excellent way to watch a production in an intimate setting at low cost.

Seattle Shakespeare Company
Center House Theater, Seattle Center, Seattle
(206) 733-8222
www.seattleshakespeare.org

Admission: Call for ticket prices.

Students who read Shakespeare as part of their class assignments will be thrilled to actually see a production. Even much younger children will appreciate the drama and intrigue, especially if you go over in advance the basic storyline of the play. The Seattle Shakespeare Company annually stages four to six of the Bard's plays at their small theater on the lower level of the Center House at the Seattle Center. A matinee program offers special student performances of each production at a significant discount.

Every summer they offer an extensive Shakespeare in the Park production at parks throughout greater Seattle. This is a free, fun, and easy way to introduce kids to Shakespeare.

Shakespeare in the Park—GreenStage
(206) 748-1551
www.greenstage.org

Season: Summer

Admission: Free

Each summer, for over 20 years, GreenStage has presented Shakespeare's plays in Seattle public parks. Audience members are encouraged to bring lawn chairs or blankets and a picnic lunch or dinner. And if it rains? The show usually goes on; lightning will cancel a performance. The theater has a permanent home at Seattle's Sand Point Magnuson Park and offers a Shakespeare day camp every summer. As Seattle's Shakespeare in the Park Company, they are committed to presenting quality productions of classical theater in a manner that is available to all—performing for free in order to reach the largest possible audience.

Seattle Storytelling Guild
(206) 621-8646
www.seattlestorytelling.org

Founded in 1982, the Seattle Storytelling Guild is one of the strongest storytelling organizations in the country. It is a nonprofit organization of tellers and story enthusiasts who actively promote the art of storytelling for adults as well as children, at frequent events that take place at community centers, libraries, bookstores, and other venues. On its website, you can even listen to a story read by a local storyteller.

The guild also hosts performances and workshops throughout the year, including Tellabration, a worldwide celebration of storytelling in November, and assists with storytelling at the Northwest Folklife Festival in May. In addition, the Seattle Storytelling Guild publishes *In the Wind*, a quarterly newsletter.

Snoqualmie Falls Forest Theatre

36800 S.E. David Powell Rd., Fall City
(425) 736-7252 (tickets); (425) 222-7044 (business office)
www.foresttheater.org

Hours: July–Aug., Sat. 3 P.M. and 8 P.M.; Sun. 3 P.M.

Admission: $18/adults, $16/students, $8/ages 6–12, under 6 free. Optional BBQ dinners before the show $9–$16 (also $5 hot dog available).

Located just east of Issaquah in Fall City, the Snoqualmie Falls Forest Theatre has offered open-air theater productions for over 43 years. Visitors to this outdoor theater, set within 95 acres of natural forest, will also enjoy a view of Snoqualmie Falls. Optional steak, chicken, or salmon barbecue dinners are served at approximately 5:30 P.M.—either prior to the evening performance or after the matinee. Reservations are required for dinner and recommended for all theater performances. The theater is a short walk from the free parking area and is accessible for the handicapped. Be sure to bring sweaters as evenings can get chilly.

Sprouts Children's Theatre

16587 N.E. 74th St., Redmond
(425) 881-6777
www.secondstoryrep.org

Season: Year-round

Admission: $8.75/person

Sprouts knows its audience: young kids with short attention spans. That's why the musical productions, featuring songs, magic, and audience participation, are just one hour long. *The Emperor's New Clothes*, *Little Red Riding Hood*, and *Cinderella* are examples of the familiar storybook tales this theater group adapts for the stage.

Storybook Theatre

Studio East, 402 Sixth St. S., Kirkland
(425) 827-3123
studio-east.org

Admission: $9

Especially for children ages 3–9, Storybook Theatre uses professional adult actors to present original adaptations of traditional fairy tales. Shows are 55 minutes in length, and children in the audience are encouraged to use their imagination and creativity to participate in the shows. While Storybook is housed at Studio East in Kirkland, its productions are offered at several venues in the Puget Sound area, including the Carco Theatre in Renton, Edmonds Center for the Arts, and Kirkland Performance Center. Some performances are limited to school audiences.

Studio East

402 Sixth St. S., Kirkland
(425) 827-3123
studio-east.org

Season: Oct.–Aug.

Admission: Varies by show

Studio East's outstanding Eastside youth theater program, located in Kirkland, presents several shows a season, including a full-length summer musical featuring teens. Attending these productions is an excellent way to give your child a theater experience at reasonable cost.

Thistle Theatre

(206) 524-3388
www.thistletheatre.org

Season: Sept.–June

Admission: Varies by show

Thistle Theatre specializes in Bunraku, a variation of the ancient Japanese style of puppetry. The puppeteers dress head-to-toe in black and visibly move puppets on stage for an unusual and captivating theater experience. Performances are held at locations in Bellevue, Seattle, and Burien. Most shows are recommended for ages 3 and up.

Village Theatre/Kidstage

Everett Performing Arts Center, Everett, 2710 Wetmore Ave., Everett
Frances J. Gaudette Theater, 303 Front St., Issaquah
(425) 257-8600 (Everett); (425) 392-2202 (Issaquah)
www.villagetheatre.org

Season: Year-round

Admission: Varies by show. Family room tickets (Issaquah only) available.

Village Theatre presents a variety of plays, most of which are appropriate for families. The season usually includes several musicals, such as *Man of La Mancha* and *South Pacific*. The play that spans the holiday season is invariably a family-friendly show, such as *The Secret Garden*. Village Theatre productions run first at the theater in Issaquah and then move to Everett for another run. The Issaquah theater features a Family Room so even parents with infants and small children can enjoy the shows. Kidstage, a theater-arts education program, offers classes for children age 3 and up in both Everett and Issaquah. Performance opportunities are part of the program. Pied Piper, which produces shows especially for children, is part of Village Theatre.

Youth Theatre Northwest

8805 S.E. 40th St., Mercer Island
(206) 232-4145
www.youtheatrenorthwest.org

Season: Year-round

Admission: $15/person opening night, $13/all other nights

Youth Theatre Northwest on Mercer Island presents shows that are by and for children. The regular season includes a mix of shows especially for younger children, as well as those appropriate for older kids. The theater, located in a remodeled middle school, has been in operation for over 25 years. Along with the plays it produces, it offers an extensive array of theater classes and camps for kids.

....

Dance

....

Ballet Bellevue
(425) 455-1345
www.balletbellevue.org

Ballet Bellevue, a small company, has a vision of bringing world-class performances to local audiences. The company repertoire features classical ballets, contemporary masterpieces, and new works. It frequently produces a holiday dance concert as part of downtown Bellevue's Magic Season in December.

....

Cornish College of the Arts
710 E. Roy, Seattle
(206) 726-5066
www.cornish.edu

Admission: $10/adults, $7/seniors and students

The Cornish Junior Dance Company, part of the school's Preparatory Dance Division for students ages 4–18, performs a spring concert for the public in May. The dancers present a repertory of original choreography and classical pieces in modern dance as well as ballet. The company usually also offers a holiday concert in December.

Kaleidoscope Dance Company

(206) 363-7281

www.creativedance.org

The Northwest's only professional modern dance company of young people, Kaleidoscope presents several concerts each year. The company also often performs at schools and community events throughout the year. Founder Ann Gilbert has also created a strong dance education program for ages birth through adult, including the Braindance program, based on a philosophy integrating brain development with movement. Birthday parties that include a creative dance instructor to lead the group in dance fun and field trips that allows schoolchildren to experience creative dance are also offered.

Olympic Ballet Theatre

700 Main St., Edmonds

(425) 774-7570

www.olympicballet.com

Season: Dec.–May

The Edmonds-based ballet company, which also offers classes for students ages 3 and up, performs *The Nutcracker* each December and also annually presents a family production, such as *Peter and the Wolf* at various venues in the area, including Everett, Kirkland, and Seattle. The Easter Bunny Brunch features music as well as dance improvisation. The ballet company also offers several other performances during the year.

Pacific Northwest Ballet
301 Mercer St., Seattle
(206) 441-9411; (206) 441-2424 (box office)
www.pnb.org

Season: Year-round

Seattle's largest ballet company presents several performances of classic and contemporary works each year at Seattle Center's McCaw Hall and on tour. In November and December, it performs *The Nutcracker* at the Seattle Opera House, a family tradition for many Seattle families, with sets and costumes designed by Maurice Sendak.

PNB makes extensive efforts to educate youth in the community about ballet and make it accessible. Their annual Special Family Matinee Series features hour-long performances by PNB students, with programs especially suited to young children and afternoon matinees for families. Past presentations have included *Pinocchio* and *Snow White and the Seven Dwarfs*. The Eyes on Dance program includes student matinees, as well as programs in the schools to learn about the featured ballet.

Chapter 4

Harvests

In the urban and suburban world of 24-hour grocery stores and we-have-everything warehouses, it is easy for a child to grow up without knowing the real source of food and plants: **land** and **farms**. And though the convenience of being able to buy your own food, pumpkins, and even **Christmas trees** at the local supermarket is undeniable, there is much to be said for the experience of going out to the farms where these goods are grown. Luckily, you don't have to drive too far to get back to **nature,** and the minute you are out of city and suburban traffic, you'll be glad you made the effort. The sweet fragrance of a **strawberry** field, the cool frost on a **pumpkin** patch, the braying and neighing of farm animals—these rural sights, smells, and sounds are quite alluring, and the entire family will be better off for a bit of country air.

Farmers Markets

Even if you don't have the time or inclination to grow your own vegetables or drive to the real deal, you can still get fresh produce and a pleasant shopping experience at one of the area's many farmers markets. Rich in colors, sights, smells, and sounds, these markets present a plentiful array of fresh-from-the-garden vegetables, fruits, and flowers, as well as clothes, jewelry, and other items made by local craftspeople and street artists. Just about every neighborhood in the area seems to be getting their own farmers market, and many now continue year-round. For the most up-to-date information about farmers markets, including hours and locations, as well as what produce is in season, go to *www.pugetsoundfresh.com.*

- **Ballard Farmers Market**, 5300 Ballard Ave. N.W., Seattle; year-round, Sun., 10 A.M.–3 P.M.

- **Bothell Country Village Farmers Market**, Country Village, 23732 Bothell–Everett Hwy., Bothell, (425) 483-2250; June–Sept., Fri., noon–6 P.M.

- **Broadway Farmers Market**, 10th Ave. E. and E. Thomas, Seattle; May–Nov., Sun., 11 A.M.–3 P.M.

- **Burien Farmers Market**, Fourth Ave. S.W., between 150th and 152nd, Burien, (206) 433-2882; mid-May–Sept., Thurs., 11 A.M.–6 P.M.

- **Columbia City Farmers Market**, Columbia Plaza, 4801 Rainier Ave. S., Seattle; late Apr.–late Oct., Wed., 3–7 P.M.

- **Edmonds Museum Summer Market**, Bell St., between Fifth and Sixth, Edmonds, (425) 775-5650; July–Oct., Sat., 9 A.M.–3 P.M.

- **Everett Farmers Market**, 1600 W. Marine View Dr., Everett, (425) 258-3356; June–end of Sept., Sun., 11 A.M.–4 P.M.

- **Issaquah Public Market**, Pickering Barn, 1730 10th Ave. N.E., Issaquah, (425) 837-3311; mid-Apr.–mid-Oct., Sat., 9 A.M.–2 P.M.

- **Kirkland Wednesday Market**, Park Ln. E., between Third and Main, Kirkland, (425) 893-8766; May–mid-Oct., Wed., 2–7 P.M.

- **Lake City Farmers Market**, N.E. 127th St. and 30th Ave. N.E., Lake City, (206) 632-5234; June–mid-Oct., Thurs., 3–7 P.M.

- **Magnolia Farmers Market**, Magnolia Community Center, 2550 34th Ave. W., Seattle, (206) 632-5234; mid-June–mid-Oct., Sat., 10 A.M.–2 P.M.

- **North Bend Farmers Market**, North Bend Senior Center, Main and Park at Hwy 202, North Bend, (425) 888-3434; June–Sept., Thurs., 4–8 P.M.

- **Phinney Farmers Market**, Phinney Neighborhood Center, 67th and Phinney Ave. N., Seattle; Fri., 3–7 P.M.

- **Pike Place Market**, First Ave. and Pike St., Seattle, (206) 682-7453; year-round, Mon.–Sat., 9 A.M.–6 P.M.; Sun., 10 A.M.–5 P.M.

- **Redmond Saturday Market**, 7730 Leary Way at Bear Creek Pkwy., Redmond, (425) 556-0636; May–Oct., Sat., 9 A.M.–3 P.M.

- **Renton Farmers Market**, S. Third St., at the piazza between Logan and Burnett, Renton, (425) 226-4560; mid-June–early Sept., Tues., 3–7 P.M.

- **Snohomish Farmers Market**, First Ave., two blocks west of bridge, Snohomish, (360) 668-5599; May–end of Sept., Thurs., 3–8 P.M.

- **Tacoma Farmers Market**, Broadway between S. Seventh and S. Ninth, Tacoma, (253) 272-7077; June–mid-Oct., Thurs., 9 A.M.–2 P.M.

- **Tacoma-Proctor Farmers Market**, N. 27th St. at Proctor, Tacoma, (253) 961-3666; Apr.–mid-Nov., Sat., 9 A.M.–2 P.M.

- **University District Saturday Market**, N.E. 50th St. and University Way N.E., Seattle, (206) 633-5234; year-round, Sat., 9 A.M.–2 P.M.

- **West Seattle Farmers Market**, Alaskan Way and California St., Seattle, (206) 632-5234; year-round, mid-May–Nov., Sun., 10 A.M.–2 P.M.

Parent Tips

Puget Sound Fresh is a buy-local program presented by the Cascade Harvest Coalition. It supports farms in 12 counties in Washington State. It distributes a printed guide, *Farm Fresh*, in the spring that lists names, addresses, crops, and hours of operation for many of the U-pick farms throughout King, Pierce, Skagit, and Snohomish counties. The guide is available free at public libraries and chamber of commerce offices.

For the most up-to-date information on U-pick farms, farmers markets, harvest schedules, and farm-fresh recipes from local farmers as well as information about the CSAs—a weekly farm delivery system for getting fresh, local food delivered to your neighborhood or house—see the Puget Sound Fresh website *(www.pugetsoundfresh.com)*.

- **White Center Farmers Market**, 15th St. S.W., Seattle, (206) 694-1082; June–Oct., Sat., 10 A.M.–2 P.M.

- **Woodinville Farmers Market**, 14700 NE 145th, Woodinville, *www.woodinville farmersmarket.com*; (425) 546-7960; mid-Apr., May.–mid-Oct., Sat., 9 A.M.–3 P.M.

....

Farms to Visit

....

Biringer Farm
4625 40th Pl. N.E., Everett
(425) 259-0255
www.biringerfarm.com

Families can pick berries in the summer, select pumpkins, and puzzle their way out of a maze in the fall. This family-friendly working farm also offers tours and a picnic area. Call for information about seasonal hours and special events.

....

Fall City Farms
3636 Neal Rd., Fall City
(425) 222-4533
www.fallcityfarms.com

You can pick your own produce or buy it at the farm store, which opens in mid-July and features a wide variety of vegetables, fruits, herbs, and flowers. Owners Debbie and Rob Arenth believe that their farm serves as an agricultural education—and culinary—resource. Tours are offered for all ages. Special events include Apple Day (the farm's orchard has 15 varieties of apples) and a variety of October activities. Wagon rides, a petting zoo, and a picnic area are available. Call for information on special events before you go.

Fosters Produce, Corn Maze, and Pumpkin Patch

5818 SR 530 N.E., Arlington
(360) 435-5095
www.fosterscornmaze.com

It's no surprise, given its name, that this farm offers a corn maze in the fall. But there's more here, including the Flower Field Festival in the spring with U-pick daffodils and tulips, National Dairy Month in June, and Apple Cider Pressing Days in the fall—along with that corn maze and a pumpkin patch. The farm barn features milking stalls (Fosters was originally a dairy farm) and antiques. Visit the "goat walk" and old Western town, and enjoy seeing farm animals, including rabbits, goats, sheep, chickens, pigs, and cows. Antiques, gifts, and ice cream are also available, along with plenty of produce.

Remlinger Farms

32610 N.E. 32nd St., Carnation
(425) 333-4135
www.remlingerfarms.com

If there is a farm that has it all, Remlinger is surely it. Remlinger caters to families in a big way, offering a petting zoo, many U-pick opportunities, wagon rides, steam train rides, a Country Fair Fun Park, pony rides, performances especially for children, and a country store and restaurant. Special events include a U-pick Strawberry Festival in June, a U-pick Raspberry Festival in July, and a U-pick Pumpkin Festival in October. Seasonal theme tours—such as the Spring Planting and Bee Tour, and the Pony and Baby Animal Tour—are offered, and if your child really loves this farm, he can have his birthday party here. The store is large and offers gifts as well as produce. Be sure and stop by the restaurant and bakery for delicious, wholesome fare.

Serres Farm

20306 N.E. 50th St., Redmond
(425) 868-3017

Enjoy U-pick strawberries in June, a corn maze and pumpkin patch in the fall, and U-cut Christmas trees in December at this low-key farm. The property includes a big red barn and a pretty creek.

South 47 Farm

15410 N.E. 124th St., Redmond
(425) 869-9777
www.south47farm.com

This 47-acre farm is a project of FARM LLC, a group working to preserve farm-land and support sustainable agriculture in the fertile Sammamish Valley. Six farmers, along with P-Patchers (see next page), lease space here and grow ber-ries, vegetables, herbs, and flowers. Some land is available for U-pick. Special events include a pumpkin patch, corn maze, and hay rides.

Parent Tips

Farm Tots is a fun chance for little ones, accompanied by a grown-up, to explore the South 47 Farm (*www.south47farm.com*) at their own pace. Kids get to take a wagon ride, do an art or nature activity, and pick a child-sized portion of seasonal U-pick crops. Open to children ages 5 and under with a parent or guardian. No reservations necessary.

The Frequent Farmer punch card ($33) is good for six Farm Tots vis-its for one child. For more information on the Farm Tots program, call (425) 753-0756.

Gardening Programs

Seattle P-Patch Community Gardening Program
City of Seattle, Department of Neighborhoods
(206) 684-0264
www.cityofseattle.net/neighborhoods/ppatch

If visiting a farm has whet your appetite for growing things, but you don't have space of your own, consider participating in a community P-Patch program. The Seattle Department of Neighborhoods in conjunction with the nonprofit Friends of P-Patch, allows Seattle residents to organically grow vegetables, small fruits, and/or flowers in one of 44 neighborhood garden sites. The P-Patch Program also serves refugees, low-income, disabled (some gardens are wheelchair accessible), and youth gardeners.

The P-Patch plots range in size from 100 to 400 square feet; there is a nominal annual fee. Many P-Patch communities set aside a plot to grow produce for food banks; most also donate excess produce (to the tune of a collective 10 tons a year) to food banks. There is a waiting list for P-Patches; currently the city estimates that 1,800 gardeners participate in the program.

Each year, 10 to 20 percent of the P-Patches turn over, but waiting lists exceed that turnover rate, so you may have to wait a while before you can claim a patch. While you're waiting for a patch, consider volunteering—many P-Patch communities hold work parties or seek volunteers to help with communal herb and flower beds. Check out the website for detailed information about the program, exact location of P-Patch garden sites, information on signing up for your own patch, and volunteer opportunities.

Seattle Tilth Children's Garden
4649 Sunnyside Ave. N., Seattle
1730 10th Ave. N.W., Issaquah
(206) 633-0451
www.seattletilth.org

The Seattle Tilth Association, located in the Wallingford neighborhood, promotes organic gardening, conservation of natural resources, and support for local food systems. It teaches children about gardening and fosters an appreciation for our connection to all living things. The Association offers a variety of classes and camps during the summer for children ages 1–14. Children learn about insects and soil, tend gardens, and grow food. Children can also participate in activities during the annual Organic Harvest Fair in September.

U-Pick Farms

Berry picking in early summer, pumpkin harvesting in October, and cutting Christmas trees in December are all fine family traditions and good excuses for a trip to the countryside.

The following are some of the best places to U-pick, as well as tips for a successful outing.

Berry Picking

Just about the time summer vacation begins, ripe strawberries, raspberries, and blueberries are ready for picking. Boxes are usually supplied at U-pick farms. A staff member will assign you and your kids a row where you can pick to your heart's content. When you're finished, someone weighs your berries and you pay by the pound. Reservations are not necessary, but call ahead to make sure berries are available. Try to go early in the day, when the selection is best. Many fields are pretty bare by the end of the day. It's hard work, but the rewards are immediate.

When berry picking, use sunscreen and hats and bring food and plenty of drinks. Also, show the kids how to maneuver between the rows of plants carefully. Make sure they understand which berries are ripe for picking (there are little secrets the farms might share), and don't pick more than your family can eat or process in a day or two, because berries spoil quickly.

- **Aarstad Blueberry Farm**, 6201 163rd Ave. S.E., Snohomish, (360) 568-6067; blueberries
- **Biringer Farm**, Hwy. 529, north of Everett and south of Marysville, (425) 259-0255, *www.biringerfarm.com*; strawberries, raspberries
- **Blue Dog Farm**, 7125 W. Snoqualmie Valley Rd. N.E., Carnation, (425) 844-2842; blueberries
- **Bryant Blueberry Farm and Garden**, 5628 Grandview Rd., Arlington, (425) 474-8424; blueberries
- **Bybee-Nims Farms**, 42930 S.E. 92nd St., North Bend, (425) 888-0821; blueberries
- **Cottage Gardens Blueberry Farm**, 14510 Kelly Rd. N.E., Duvall, (425) 947-4523; blueberries
- **Due's Berry Farm**, 4604 152nd St. N.E., Marysville, (360) 659-3875; strawberries
- **Harvold Berry Farm**, 32325 N.E. 55th, Carnation, (425) 333-4185; strawberries, raspberries
- **John Hamakami Strawberry Farm**, 14733 S.E. Green Valley Rd., Auburn, (253) 833-2081; strawberries
- **Kennydale Blueberry Farm**, 1733 N.E. 20th St., Renton, (425) 228-9623; blueberries
- **Paradise Berry Farms**, 832 Valley Ave. N.W., Puyallup, (253) 435-1300; strawberries, raspberries
- **Remlinger Farms**, 32610 N.E. 32nd St., Carnation, (425) 333-4135, *www.remlingerfarms.com*; strawberries, raspberries
- **Serres Farm**, 20306 N.E. 50th St., Redmond, (425) 868-3017; strawberries
- **South 47 Farm**, 15410 124th St., Redmond, (425) 869-9777, *www.south47farm.com*; strawberries, raspberries

Christmas Trees

Bundle up the family and visit one of the area's Christmas tree farms for a special outing during the winter holidays. Many farms offer hot cider, coffee, and holiday goodies, as well as special attractions, such as tractor rides and visits with Santa. Each year, the Puget Sound Christmas Tree Association publishes a guide with its member Christmas tree farms including addresses, phone numbers, and hours of operation for each farm, as well as special amenities. This free guide is available during November and December at chamber of commerce offices and public libraries throughout the Puget Sound area. It's also available at *pscta.org*. We list just a few of the local tree farms below.

The Pacific Northwest Christmas Tree Association also publishes a guide covering Washington and Oregon, which is available locally during the holidays. Call (503) 364-2942 to receive a free copy or for more information, or go to *nwtrees.com/washington.htm*.

Before leaving on your outing, it's a good idea to check with the farm you hope to visit, to make sure trees are still available. In some years, stock may be low at a particular tree farm, causing it to close early—or in some cases—never open that year. Be sure to bring boots along, as well as other wet-weather gear. This is a damp time of year.

Another option for those who like to get a really fresh tree, is to get a permit from the U.S. Forest Service. The Forest Service issues permits for $10, allowing the permit holder to cut a tree in a specified area. Call the local ranger station for areas and permit information: Darrington, (360) 436-1155; Mt. Baker at Sedro-Woolley, (360) 856-5700; REI Lynnwood, (425) 774-1300; Skykomish, (360) 677-2414; Snoqualmie at Enumclaw, (360) 825-6585; and Snoqualmie at North Bend, (425) 888-1421. Tree permit sales usually begin in mid-November. A limited number of permits are available.

This can be a wonderful adventure for your family. But be forewarned. The areas designated by the Forest Service can be quite remote, requiring that you drive on primitive roads. You may be directed to an area at a fairly high elevation, making it more likely that there will be snow on the road. Be sure you carry chains in your car, a snow shovel into the trunk, extra warm clothing along for everyone, and a few snacks.

As romantic as they sound, family outings to find a Christmas tree have the potential to turn into a tortured experience in failed group decision-making. Whether you search for your tree at a Christmas tree lot in the city or venture out to a tree farm, discuss in advance how the group will choose a tree (a lesson in compromise or dictatorship). It's also a good idea to measure the height of the room the tree will stand in, before leaving the house—and then bring a tape measure along with you. Trees always look much smaller in the great outdoors than they do when you bring them into your house.

Carnation Tree Farm
31523 N.E. 40th St., Carnation
(425) 333-4510
www.carnationtreefarm.com

A designated historic landmark, this tree farm has been in the same Norwegian family for more than a century. Shop for ornaments, handcrafted gifts, wreaths, and tree stands in the old barn. There's also complimentary hot cider, which can be enjoyed with the baked goods that are for sale. Kids can visit Santa on the weekends and take a pony ride. Oh—and don't forget the tree!

Christmas Creek Tree Farm
15515 468th Ave. S.E., North Bend
(425) 488-2099
www.yourchristmastree.com

Enjoy a hayride with Santa on the weekends at this tree farm, which also features a warming shelter with fire, cookies, complimentary hot cider, and a Christmas shop. Trees, wreaths, boughs, and holly are the main attractions.

Mountain Creek Tree Farm
6821 440th Ave. S.E., Snoqualmie
(425) 888-1770

Tromp through the trees that grow along a creek and up a hill at this tree farm, which also offers a gift shop with handcrafted items.

Pilchuck Secret Valley Christmas Tree Farm
9533 Mose Rd., Arlington
(360) 435-9799

A wide variety of U-cut trees are available. After you cut your tree, enjoy hot drinks around a fire and browse through a selection of gifts and decorations.

Redmond Tree Farm
14001 Redmond-Woodinville Rd., Redmond
(425) 487-3447

Cut your tree, or choose one from those that have been freshly cut. Then enjoy a hayride, free candy canes, and hot drinks.

Red-Wood Farm
13925 Redmond-Woodinville Rd. N.E., Redmond
(425) 482-6798
www.red-woodfarm.com

Hayrides and hot beverages round out the U-cut experience at this Redmond farm. Many related products—wreaths, swags, and holly—are also available.

Trinity Tree Farm
14237 228th Ave. S.E., Issaquah
(425) 391-8733

After selecting and cutting a tree, you can enjoy complimentary hot drinks by a bonfire, visit Santa on weekends, and buy decorations and ornaments from the gift shop.

Pumpkin Patches and Mazes

Just when the fallen leaves have been drained of their last vestiges of color and the dreary drizzle of autumn has settled in, Halloween comes along and rejuvenates our spirits (quite literally according to some). Children adore this holiday: creating fun costumes, trick-or-treating, and, of course, carving their jack-o'-lanterns for display on the windowsill or porch.

Many pumpkin farms offer an array of special activities throughout October, including hayrides, haunted houses, scarecrows, hay mazes, and costumed characters. Corn mazes are a new and popular twist, and often open at the end of August or early September. Sometimes these are located at a farm in conjunction with pumpkin patches, and sometimes created at a different location. These mazes are often quite amazing and provide the whole family with some wholesome entertainment, but be careful—it is easy to lose a child in the twists and turns.

With both pumpkin patches and corn mazes, be sure to call ahead for hours of operation; many farms are not open every day, and some are only open on weekends. Also verify special events since they're apt to change from year to year.

At most farms, pumpkins have already been cut from the vine and are lying free in the fields. The cost of the pumpkins varies from farm to farm but is usually determined individually by weight. Remember to dress for the weather, wear your boots, and bring the camera!

The following are just a few of the farms in the area with pumpkins to pick and fun October harvest activities. For a more complete list, go to *www.puget soundfresh.com.*

....

Biringer Farm

Hwy. 529, north of Everett and south of Marysville
(425) 259-0255
www.biringerfarm.com

The month-long schedule of activities and attractions during October includes a pumpkin village, "boo barn," tumbling tunnel, miner's cabin, wood tepee, goat climb—and of course, a pumpkin patch. There is a fee—around $6; or combine your visit with a trip through the farm's corn maze for around $9 for all attractions. You can also choose to just visit the maze (also around $6—kids under 40 inches tall get in free). The maze usually opens at the end of August.

....

Charlie's Organic Gardens

15001 Old Snohomish Rd., Snohomish
(360) 794-8434

During Fall Harvest Days at this farm, you can take a bumpy hayride, find your way through the corn and sunflower maze, and pick a bunch of pumpkins.

Craven Farms
13817 Short School Rd., Snohomish
(360) 568-2601
www.cravenfarm.com

There's a lot going on in October at Craven Farms. Some events have fees; others are free. For the children's Storytime Tour, kids are greeted by an orange pumpkin and given a cookie, and then hear the story of life on the farm. They also visit baby farm animals. The farm features a collection of about a dozen pumpkin-themed scenes, such as Snow White and the Seven Pumpkins. Other attractions include pumpkin picking, the pumpkin slinger, scarecrow building, the Harvest Market, and a corn maze.

Fall City Farm
3636 Neal Rd., Fall City
(425) 222-4553

Tours are available for all ages, and special activities are always planned in October. You'll also find U-pick and pre-picked pumpkins, and a store with produce and prepared foods.

Foster's Produce, Corn Maze, and Pumpkin Farm
5818 SR 530 N.E., Arlington
(360) 435-5095
www.fosterscornmaze.com

The farm offers a corn maze, pumpkin patch, and Pumpkin Puppet Theater, featuring a show and storytime in October. The corn maze opens in early September, with a new theme each year. There are also pigs and chickens to visit, fantastic frozen pies for sale, and even a goat that does a trick for a treat.

Remlinger Farms

32610 N.E. 32nd St., Carnation
(425) 333-4135
www.remlingerfarms.com

The granddaddy of pumpkin patches, Remlinger claims to have the largest pumpkin harvest festival in the Northwest. Along with acres of U-pick pumpkins, there's a Pumpkin Harvest Festival Park with 25 rides and amusements, a hay jump, hay maze, corn maze, wall climb, pony rides, and steam train ride. Some events are held weekends only; there is an admission fee ($10.50/person). The festival usually begins the last weekend in September and continues through October.

South 47 Farm

15410 N.E. 124th St., Redmond
(425) 869-9777
www.south47farm.com

Pick pumpkins and gourds, enjoy seeing farm animals and taking hayrides, and don't miss the spectacular corn maze.

Stocker Farms

10622 Airport Way, Snohomish
(360) 568-7391
www.stockerfarms.com

Across Highway 9 from the farm market, you'll find a 10-acre pumpkin patch and a field full of fun activities, including hayrides, storytellers, face painting, air jumpers, straw crawl, pumpkin launching, casting ponds, and craft booths. Admission is $5 (kids ages 2 and under are free). A trip through the 10-acre corn maze (the maze theme changes each year) rounds out the day at Stocker Farms. Both U-pick and pre-picked pumpkins are available. The corn maze usually opens mid-September; other activities are in October.

Chapter 5

Indoor Fun

The mid-January post-holiday crash has hit. Or maybe **summer vacation** started a week ago and it hasn't stopped **raining** since the last school bell rang. The kids are swinging from the light fixtures. You can't face another craft project—so now what? Insist the little critters clean their closets? Consider recruiting another family for some sanity-preserving adult company, and trying out one of these activities that will **get everyone out of the house.** The kids will burn off some of their energy and everyone will likely return home a little more mellow. The places listed range from **art studios** to **disco bowling alleys** and everything in between, but what they hold in common is that they offer activities that take place inside and that you can just drop in for some fun—no advance planning or registration required, unless indicated.

Arts & Exploration

Blue Highway

2203 Queen Anne Ave. N., Seattle

(206) 282-0540

www.bluehighwaygames.com

These days if you hear the description "game store" you are likely to think electronic, but this busy place on Queen Anne Hill is all about the kind of games that are off-screen. The founders met while working at the computer games division of Microsoft. They shared in common good memories of hours spent playing board games as kids, so they decided to open Blue Highway to encourage families to enjoy the pleasures of fun and challenging board or card or action games. The motto for the business says it all: "unplug and reconnect."

At Blue Highway you'll find demo tables to try out new games, plus regularly scheduled Scrabble, chess, Xeko, and mahjong tournaments and open Game Night every Saturday night.

In addition, they offer School Game Nights, where they work with a school's PTA to host an event with games emphasizing math, reading, memory skills, and abstract thinking. Birthday parties for ages 8 and up are also available in the loft at the store.

Creation Station

19511 64th Ave. W., Lynnwood

(425) 775-7959

www.creationstationinc.com

Admission: $6.95/child for two hours of "drop-in" creating

As every parent knows, stuff we consider junk is often, in the eyes of a child, material for creation. Creation Station is chock-full of unusual, unused, uncontaminated recyclable materials, including cones, tubes, fabrics, plastic, foam, and wood as well as more conventional craft materials such as glitter, clay, felt, stencils, tumbled mosaic glass, and pompoms. This is a place for therapists, kids, engineers, and teachers. The staff has tables set up with loads of interesting material to spur creativity. If your children would rather work at home, the store sells materials to take home.

Children (or adults) can drop in any time during open hours and create at their own pace. Recommended age is 4 years and up for the "drop-in" creating time, but parents can decide. Groups of five or more need a reservation. Group sessions are limited to 1.5 hours. The staff recommends you call ahead to see how busy the store is before you bring your children in for a creation session.

....

Dig It: The Fossil Workshop
1402 S.E. Everett Mall Way, Everett
(425) 423-8506
www.digitfossils.com

Admission: $8.99 for one specimen; up to $34.99 for six

This "interactive learning center" located in Everett Mall is the flagship in a new franchise started by a mom with fond memories of digging fossils with her father. It provides three "quarries"—Shark Bite Bay, with sea fossils; Excavation Station, with land fossils; and Prospector's Pit, with rocks and minerals—where kids (or adults) can dig up and learn about authentic fossils, then clean and take them home. There are also geodes buried in the sand that can be cracked open with a hammer—a favorite with preschoolers who usually are underwhelmed by the 5- to 600-million year-old fragments of fossils.

"Learn It! Play It! Dig It!" is a Dig It education program available for school and other group field trips. There's also a gift shop on the website for the geologically minded birthday child in your life.

The Little Artist
4740 California Ave. S.W., Seattle
(206) 935-4185
www.littleartiststudio.com

In the Parent and Tot Studios, for parents and ages 1–3, the Open Art Studio and Preschool Art Studio drop-in open art times are offered several times a week at this charming West Seattle studio located above the Curious Kid Stuff toy store. The studio is stocked with washable paints, brushes, and painter's smocks. Kids can have fun with paints, without parents worrying about a mess to clean up. Drop-in open art times are limited to 5–8 children, depending on their ages. Check with the studio for times; registration is not required.

Moonpaper Tent
918 N.E. 64th St., Seattle
(206) 779-4541
www.moonpapertent.com

When young children naturally explore dance and drama, they bring their imaginations along. Moonpaper Tent is a magical place where the stuff of fairy-tales, with adventures of heroic rescue and acts of fantastic kindness, are woven into learning about music, dance, storytelling, and acting. Classes range from "Storybook Adventures" to "Fashion Passion" and are offered for ages 3–14.

The third Friday of every month is Parents Night Out. Parents can drop children ages 4 and older off from 6–10 P.M. ($8/hour) so they can go have fun while the kids have fun.

....

Scratch Patch
6410 Latona Ave. N.E., Seattle
(206) 523-6164
www.scratchpatchusa.com

Admission: $2/person plus cost of stones

Searching for a pretty rock is soothing for all ages, and at the Scratch Patch over two tons of semi-precious gemstones are waiting for the discerning eye to notice their special gleam and take them home. Stones are sold by the bagful— $8 for a medium sack, $15 for large, and $25 for extra large. It is a soothing and satisfying activity, but sitting on a pile of stones is not comfortable for some grown-ups, so if you suspect your young child will want to be searching for that certain gem for a long stretch, consider bringing along an older child who will be happy to sit with them digging through the beautifully polished rocks for their own sack of favorites. Founder Amanda Lambrecht is a native South African who brings the "scratch patch" idea from her homeland. After just one year, the Scratch Patch moved to a new space that is double the original size.

Ceramics/Pottery

Kids can create a personalized present or keepsake at a ceramics studio. All these places are well stocked with all manner of pottery—mugs, figurines, plates, and bowls and you can drop in—registration not required. Just pick out a ceramic piece, paint it, and the studio will fire and glaze it. You pay for the piece and studio time. This is an easy way for your child to make a personalized present for mom or dad or grandparents, but expect it to take at least a couple of days for the piece to be fired in the kiln. Especially at the busy holiday season, plan your visit early so gifts are ready on time. These ceramic studios are also popular birthday-party destinations.

- **Ceramic Gallery, Etc.**, 418 Park Place Center, Kirkland, (425) 822-1222
- **Earth, Ware & Fire Ceramics Studio**, 13018 S.E. Kent–Kangley Rd., Kent, (253) 630-6645

- **Glaze Cottage**, 2539 Gateway Center Blvd. S., Federal Way, (253) 946-4502
- **Paint N Place**, 2226 Queen Anne Ave. N., Seattle, (206) 281-0229
- **The Paint Patch**, 5405 Ballard Ave. N.W., Seattle, (206) 789-7160
- **Paint the Town**, University Village, Seattle, (206) 527-8554
- **Paint Yourself Silly**, 2132 S.W. 336th St., Federal Way, (253) 661-6067
- **West Side Ceramics and More**, 9447 35th Ave. S.W., Seattle, (206) 933-8999

For more Indoor Arts and Exploration ideas, see also entries for Chapter 2, Woodland Park Zoo: Zoomazium, and Chapter 3, Museums.

Batting Cages and Ranges

If you have a youngster in your house with a love of baseball, the following places will give him or her a chance to practice baseball skills while having fun. Some places allow drop-ins and are a good spot to host a birthday party for little sluggers, others are for those seeking serious practice and may require advance registration for skills clinics.

- **Big League Connection**, 15015 N.E. 90th St., Redmond, (425) 885-2862
- **Bleacher Reachers**, 18366 Eighth S., Sea-Tac, (206) 431-5995
- **Family Fun Center/Bullwinkle's**, 7300 Fun Center Way, Tukwila, (425) 228-7300
- **Funtasia Family Fun Park**, 7212 220th St. S.W., Edmonds, (425) 774-GAME
- **Mini Mountain**, 1900 132nd Ave. N.E., Bellevue, (425) 746-7547
- **Northshore Sports Complex**, 19250 144th Ave. N.E., Woodinville, (425) 643-8384
- **Stod's Baseball Inc.**, 5629 119th S.E., Bellevue, (425) 643-8384
- **Strike Zone**, 270 S. Hanford, Ste. D, Seattle, (206) 624-8030

Bowling

Bowling with kids is fun—and even more fun in the last few years as many bowling alleys in the Seattle area have spiffed up their facilities. It is worth taking the time to look at the websites for the bowling alleys listed below to check out their new offerings, such as "disco" and "cosmic" bowl. If you have kids under 10, make sure the place is equipped with bumpers.

These clever devices are basically gutter pads that ensure almost every ball eventually makes its way down the alley to reach the pins without succumbing to the gutter. Almost always, the bumpers will guide your child's bowling ball straight to the Big Ten, ensuring at least one satisfying crash. Beware the other not-so-good-crashes, like Bowling Ball on the Toe, Child's Bowling Ball Attached to Thumb, and Bowling Ball Hurled Backwards Toward Little Sister. Bumper bowling is popular with kids; the fact it also helps parents avoid embarrassment probably doesn't hurt. Prices vary a bit from alley to alley—and not all places offer bumper bowling; some may only offer it on certain lanes. Call ahead to be sure bumpers are available. And don't forget shoe rental. If you can't find shoes small enough to fit your kids, they can bowl in their socks (adds slippery thrills).

If you have very young children, it's also a good idea to check to see if the alley you've chosen has any age restrictions. Some bowling alleys require a minimum age (such as 4) for young bowlers.

If you are looking for birthday party places, almost all bowling alleys are happy to accommodate with special birthday packages.

- **Acme Bowl**, 100 Andover Park W., Seattle, (206) 340-2263, *www.acme bowl.com*
- **Brunswick Majestic Lanes**, 1222 164th Ave. S.W., Lynnwood, (425) 743-4422
- **Cascade Lanes**, 17034 116th Ave. S.E., Renton, (425) 226-2035, *www. cascadelanes.com*
- **Hi-Line Lanes**, 15733 Ambaum Blvd. S.W., Burien, (206) 244-2272, *www. hilinelanes.com*

- **Hillcrest Family Bowling Center**, 2809 N.E. Sunset Blvd., Renton, (425) 226-1600, *www.bowlhillcrestfamily.websiteanimal.com*
- **Imperial Lanes**, 2101 22nd Ave. S., Seattle, (206) 325-2525, *www.amf.com/imperiallanes*
- **Kent Bowl**, 1234 N. Central, Kent, (253) 852-3550, *www.kentbowl.net*
- **Lynnwood Bowl & Skate**, 6210 200th Ave. S.W., Lynnwood, (425) 778-3133, *www.bowlandskate.com*
- **Magic Lanes**, 10612 15th Ave. S.W., Seattle, (206) 244-5060, *www.magiclanesbowl.com*
- **Robin Hood Lanes**, 9801 Edmonds Way, Edmonds, (425) 776-2101, *www.robinhoodlanes.com*
- **Roxbury Lanes**, 2823 S.W. Roxbury St., Seattle, (206) 935-7400, *www.roxburylanes.com*
- **Spin Alley**, 1430 N.W. Richmond Beach Rd., Shoreline, (206) 533-2345, *www.spinalley.com*
- **Sun Villa Lanes**, 3080 148th Ave. S. E., Bellevue, (425) 455-8155, *www.amf.com/sunvillalanes/*
- **Tech City Bowl and Fun Center**, 13033 N.E. 70th Pl., Kirkland, (425) 827-0785, *www.techcitybowl.com*
- **West Seattle Bowl**, 4505 39th Ave. S.W., Seattle, (206) 932-3731, *www.wsbowl.com*

Community Centers and Clubs

City Parks and Recreation, the YMCA, and the Boys and Girls Club offer an abundance of community centers that are the hub for a rich variety of reasonably priced after- and before-school activities, sports, and educational support. When looking for classes, drop-in sports opportunities, or special events, get in the habit of checking out the community center closest to your home—you might be surprised just how much fun and learning can be found practically next door.

Boys and Girls Clubs of King County

(206) 461-3890, *www.positiveplace.org*

The heart of every Boys and Girls Club is the drop-in program. For an average membership fee of $1.50 per month ($18 annually), members can visit a Club after school and on weekends and explore new games, develop social skills, get help with homework, take computer education classes, play in the games room or gym and on the ball fields, and make new friends with peers and adults. Additional structured programs are available year-round (only to members) for a nominal fee. Before- and after-school programs are often offered at elementary schools, so check the club closest to you for more program locations.

Boys and Girls Clubs in Seattle

- **Ballard Boys and Girls Club**, Main Office, 1767 N.W. 64th St., Seattle, (206) 436-1878, *www.ballard-bgc.org*. Extensive before- and after-school programs in numerous school locations.

- **Iwasil Boys and Girls Club**, 2524 16th Ave. S., Seattle, (206) 325-3942. The first Boys and Girls Club in the country dedicated to serving Native American youth.

- **North Seattle Boys and Girls Club**, Main Office, 8635 Fremont Ave. N., Seattle, (206) 436-1850. Extensive before- and after-school programs in numerous school locations.

- **Rainier Boys and Girls Club and Teen Center**, 4520 Martin Luther King Jr. Way S., (206) 436-1890, *www.rainiervistabgc.org*. A new 40,000-square-foot club with separate facilities for the Girls Club, Boys Club, and Teen Center, plus a music and art studio and industrial kitchen, opened in fall of 2008.

- **Southwest Boys and Girls Club**, 9800 Eighth Ave. S.W., Ste. 105, Seattle, (206) 436-1910

- **Wallingford Boys and Girls Club**, Main Office, 1310 N. 45th St., Seattle, (206) 436-1930, *www.wallingfordboysandgirlsclub.org*. Extensive before- and after-school programs in numerous school locations.

- **Federal Way Boys and Girls Club**, 30815 Eighth Ave. S., Federal Way, (253) 681-6510, *www.fw-bgc.org*
- **Kirkland Boys and Girls Club**, 10805 124th Ave. N.E., Kirkland, (425) 250-4750, *www.onepositiveplace.org*
- **Mercer Island Boys and Girls Club**, 2825 W. Mercer Way, Mercer Island, (206) 436-1940, *www.mipositiveplace.org*
- **Redmond/Sammamish Boys and Girls Club**, Main Office, 7300 208th Ave. N.E., Redmond, (425) 836-9295, *www.positiveplace.org*. Before- and after-school programs in numerous school locations.
- **Renton/Skyway Boys and Girls Club**, 12400 80th Ave. S., Seattle, (206) 436-1920

City of Seattle Parks Department Community Centers

Kids are always welcome to drop in at parks department community centers, either to join a class, enjoy a special event, or just join a pick-up game in the gym. Visit *www.seattle.gov/PARKS/* for more information and details on the following parks.

- **Alki Community Center**, 5817 S.W. Stevens St., (206) 684-7430
- **Ballard Community Center**, 6020 28th Ave. N.W., (206) 684-4093
- **Bitter Lake**, 13040 Greenwood Ave. N., (206) 684-7524
- **Delridge**, 4501 Delridge Way S.W., (206) 684-7423
- **Garfield**, 2323 E. Cherry St., (206) 684-4788
- **Green Lake**, 7201 E. Green Lake Dr. N., (206) 684-0780
- **Hiawatha**, 2700 California Ave. S.W., (206) 684-7441
- **High Point**, 6920 34th Ave. S.W., (206) 684-7422
- **International District/Chinatown**, 719 Eighth Ave. E., (206) 233-0042

- **Jefferson**, 3801 Beacon Ave. S., (206) 684-7481
- **Laurelhurst**, 4554 N.E. 41st St., (206) 684-7529
- **Loyal Heights**, 2101 N.W. 77th St., (206) 684-4052
- **Magnolia**, 2550 34th Ave. W., (206) 386-4235
- **Magnuson**, 71110 62nd Ave. N.E., (206) 684-7026
- **Meadowbrook**, 10517 35th Ave. N.E., (206) 684-7522
- **Miller**, 330 19th Ave. E., (206) 684-4753
- **Montlake**, 1618 E. Calhoun St., (206) 684-4736
- **Northgate**, 10510 Fifth Ave. N.E., (206) 386-4283
- **Queen Anne**, 1901 First Ave. W., (206) 386-4240
- **Rainier Beach**, 8825 Rainier Ave. S., (206) 386-1944
- **Rainier Community Center**, 4600 38th Ave. S., (206) 386-1919
- **Ravenna-Eckstein**, 6535 Ravenna Ave. N.E., (206) 684-7534
- **South Park**, 8319 Eighth Ave. S., (206) 684-7451
- **Southwest**, 2801 S.W. Thistle St., (206) 684-7438
- **Van Asselt**, 2820 S. Myrtle St., (206) 386-1921
- **Yesler**, 835 E. Yesler Way, (206) 386-1245

Eastside City Community Centers

- **Crossroads**, 6000 N.E. 10th St., Bellevue, (452) 452-4874
- **Highland**, 14224 Bel-Red Rd., Bellevue, (425) 452-7686
- **Issaquah**, 301 Rainier Blvd. S., Issaquah, (425) 837-3300
- **Mercer View**, 8236 S.E. 24th St., Mercer Island, (206) 236-3537
- **North Bellevue**, 4063 148th Ave. N.E., Bellevue, (425) 452-7681
- **North Kirkland**, 12421 103rd Ave. N.E., Kirkland, (425) 828-1105
- **Old Redmond Schoolhouse**, 16600 N.E. 80th St., Redmond, (425) 556-2300
- **Si View**, 400 S.E. Orchard Dr., North Bend, (425) 831-1900

South End Community Centers

- **Highland Neighborhood Center**, 800 Edmonds Ave. N.E., Renton, (425) 430-6700
- **Kent Commons**, 525 Fourth Ave. N., Kent, (253) 859-3350
- **North SeaTac Park**, 13735 24th Ave. S., Sea-Tac, (206) 973-4680

North End Community Centers

- **Frances Anderson Cultural and Leisure Center**, 700 Main St., Edmonds, (425) 771-0230
- **Lynnwood**, 18900 44th Ave. W., Lynnwood, (425) 771-4030
- **Mountlake Terrace**, 5303 288th St., Mountlake Terrace, (425) 776-9173
- **Shoreline Center**, Spartan Gym, 18560 First Ave. N.E., Shoreline, (206) 546-5041

YMCA of Greater Seattle

- **Auburn Valley YMCA**, 1005 12th St., Auburn, (253) 833-2770, *www.seattleymca.org/page.cfm?id=av*. Serving Auburn, Kent, Pacific, and Enumclaw Plateau.

- **Bellevue Family YMCA**, 14230 Bel-Red Rd., Bellevue, (425) 746-9900, *www.seattleymca.org/page.cfm?id=bv*. Serving Bellevue, Kirkland, Redmond, and surrounding areas.

- **Dale Turner Family YMCA**, *www.seattleymca.org/page.cfm?id=DTFY*. Serving North King County and south Snohomish County; opened late 2008.

- **Federal Way Norman Center YMCA**, 33250 21st Ave. S.W., Federal Way, (253) 838-4707, *www.seattleymca.org/page.cfm?id=fw*

- **Highline**, 17874 Des Moines Memorial Dr., Seattle, (206) 244-5880, *www.seattleymca.org/page.cfm?id=hl*. Also serving Burien, Des Moines, Normandy Park, Sea-Tac, and Tukwila.

- **Lake Heights**, 12635 SE 56th St., Bellevue, (425) 644-8417, *www.seattleymca.org/page.cfm?id=lh*. Serving south Bellevue, Newcastle, Renton, and Mercer Island.

- **Meredith Mathews East Madison**, 1700 23rd Ave., Seattle, (206) 322-6969, *www.seattleymca.org/page.cfm?id=mm*

- **Northshore**, 11811 N.E. 195th, Bothell, (425) 485-9797, *www.seattleymca. org/page.cfm?id=ns*. Serving Bothell, Kenmore, and Duvall.

- **Sammamish**, 4221 228th S.E., Issaquah, (425) 391-4840, *www.seattleymca. org/page.cfm?id=sm*. Serving Sammamish, Issaquah, North Bend, Fall City, Carnation, Snoqualmie, and Maple Valley.

- **Seattle Downtown**, 909 Fourth Ave., Seattle, (206) 382-5010, *www.seattle ymca.org/page.cfm?id=dt*. Serving all of Seattle and Bainbridge Island.

- **Shoreline/South County Family YMCA**, 1220 N.E. 175th St., Shoreline, (206) 364-1700, *www.seattleymca.org/page.cfm?id=sh*

- **University Family YMCA**, 5003 12th Ave., Seattle, (206) 524-1400, *www. seattleymca.org/page.cfm?id=uv*. Also serving north Seattle, Sand Point, Ballard, Greenlake, and Lake City.

- **West Seattle & Fauntleroy Family YMCA**, 4515 36th Ave. S.W., Seattle, (206) 935-6000; 9140 California Ave. S.W., (206) 937-1000, *www.seattleymca. org/page.cfm?ID=0059*

....

Family Entertainment Centers

The atmosphere is "indoor carnival." It's noisy, crowded—and most kids love the scene. Besides video and redemption games, most offer activities such as laser tag, miniature golf, go-karts, and batting cages. All accommodate birthday parties and offer packages. A number of these places offer both indoor and outdoor seasonal activities. Often, you aren't charged admission; instead you buy tickets or tokens for various activities or packaged deals. Snack bars are usually available, selling hot dogs, pizza, and popcorn.

Chuck E. Cheese
2239 148th Ave. N.E., Bellevue, (425) 746-5000
25817 104th Ave. S.E., Kent, (253) 813-9000
3717 196th Ave. S.W., Lynnwood, (425) 778-6566
www.chuckecheese.com

Hours: 9 A.M.–10 P.M.

Games, kiddie rides, tube, and ball play area plus pizza.

Family Fun Center/Bullwinkle's
7300 Fun Center Way, Tukwila
(425) 228-7300
www.fun-center.com

Hours: Mon.–Thurs., 10 A.M.–10 P.M.; Fri., 11:30 A.M.–9 P.M.; Sat., 11 A.M.–9 P.M., Sun., 11 A.M.–8 P.M.

A four-level playground with tubes, a 28-foot rock wall, a large arcade, a virtual roller coaster, and laser tag are among the indoor attractions here. Outside, you'll find batting cages, mini-golf, a maze, bumper boats, and go-karts. A number of attractions require a minimum height.

Fun Forest Amusement Park
305 Harrison St., Seattle Center, Seattle
(206) 728-1585
www.funforest.com

Hours: June–Labor Day, daily, noon–11 P.M.; Labor Day–May, Sat.–Sun., noon–11 P.M. Entertainment Pavilion open daily, year-round, Mon.–Thurs., 11 A.M.–6 P.M.; Fri., 11 A.M.–6 P.M.; Sat.–Sun., 11 A.M.–8 P.M.

The Entertainment Pavilion was open year-round as of 2008, but is slated to close in 2009 unless it gets a reprieve. Other amusements, many of which are outdoors, are seasonal. The Entertainment Pavilion recently added a 25-foot climbing wall. You'll also find a roller-coaster simulator, skee ball, laser tag, bumper cars, prize games, video games, mini-golf, and two rides for small children.

....

Funtasia Family Fun Park
7212 220th St. S.W., Edmonds
(206) 775-2174
www.familyfunpark.com

Hours: Mon.–Thurs., noon–9 P.M.; Fri., noon–11:30 P.M., Sat., 10 A.M.–11:30 P.M., Sun., 11 A.M.–9 P.M. Go-karts close an hour before closing.

This indoor-outdoor facility has bumper cars, laser tag, and video games inside—plus a 4,000-square-foot Fun Fortress for kids under 57 inches. Outdoors, you'll find batting cages, bumper boats, and go-karts. A number of items do require a minimum height.

The indoor half of the 18-hole mini-golf course has a lost civilization theme, with tropical tiki statues, palm trees, and a cave with an overhead waterfall. Go outside for the remaining nine holes and there's a pirate theme that includes an elevated fort with 12-foot cannons overlooking a water lagoon, a replica of a pirate ship, a waterfall, and more palm trees.

Whirley Ball Inc.
23401 Hwy. 99, Edmonds
(425) 672-3332
www.whirlyball.net

Admission: $180/1–10 people for 1.5 hours

Described as a combination of basketball, hockey, and jai alai played while riding an electrically powered machine similar to a bumper car, Whirley Ball is a team sport, so bring your team of 8 or more. Kids as young as 8 are allowed to play. There is a snack bar on the premises.

Libraries

Storytimes, summer reading programs, after-school homework help: these are some of the things that our local public libraries offer. And don't forget about the opportunity to check out all sorts of wonderful materials including books, CDs, DVDs, and periodicals. Libraries also offer access to computers and the Internet. Most branch libraries have children's librarians who can suggest books for different ages or steer a child to resources he needs to complete a school report. Many libraries also have occasional special programming for kids and families—including performances by local children's entertainers.

In the Seattle area, the two largest library resources are the King County Library System, which has branch libraries in cities throughout the county, and the Seattle Public Library, which has branch libraries throughout the city. In May 2004, the SPL opened its spectacular new Central Library in downtown Seattle at 1000 Fourth Avenue. Designed by internationally renowned architect Rem Koolhaas, the dramatic glass and steel structure is a new landmark for downtown Seattle. In the last few years, all 22 Seattle branch libraries have been undergoing renovations and improvements, thanks to a bond measure approved by voters in 1998.

All library systems have websites, which offer extensive information on library programming and resources. The King County Library System offers a variety of resources, including books and videocassettes, centered on different themes.

- **Seattle Public Libraries**, (206) 386-4190 (Central Library), (206) 386-4675 (children's services), *www.spl.org*
- **King County Library System**, (425) 462-9600 (information), (425) 369-3322 (children's department), *www.kcls.org*
- **Bellevue Regional Library** (part of KCLS), (425) 450-1765
- **Pierce County Public Libraries**, (253) 536-6500, *www.pcl.lib.wa.us*
- **City of Renton Libraries**, (425) 430-6610 (downtown), (425) 430-6790 (Highlands), *www.ci.renton.wa.us/commserv/library*
- **Sno-Isle Libraries** (Snohomish/Island Counties), (360) 651-7000, *www.sno-isle.org*
- **Tacoma Public Libraries**, (253) 591-5666, *www.tpl.lib.wa.us*

Go to the Movies

While watching movies at home is hands-down more convenient, an outing to the local movie theater makes movie viewing more of an event. The following movie theaters are listed because of their bargain rates—more family affordable—and/or special accommodations for parents. We've listed theaters with crying rooms—not the finest way to watch a movie but a welcome sanctuary if a noisy baby won't let you stay in the main theater—as well as theaters that designate certain days/times as "babies-at-the-movies" time.

Good Deal Movies

- **Admiral Movie Theater**, 2347 California Ave. S.W., Seattle, (206) 938-3456, $5/person
- **Crest Movie Theater**, 16505 Fifth Ave. N.E., Seattle, (206) 781-5755, $3/person

Crying Rooms

The following theaters offer crying rooms—glassed-in areas where the kids can do some primal therapy without disrupting other movie-goers—or special accommodations at certain times/days for parents yearning to see a movie on the big screen but not ready to leave baby at home yet. Since all these cinema houses have several theaters, finding out if the feature that you wish to see is being shown in the theater equipped with a crying room is no easy task. For the three Landmark movie theaters listed below, call (206) 781-5755 or go to *www.landmarktheatres.com* to find out what movies are playing in the theaters with the crying rooms. Also get there early, these small rooms fill up fast.

- **Landmark Guild 45**, 2115 N. 45th St., Seattle, (206) 633-3353. Crying room in theater #2 (the "blue" theater).
- **Landmark Metro Cinema**, 4500 N.E. Ninth Ave., Seattle, (206) 633-0055. Crying room in theater #1.
- **Landmark Varsity Theatre**, 4329 University Way, Seattle, (206) 632-3131. Crying room in main, first-floor theater.
- **North Bend Theatre**, 125 Bendigo Blvd. N., North Bend, (425) 888-1232, *www.northbendtheatre.com*. Located in downtown North Bend, a small town 30 minutes east of Seattle on I-90.

Babies at the Movies Day

The following theaters offer special days/times when parents are encouraged to bring babies to the movies. The features being shown are not specifically family-friendly—so little ones who attend are expected to be babes-in-arms, not kids actually watching the movies.

- **Columbia City Cinema**, 4816 Rainier Ave. S., (206) 721-3156, *www.columbia citycinema.com*. On Cry Baby Tuesday, you can bring a baby to any matinee movie before 6 P.M., every Tuesday.
- **Kirkland Parkplace Cinema**, 404 Parkplace Center, Kirkland, (425) 827-9000, *www.kirklandparkplace.com/cinema*. At Baby's Day at the Movies, parents can bring the baby along and choose from up to six movies at 9:45 A.M. every Friday.

- **Lincoln Square Cinema**, 700 Bellevue Way N.E., Bellevue, (425) 450-9100, *www.lincolnsquarescinema.com*. Mother's Days Thursdays happens every Thursday at 10 A.M. Moms or dads are encouraged to bring infants (and a stroller, if you prefer). First-run movies are offered in multiple theaters so you have a good selection of movies. This is a new, large theater just east of Bellevue Square with easy parking in the building.

- **North Bend Theatre**, 125 Bendigo Blvd. N., North Bend, (425) 888-1232, *www.northbendtheatre.com*. Located in downtown North Bend, a small town 30 minutes east of Seattle on I-90. Offers Mommy Matinee for parent and baby every Monday at 11 A.M.

Indoor Play Spaces

These indoor play facilities are wonderful—especially during Seattle's rainy season, when it can be hard to get outside for play to burn off energy. They're also great opportunities for parents to meet and socialize while the kids are playing. Most city parks and recreation departments in the Seattle area offer drop-in indoor playgrounds for toddlers and preschoolers, usually at community center locations. Hours change frequently, so check websites or call before you go. Drop-in fees are usually in the $1–$2 range; at some centers, you can get a discount if you pay for a certain number of visits ahead of time. Most indoor play areas are designed for children ages 1–5 unless otherwise noted and children must always be accompanied by a parent or caregiver.

In addition, there are several businesses offering drop-in indoor playground programs.

The Arena Sports Fun Zones
Redmond Fun Zone, (425) 885-4881
Magnuson Park Fun Zone, (206) 985-8990
SODO Seattle Fun Zone, (206) 762-8606
www.arenasports.net/fun-zone-indoor-inflatable-playground

Admission: $5/child for members, $7/child for nonmembers. Annual and monthly family passes available. Parents play for free with child.

The Arena Sports Fun Zones indoor inflatable playgrounds are play spaces filled with large inflatable play equipment that gives kids the chance to jump and bounce, slide and jump. Hours vary, so call in advance.

....

The Bouncy Place
21224 84th Ave. S., Kent
(253) 395-5572
www.thebouncyplace.com

This indoor party facility features inflatable games, slides, and obstacle courses and is located in the Kent Valley. Though primarily intended as a place for birthday parties, they offer numerous times during the week when children can drop in to play. Check the website for current drop-in schedule and costs.

....

Great Play
16510 Cleveland St., Suite N., Redmond
(425) 885-3800, Redmond@greatplay.com
www.greatplay.com

Great Play is a creative and exciting concept. The company's proprietary Interactive Arena™—a patent-pending network of computers, projectors, video sensors, and sound systems—allows kids ages 6 months to 12 years to develop motor skills and sport skills via instruction and playing specially designed age-appropriate games. Drop-in play is not offered, but free trial classes are available.

Playmatters
7720 Greenwood Ave. N., Seattle
(206) 784-0122, info@playmatters.com
www.playmatterseattle.com

Admission: $10/one adult, up to two kids, $5 extra for more than two kids. Monthly and yearly passes available.

Hours: Closed some days for birthday parties. Opens 10 A.M. Closing time varies. Check website.

Located in the Phinney Ridge/Greenwood neighborhood, Playmatters is a 1,000-square-foot indoor play space geared to children 5 and under and their parents and caregivers. Snacks are available for purchase, or it is OK to bring your own food. Workshops for parents and caregivers are also offered.

City of Seattle Parks and Recreation Indoor Playgrounds
www.seattlegov/Parks/Children/play.htm

By opening up its community center gyms or other spaces and stocking them with play equipment, the city provides a much needed, low-cost space for parents and kids to congregate on the many rainy days in Seattle. Check the website above for the most current list of locations and hours. There is usually a charge of $2/child or $5/family.

King County Community Center Indoor Playgrounds

- **Crossroads**, 16000 N.E. 10th St., Bellevue, (452) 452-4874
- **Highland**, 800 Edmonds Ave. N.E., Renton, (425) 430-6700
- **Issaquah**, 301 Rainier Blvd. S., Issaquah, (425) 837-3300

- **Kent Commons**, 525 Fourth Ave. N., Kent, (253) 859-3350
- **North Kirkland**, 12421 103rd Ave. N.E., Kirkland, (425) 828-1105
- **Old Redmond Schoolhouse**, 16600 N.E. 80th St., Redmond, (425) 556-2300
- **Shoreline**, Spartan Gym, 18560 First Ave. N.E., Shoreline, (206) 801-2600

....

Seattle Gymnastics Indoor Playground
12535 26th Ave. N.E., Seattle
12745 28th Ave. N.E., Seattle
(206) 362-7447
www.seattlegymnastics.com/indoorplayground2.html

Admission: $6/child, $4/child if currently enrolled in class at Seattle Gymnastics.

Children ages 1–5, accompanied by a caregiver or parent, are under supervision of gymnastics instructors. Kids can play on SGA's gymnastic equipment, including the trampoline, balance beam, huge foam pit, and child-sized climbing wall. Location varies between Shively Gymnasium (12535 26th Ave. N.E., Seattle, 206-362-7447) except during the summer, when it moves to Glade Training Gymnasium (12745 28th Ave. N.E., Seattle).

....

Pump It Up
11605 NE 116th St., Kirkland, (425) 820-2297
18027 Hwy. 99, Lynnwood, (425) 774-2297
www.pumpitupparty.com

Admission: $6/child, $4/ each additional child—parents free!

At Pump It Up, kids enjoy the 12,000-square-foot facility's eight inflatable toys, which include 20-foot slides, obstacle courses, and bounce houses. The spaces are used most of the time for birthday parties, but open playtimes are available for a 75-minute sessions. Parents are welcome to climb and bounce along with kids.

Rock Climbing

If you have a tree in your backyard, it's likely your kids have tried to climb it. It's almost instinctual. Most kids love to climb—trees, furniture, fences, walls, rocks. Adults like to climb, too. One result of this has been the opening of a number of indoor climbing facilities where kids and adults can learn skills and test themselves in a safe environment.

Cascade Crags Indoor Climbing Gym
2820 Rucker Ave., Everett
(425) 258-3431

This gym contains more than 10,000 square feet of climbing wall. It also offers kids' programs, classes, and family discounts. Ages 4 and up.

REI
222 Yale Ave. N., Seattle, (206) 223-1944
3000 184th St. S.W., Alderwood, (425) 640-6200
Redmond Town Center, 7500 166th Ave. N.E., Redmond, (425) 882-1158

The rock Pinnacle at three REI stores in and around Seattle are a fun and easy way to show your child rock climbing without leaving town. There are usually a few climbers attempting to reach the peak by different routes. It's even more fun to try it yourself, and no doubt your kids will be clamoring to do the same.

Kids can try to climb the Pinnacle during the times it's open to the public, but there are minimum height requirements and parents must sign a release waiver for children age 18 and under. The Pinnacle has become very popular; reservations are taken on a first-come, first-served basis and can be made in advance by phone. There are charges for classes and for climbing the Pinnacle ($5/members, $15/nonmembers).

Stone Gardens

2839 N.W. Market St., Seattle
(206) 781-9828
www.stonegardens.com

This center offers regular climbing sessions for kids ages 6 and up on some weekday evenings and weekend mornings. There are also junior climbing programs and summer camps.

Vertical World

2123 W. Elmore St., Seattle, (206) 283-4497
15036B N.E. 95th St., Redmond, (425) 881-8826
2820 Rucker Ave., Everett, (425) 258-4159
5934 Hwy. 303 N.E., Bremerton, (360) 373-6676
www.verticalworld.com

Vertical World gyms offer climbers a variety of youth climbing classes, family climbs, and homeschool instruction.

Skating

Ice Skating

Most youngsters more or less crawl around the ice rink on their first few ice-skating attempts, so be sure to encourage plenty of hot chocolate breaks. Mittens are also essential.

Also, you might mention to the kids that although Olympic skaters make it look really easy, they devote pretty much all their waking hours to perfecting that graceful form. If possible, make sure that at least one adult in your party has enough control on the ice to support the wobbly skaters.

If your child is really taken with ice skating, most rinks offer lessons. And for those more attracted to another form of skating—ice hockey—there are local leagues at many rinks. Or for something completely different—check out broomball at Castle Ice Arena. The following are open daily year-round; call or visit their websites for information on public sessions.

....

Castle Ice Arena
2620 164th Ave. S.E., Renton
(425) 254-8750
www.castleice.com

Admission: $8/ages 12 and up Fri.–Sun., $7.50/ages 12 and up Mon.–Thurs., $7/ages 6–12, $5/ages 5 and under, $3 skate rentals. Walker rentals to assist preschool skaters, available for $3, first-come, first-served basis.

....

Highland Ice Arena
18005 Aurora Ave. N., Shoreline
(206) 546-2431
www.highlandice.com

Admission: $6/ages 13 and up, $5.50/ages 6–12, free/ages 5 and under, $3 skate rental. $12/per family Sun., 1:30–8 P.M.

Kent Valley Ice Center
6015 S. 240th St.
(253) 850-2400 ext. 19
www.familynightout.com

Admission: $7.62/ages 13 and up, $6.57/ages 4–12, free/ages 3 and under, $3.03/ skate rental

Lynnwood Ice Center
19803 68th Ave. W., Lynnwood
(425) 640-9999
www.lynnwoodicecenter.com

Admission: $7/adults, $6/youth 12 and under, $3/skate rental, $5/person Wed., 7–8:30 P.M.

Roller Skating

Yes, they still do the Hokey Pokey, and they still play the Top 40. But don't let your warped, disco-days memories stop you from taking the kids roller skating. Not only is it easier than ice skating, it's much warmer. Skaters can bring their own skates or rent at the rink. Rates vary depending on day and time, but the following are good gauges. Skate sessions vary, call or check websites for information. Activities for families include family skate sessions with special rates, tiny tot skates for children under age 10, teen skates, drop-in skate lessons, and birthday party packages.

Roll-a-Way Skate Center
6210 200th St. S.W., Lynnwood
(425) 778-4446
www.bowlandskate.com

Admission: $6/person, $3/in-line skates rental, $1.50/roller skates rental

Skate King
2301 140th Ave. N.E., Bellevue
(425) 641-2047
www.bellevueskateking.com

Admission: $6/person, $4/in-line skates rental, $1.50/roller skates rental

TCL Family Skating Center
10210 S.E. 26oth St., Kent
(253) 852-9379

Admission: $3.75–$6, many sessions include skate rentals; $4/in-line skates rental, $1.50/rollerskate rental

Skate Parks

In the last years, many park departments have built skate parks for in-line skaters and skateboarders; there are also a few commercial ventures. Some facilities require helmets and knee and elbow pads; even if these aren't required, they are certainly a good idea. Most public parks don't charge fees, but there are rules—and it's a good idea to make sure your young skater understands and follows those rules. Also note that if a facility's hours vary, it is mostly to accommodate school hours. Hours expand greatly during summer vacation; during the school year, they are most likely to follow after-school hours.

Bellevue Skate Park
Highland Community Center, 14224 Bel-Red Rd., Bellevue
(425) 452-2722
www.cityofbellevue.org

Hours: Vary by season

This indoor skate park for inline skaters and skateboarders has a street course with ledges, rails, and quarter pipes. Admissions, with skate park ID card, are $5/resident, $8/nonresident; and per session, $3/resident, $5/nonresident.

Inner Space Skatepark
3506-½ Stone Way N., Seattle
(206) 634-9090
www.innerpaceskateboarding.com

Seattle's only indoor skate park is on a quiet street on the east side of Fremont. They have about 7,000 square feet of skateable indoor space, plus a shop with skateboards, accessories, helmets, rentals, snacks, and sodas.

Ramp 'n Roll
13317 Ash Way, Bldg. 2A, Everett
(425) 741-3926
www.rampnroll.com

Hours: Vary by season

This is an indoor skate park with roll-ins, pyramids, hips, and a 14-foot vertical wall.

Skate Barn West
2900 Lind Ave. S.W., Renton
(425) 656-2863
www.skatebarn.com

Hours: Vary by season

This indoor skate park has sessions for bikes, blades, and boards, as well as a skate camp and skate team. The fees are $6/session for members, $10/session nonmembers.

Swimming

An indoor swim in the middle of winter soothes kids and gives parents a chance to sneak in a few laps. The public pools in the area have designated family swim times, and the admission fees are very reasonable. All pools listed below are indoors and all offer family swims and lessons.

Seattle Parks and Recreation Pools

Admission is $3.25/adults and $2.25/children age 18 and under. Swim cards are available at a discounted rate. Schedules are posted at *www.cityofseattle.net/parks/aquatics/poolmap.htm*.

- **Ballard**, 1471 N.W. 67th St., (206) 684-4094
- **Evans**, 7201 E. Green Lake Dr. N., (206) 684-4961
- **Madison**, 13401 Meridian N., (206) 684-4979
- **Meadowbrook**, 10515 35th Ave. N.E., (206) 684-4989
- **Medgar Evers**, 500 23rd St., (206) 684-4766

- **Queen Anne**, 1920 First Ave. W., (206) 386-4282
- **Rainier Beach**, 8825 Rainier S., (206) 386-1944
- **Southwest**, 2801 S.W. Thistle St., (206) 684-7440

King County Pools

Admission to public swim is $3.25. Schedules are at *www.metrokc.gov/parks/pool/pools.aspx*.

- **Evergreen (Burien)**, 606 S.W. 116th St., Seattle, (206) 296-4410
- **Weyherhaeuser King County Aquatic Center**, 650 S.W. Campus Dr., Federal Way, (206) 296-4444
- **Tahoma**, 18230 S.E. 240th St., Kent, (206) 296-4276

Other City Pools

- **Auburn**, 516 Fourth St. N.E., Auburn, (253) 939-8825; $3.25/person
- **Bellevue Aquatic Center**, 601 143rd Ave. N.E., Bellevue, (425) 452-4444; $4/adults, $3/youth 12 and under
- **Julius Boehm Pool**, 50th S.E. Clark St., Issaquah, (425) 837-3350; $4/adults, $3/ages 3–17, free/ages 2 and under
- **Kenneth Jones Pool**, 30421 16th Ave. S., Federal Way, (253) 839-1000; $3/person
- **Kent Meridian Pool**, 25316 101st Ave. S.E., Kent, (253) 854-9287; $3.25/person
- **Lynnwood Recreation Center**, 18900 44th Ave. W., Lynnwood, (425) 771-4030; $2.75/adults, $2/youth, free/ages 2 and under
- **Mercer Island**, 8815 S.E. 40th St., Mercer Island, (206) 296-4370; *www.nwcenter.org/pool*; $3/adults, $2.70/youth

- **Mountlake Terrace**, 5303 228th St. S.W., Mountlake Terrace, (425) 776-9173; $3.25/adults, $2.25/ages 15 and under
- **Mount Rainier**, 22722 19th Ave. S., Des Moines, (206) 824-4722; $3.25/person
- **Northshore**, 9815 N.E. 188th St., Bothell, (206) 296-4333; *www.nwcenter.org/pool*; $3/adults, $2.70/youth
- **Redmond**, 17535 N.E. 104th St., Redmond, (206) 296-2961; $3/adults, $2.70/youth
- **Renton**, 16740 128th Ave. S.E., Renton, (206) 296-4335; $2.50/adults, $2/youth
- **Shoreline**, 19030 First Ave. N.E., Shoreline, (206) 362-1307; $3.25/adults, $2.25/ages 5–17, free/under 5
- **Si View Pool**, 400 S.E. Orchard, North Bend, (425) 888-1447; *www.nwcenter.org/pool*
- **St. Edward Pool**, 14445 Juanita Dr. N.E., Bothell, (425) 823-6983; *www.nwcenter.org/pool*; $3/adults, $2.70/youth
- **Tukwila/South Central Pool**, 4414 S. 144th St., Seattle, (206) 267-2350; $3/adults, $2/youth

Parent Tips

In 2008, parents on both sides of Lake Washington organized to have more public pools built in their communities. Project Seattle Pools *(www.seattlepools.org)* seeks to get an outdoor pool built in both northeast and southeast Seattle. SPLASH for All *(www.splashforall.org)* is working to build an extensive aquatic center in Bellevue. Check the websites for progress reports and information on how to get involved in these efforts.

Chapter 6

Outdoor Fun

Every season brings a new array of **outdoor** opportunities for Seattle families. In a city surrounded by **water** and **mountains**, within minutes you can find a way to have both exercise and good times. And don't let a lack of experience or equipment stop you—**classes** and **rentals** for all skill levels and activities are easy to find.

Walking/Hiking

Forget the old adage about how getting somewhere is half the fun. On a hike with kids, getting there has to be all the fun. Picking up slugs, climbing stumps, crossing bridges, dipping toes into freezing cold streams—those are the reasons kids like to hike.

Urban Trails

These trails are close enough to require just a short drive (under one-half hour from most neighborhoods in Seattle), but you'll feel like you've escaped for some good time with Mother Nature.

Bridal Trails State Park
Bellevue
(425) 649-4276
www.bridletrails.org

Directions: From I-405 northbound, take Exit 17. At end of off-ramp, turn right and head south on 116th Avenue N.E. At the four-way stop, continue straight ahead. The park entrance is located at the first opening in the trees on the left. From I-405 southbound, after taking Exit 17, turn right, crossing over freeway. At the first light, turn right again, heading south on 116th Avenue, and follow same directions as above.

Best known for its equestrian trails and horse shows, this park's 28 miles of trails are also open to pedestrian use—although horses do have the right-of-way. The park is almost 500 acres, and mostly forested. The trails are easy to navigate, with dirt/gravel surfaces, and flat to moderate inclines. There are guided nature walks offered—check website for details.

During the summer, a number of horse shows take place in the park, which can be a fun diversion if your kids are interested in horses and riding. The shows are free; check the park's website for a schedule, or look on the bulletin boards at the horse show facilities when you're at the park. The two biggest horse shows are hunter-jumper, on the third weekend in May and the fourth weekend in June. There's a $5 parking fee—whether you are just enjoying the trails or stopping by to watch a show.

Cougar Mountain Regional Wildlife Park

Bellevue

(206) 296-4171

www.metrokc.gov/parks/parks/cougarmountain.html

Directions: Take Exit 13 from I-90 and drive south up the hill on Lakemont Boulevard S.E. for 3.1 miles. Look for the gravel entrance to the Red Town Trailhead on the left side of the road.

Hiking at Cougar Mountain—King County's largest park—you'll find it hard to believe you're only a few minutes from the bustling Eastside. The 3,082-acre county park, part of the foothills known as the Issaquah Alps, features more than 36 miles of trails through forests of Sitka spruce, cedar, hemlock, and Douglas fir. Prospectors and coal miners worked Cougar Mountain for a century, finally leaving it alone in 1963. Most of the old-growth forests were logged, but some fragments can still be found near Wilderness Peak.

Trail destinations lead to and by a wide variety of sights, including a Nike missile site left over from the Cold War, coal-mining shafts, waterfalls, a restored meadow that was used as a baseball field in the 1920s, caves, glacial boulders, and mountaintop viewpoints.

The park's most popular entry point, Red Town Trailhead, is the site of a former mining town that had 750 residents in 1883. Coal miners worked in the area for around 100 years.

Some easier trails to try include Coal Creek Trail, a two-mile round-trip on level ground, and the Wildside/Mill Pond Loop, a level 1.5 miles. Both begin at the Red Town Trailhead.

Discovery Park

3801 W. Government Way, Seattle

(206) 386-4236

www.seattle.gov/Parks/Environment/discovparkindex.htm

The trails that penetrate this huge and beautiful city park each offer a different experience. Nature lovers will enjoy the Loop Trail, a 2.8-mile loop full of curves and twists, through wood and meadow. A great walk for families is the Wolf Tree Nature Trail, a lovely half-mile path through one of the least disturbed areas (last logged in the 1860s). Half a dozen bridges, raised wooden walkways, and numbered posts will keep kids interested in trudging along. To get to the trail from the main east gate entrance, follow the park road to the north parking lot. At the southwest corner of the lot is an information sign with a map of the park. The Wolf Tree Nature Trail begins at the northwest corner of the lot. At the south parking lot you'll find a trail leading across a large meadow with a spectacular view of the Puget Sound and the Olympic mountain range, and eventually the trail will take you down to the beach below.

There are also free drop-in nature walks led by knowledgeable and enthusiastic park rangers on many weekends, and a Junior Naturalist program for teens is offered, along with an extensive summer day camp program.

....

Juanita Bay Park
2201 Market St., Kirkland
(425) 828-1217
www.ci.kirkland.wa.us/depart/parks/tours.htm

The 113-acre park features trails, boardwalks, observation areas, and interpretive signs that help identify plants and animals in the wetlands. Kids will enjoy crossing bridges and raised wooden walkways. Volunteer rangers offer a free one-hour interpretive tour of Juanita Bay Park on the first Sunday of each month at 1 P.M., beginning in the parking lot. Registration is not required. Bring binoculars. The park is an impressive wildlife enclave, boasting a huge variety of birds, mammals, and reptiles. You can download a wildlife and park guide from the website.

....

Kubota Gardens
9817 55th Ave. S., at Renton Ave. S., Seattle
(206) 684-4584

Trails run through this 20-acre display garden, leading to waterfalls, prayer stones, and lush lawns. Kids will like the steep, brightly colored bridges (you can make your walk even more fun by suggesting trolls live underneath). Be sure to tell kids to stay on the trails, to protect planted areas. The high point of the property offers a view of the gardens, the Cascade mountain range, and the Eastside. The gardens, originally part of the Kubota Gardening Company, are now owned by the City of Seattle and received national historical landmark status in 1981. Admission is free.

Lake Hills

Ranger station, 15416 S.E. 16th St., Bellevue
(425) 452-7225

The 2-mile-long Lake Hills Greenbelt Trail threads through 150 acres of woods and wetlands. One place to access the trail is at the Lake Hills Ranger Station. You'll find information about vegetation and wildlife at the ranger station. Take time to explore the demonstration garden, which is immediately adjacent to the station. Rangers lead walks every Saturday at 11 A.M. from the ranger station. The trail is linked to the Phantom Lake Walkway, a 2.5-mile paved loop that is great for walking, biking, or jogging. The Phantom Lake Walkway intersects the Spiritridge Trail, a 2.5-mile wooded loop around the Boeing Service Center. Park at Spiritridge Park (16100 S.E. 33rd Pl.).

Marymoor Park

6064 W. Lake Sammamish Pkwy. N.E., Redmond

With all the action at Marymoor, it is easy to overlook the Marymoor Interpretive Trail, a short (just under one mile) hike to the Lake Sammamish overlook, featuring informative signs about the plants, animals, and birds that thrive in this wildlife preserve (no dogs allowed). The walk can be lengthened by taking the boardwalk north along the Sammamish River and walking over open fields to the parking lots for a loop almost two miles long.

As you walk along the trail, impress your kids by telling them that between 1964 and 1970, archaeologists from the University of Washington identified four pre-Columbian sites—two in Marymoor Park and two more just outside the park along the river. The oldest tools found there were made 6,000 years ago, the rest around 3,000 years ago.

Mercer Slough Nature Park

2102 Bellevue Way S.E., Bellevue
(425) 452-2752

Directions: To reach Winters House, from I-90, take the Bellevue Way exit and head north, past the South Bellevue Park and Ride lot. Look for the blue Winters House sign on the right. To get to the Environmental Education Center and the Bellefields Trailhead, from I-405, take the S.E. Eighth Street exit and turn west. Turn left on 118th. They are on the right before crossing I-90.

Covering 320 acres, this nature park encompasses the largest remaining wetland on Lake Washington and Bellevue's largest park. It offers more than seven miles of year-round trails through marshes, meadows, and forests, as well as a canoe trail and a blueberry farm that sells blueberries during season. Wildlife-watchers can try to spot more than 100 species of birds, plus coyotes, beavers, and muskrats. The park is a nesting area for blue herons. Free guided nature walks are offered May through September 2–3 P.M.; meet at Winters House, pre-registration not required.

The Environmental Education Center at the park is a partnership with Pacific Science Center focusing on freshwater wetland ecology. Classes and day camps, as well as school programs are offered (1625 118th Ave. S.E., 425-450-0207).

....

Ravenna Park
5520 Ravenna Ave. N.E., Seattle

This forested ravine just north of the University of Washington is hidden from the cars zipping along nearby on 15th Avenue N.E. Easy walking paths follow both sides of a little stream; steeper trails lead up to a picnic area and play fields off N.E. 55th Street, on the west end of the park. Recent daylighting of the creek, elimination of a soccer field, and the addition of a wheelchair-accessible path have added to the park's popularity in recent years.

....

Schmitz Preserve
5551 S.W. Admiral Way, Seattle

Home to one of the last stands of old-growth forest in Seattle, 50-acre Schmitz Preserve in West Seattle is a good place to hike if nearby Alki gets too windy or the kids have gotten too much sun. Rustic paths follow a stream through lush forest and over several bridges.

Washington Park Arboretum

Lake Washington Blvd. E. between E. Madison and Hwy. 520, Seattle
Graham Visitor's Center, 2300 Arboretum Dr. E., Seattle
(206) 543-8800

The University of Washington Botanical Gardens at the Washington Park Arboretum are a vast and wonderful display of native plants in a setting that allows you to forget that you are in a busy city. Kids may only have a passing interest in plants and flowers, but they are sure to be impressed with the breathtaking display of color on Azalea Way if you visit in spring, when you'll catch a wide variety of azaleas and rhododendrons in bloom. The 200-acre arboretum features miles of walking paths, mossy ponds, and the finest display of native Northwest plants found anywhere in the region. A definite kid-pleaser is the Waterfront Trail, a half-mile trail that crosses bridges and features extensive wooden walkways to get from Marsh Island to Foster Island. The trailhead begins near the Museum of History and Industry, or near the western entrance to the gated Broadmoor neighborhood. Kids will also like watching the boat traffic on Lake Washington. Wear rainboots and watch small kids closely—there are many places on this trail where it is easy to tumble into the water.

The UW Botanical Gardens at the Arboretum provide an extensive educational program for families and schools. For a $7 fee, families can check out Family Adventure Packs for two hours. Larger backpacks, intended for 6–15 people are also available for larger groups. These seasonal backpacks are full of equipment, field guides, scavenger hunts, and tools; reservations are necessary. For classroom visits there's also the Seedlings Preschool Programs and Saplings School Programs. An excellent Arboretum Summer Sleuths program is available for grades K–6. For more information or to make an appointment, call (206) 543-8801 or e-mail at *uwbgeduc@u.washington.edu*.

Another fun way to explore the arboretum is by rowboat or canoe, available for rent from the UW Waterfront Activities Center (see "Boating" elsewhere in this chapter).

The Japanese Garden, across from the southwest end of the arboretum, offers a peaceful reprieve from city activity. This authentic Japanese stroll garden, designed by Japanese landscape designer Juki Iida and maintained by the Seattle Department of Parks and Recreation, is open from March through November. Visitors are welcome to pick up a brochure at the garden entrance and walk through the fenced area on their own or take a guided tour from a trained docent (call for reservations). Each season offers something new in the garden, from blooming cherry trees in the early spring to rhododendrons and azaleas throughout the summer to colored foliage during the fall. Turtles and 50 carp can be spotted in the landscaped ponds.

Garden tours at the Japanese Garden are offered at noon and 12:30 P.M. most Sundays, and a number of events—including a teahouse tour and tea service—are offered at various times during the year. A schedule is posted at the garden's website: *www.seattlejapanesegarden.org*.

The Japanese Garden is located on Lake Washington Boulevard between E. Madison and 23rd Avenue S. Admission is $5/adults, $3/children ages 6 and up, free/5 and under. Groups are always welcome; special discount rates apply. Hours vary according to the season. Call (206) 684-4725 for more information.

Out-of-Town Trails

If you want to get out of the city, here are some suggestions for short hikes within easy driving distance of Seattle.

....

Asahel Curtis Nature Trail

Directions: Take Exit 47 from I-90, and turn right at the stop sign. Turn left at Road 55 and drive 0.5 mile to a large parking lot; the trail begins at the east end.

The 1.25-mile loop is an easy walk on a dirt and gravel path through one of the last stands of old-growth forest in the Snoqualmie Valley. Kids will enjoy the bridges as the trail crosses the Humpback Creek several times. Interpretive signs and plant labels add interest.

....

Franklin Falls

Directions: Take Exit 47 from I-90. Turn left at the stop sign, then right at the T. In 0.25 mile, turn left onto Denny Creek Road No. 58 and follow it for 2.5 miles. Turn left on a paved road just past the campground. In 200 feet, you'll find parking on the left; the trailhead is on the right.

This is an easy 2-mile round-trip walk along the South Fork of the Snoqualmie River leading through the forest to Franklin Falls. It's a nice place, especially on a warm, sunny summer day, for a picnic or sunbathing. The rocks around the falls can be slippery—be sure to warn children to be cautious.

....

Twin Falls Hike

Directions: Take Exit 34 off I-90, and turn right onto Edgewick Road. After 0.5 mile, right before a bridge, turn left onto S.E. 159th Street. The road dead-ends at the trailhead in 0.75 mile.

This 2.6-mile round-trip trail follows the South Fork of the Snoqualmie River, then climbs to an overlook at 0.8 mile. It then heads up for an up-close view of both the lower and upper falls; a wooden bridge crosses between them. Some portions of the trail drop off steeply, so watch small children.

Hiking Resources

....

Evergreen State Volkssport Association
(253) 840-1776
www.ava.org/clubs/esva

Children are welcome at volkssporting events, usually five- or 10-kilometer organized walks, though some clubs also sponsor bike rides and swims. Walks are rated by difficulty and information is available on whether the trails are suitable for strollers or wheelchairs. The free events are open to anyone. Promoting well-being and good health by providing safe exercise in a stress-free environment is the hallmark of volkssporting. Call the state organization for information about the club nearest you.

....

Issaquah Alps Trails Club
Issaquah Trails Center, First and Bush, Issaquah
www.issaquahalps.org

This family-friendly club leads free guided hikes on trails in the Issaquah Alps, including Cougar, Tiger, and Squak Mountains. Some are designated as family hikes, but all hikes are rated by length and climbing difficulty, so hikers can tell if a particular outing will be appropriate for their children. Parents should also check with the hike leader. Hikers meet at the Issaquah Trails Center, a two-story yellow house (across the street from the community center) at an appointed time, and then carpool to the trailhead. Visit the website for a complete hike schedule and more information.

The club offers a booklet, *Eastside Family Hikes*, for $3. The booklet describes family hikes and notes whether strollers are appropriate. Information on ordering this booklet, and other books, is available at the website under "Ordering."

....

The Mountaineers
300 Third Ave. W., Seattle
(206) 284-6310
www.moutaineers.org

The Mountaineers is the largest outdoor organization in the region, with headquarters in Seattle and branches in Tacoma, Everett, Bellingham, and Wenatchee. The club is dedicated to offering a wide array of outdoor activities for all ages, including hiking, cross-country skiing, backpack trips, and kayaking. A family activity committee organizes hikes and backpack trips geared for families. Individual and family memberships are available.

Mountaineer Books publishes two excellent guides: *Best Hikes With Children in Western Washington & the Cascades*, volumes 1 and 2. These guides are available at local bookstores or by contacting The Mountaineers.

The club also maintains four mountain lodges near ski areas where members can stay with children (although parents are discouraged from bringing children ages 2 and under).

Wilderness Awareness School

26425 N.E. Allen St., Ste. 203, Duvall
(425) 788-1301
www.wildernessawareness.org

This not-for-profit environmental education program offers tracking and nature awareness classes and camps for children and families that will enhance your outdoor experience.

Biking

Special family bicycling events are scheduled by various organizations throughout the Puget Sound area, especially during the summer months. The 5,000-member Cascade Bicycle Club (206-522-2407, *www.cascade.org*) offers loads of information for novice and experienced bicyclists, as well as classes and group events. Its website includes tips for riding with children.

From May through September, the Seattle Parks Department designates one Bicycle Saturday and Bicycle Sunday per month. With the help of the Seattle Engineering Department, Lake Washington Boulevard from Seward Park to Mount Baker Beach is closed to vehicle traffic between 10 A.M. and 6 P.M. on these days. Bicycle safety checks and first-aid stations are set up along the route. For more information, check the website at *www.seattle.gov/PARKS/Athletics/bikesatsun*.

Whatever bike route you choose, try not to rush it. Pack a lunch and, instead of setting a distance goal, just ride for the fun of it, stopping along the way to relax and unwind.

Before starting on a bicycle outing, make sure you have helmets for all riders, which are required by law in Seattle and King County.

Many of the following trails are utilized by bicyclists, in-line skaters, runners, and walkers. Some separate wheeled and non-wheeled users; use extra caution on all trails that are heavily traveled.

....

Alki Avenue
Harbor Ave. S.W. to 64th Ave. S.W., Seattle

One way to enjoy beautiful Alki Beach is to hop on bikes and take a delightful ride on the bicycle trail that parallels the beach. Along Alki Avenue there are lanes for bicyclists, walkers, and skaters on the flat, scenic 2.6-mile route. The safe, 12-foot-wide trail features a separate path for pedestrians, and varies from 6 to 12 feet wide. The faster riders and racers tend to stay on the roadway, making the bicycle path pretty safe for kids.

Families with older children can stretch their trip to 14 miles one-way by taking a street route west along Alki Avenue S.W. and south along Beach Drive S.W. to Lincoln Park. There isn't a designated bike path, but signs mark the route.

....

Burke Gilman Trail/Sammamish River Trail
Eighth Ave. N.W. in Seattle to Marymoor Park in Redmond

This amazing, 27-mile-long trail makes local bicyclists the envy of bicyclists in every other Northwest city. The route takes you on a level, scenic path from Eighth Avenue N.W. (Gas Works Park is the easiest place to start, however), past the University of Washington, around the north end of Lake Washington, through Kenmore and Woodinville, to Marymoor Park in Redmond. Although too far for most young children (and many adults), the route gives riders many shorter options and allows you to start wherever is the most convenient. One nice family ride is the 10-mile round-trip stretch from Marymoor Park to the wineries in Woodinville. The segment from Gas Works Park to Matthews Beach is about 15 miles round-trip. The Burke Gilman Trail (Seattle to Kenmore) and the Sammamish River Trail (Kenmore to Marymoor) are paved and often heavily traveled, especially on weekends. Plan to make a park your starting and end point, so you have access to bathrooms and a place for kids to play after the ride.

Cedar River Trail
Mouth of the Cedar River in Renton to Landsburg Trailhead

This 17-mile-long trail is paved from downtown Renton, south to 196th Avenue S.E./Jones Road—about 6 miles; south of there the trail is crushed gravel.

One segment of the trail follows the Cedar River through downtown Renton to where it eventually spills out into Lake Washington. Fans of airplanes will enjoy going past one of Boeing's fields (be warned, it can be noisy); pick up this portion of the trail from Renton Memorial Stadium. The trail can also be accessed from the Renton Community Center (1717 Maple Valley Hwy.). Bicycling is discouraged (but not prohibited) on the section through the downtown area. Heading the other direction, the trail mostly parallels SR 169 (Maple Valley Hwy.), with a cleared parking area off SR 169 north of its junction with SR 18. The trail becomes crushed rock and continues to Issaquah–Hobart Road and 276th Avenue S.E.

Discovery Park
3801 W. Government Way, Seattle
(206) 386-4236

More than 7 miles of paved roads closed to cars are great for biking. Bicycles are not allowed on dirt trails, however.

Elliott Bay Bicycle Path
Pier 70, north through Myrtle Edwards Park

This 1.25-mile-long trail is rarely crowded, except when it attracts large numbers of downtowners who are trying to get some exercise and fresh air at the lunch hour. Take the kids on a nice spring or summer evening, stop at the fishing pier, and watch the sun set over the water.

Green Lake
Between N. 59th and N. 77th, Seattle

Just northeast of Woodland Park, the 2.8-mile-long trail around the lake is flat and paved; a playground and grassy areas are scattered along the way. On almost every sunny day, however, it gets very crowded with cyclists, joggers, couples, roller skaters, baby strollers, and dogs. A line divides wheeled and non-wheeled traffic. It is more enjoyable and less risky to ride on cloudy days or weekday mornings.

Green River Trail
I-405 to S. 192nd St., Kent

The 12-mile-long Green River Trail follows the scenic Green River as it winds through the Kent Valley. A good place to park your car and pick up the trail is Briscoe Park (S. 190th St. and 62nd Ave. S., Kent), situated at one of the bends of the river. From there you can travel north or south along the flat, paved, uncrowded trail. Briscoe Park has picnic areas, a boat launch, and play fields as well, so the day can be broken up with several activities if you wish. All portions of the Green River Trail are not yet complete. When finished, it will span 30 miles from Alki Point in Seattle to King County's Auburn Narrows Park. Currently, the completed sections go through the Kent Valley, from south Seattle through Kent, connecting to a number of neighborhoods and community trails.

Interurban Trail
Strander Blvd. in Tukwila to Third Ave. in Pacific

The 14-mile-long Interurban Trail runs underneath Puget Power's power lines and is flat and paved. Parking is available at many sites along the trail, but one of the more convenient places is located at S. 182nd Street, just south of S. 180th, off the West Valley Highway on the west side of the river. You can pick up the Green River Trail or the Interurban Trail here, or take some time to relax in the park, which has a play area with swings. Another trailhead is at 259th Street, just east of Highway 167.

Iron Horse State Park/Snoqualmie Tunnel
Just east of Snoqualmie Pass

Directions: From Seattle, take I-90 to Exit 54. Turn south at exit, then turn east (left) on Highway 906. After one-half mile, turn right on Lake Keechelus boat launch road, turn right on next road. Look for the Keechelus trailhead. Follow signs to the tunnel.

The thought of pedaling through this former railroad tunnel may appeal to adventuresome kids. This 6.4-mile round-trip ride—flat and on a hard, gravel surface—is an easy one, even for novice bike riders. But beware, it is very dark in this long tunnel. If your kids are at all phobic about dark places, it may not be the best choice. In any case, be sure bikes are equipped with good bike lights before starting out. The temperature in the tunnel is also cool—even on a hot day—so be sure to bring a jacket along. It's open May 1 to October 31.

Lake Washington Boulevard Trail
Seward Park to Mount Baker Park, Seattle

The scenic, 3-mile-long paved path along the lake is popular with walkers and joggers. On a number of weekend days during the summer, Lake Washington Boulevard is closed to traffic for biking and skating. For more information, check the website at *www.seattle.gov/PARKS/Athletics/bikesatsun*.

Preston–Snoqualmie Trail
I-90 at Preston to Snoqualmie Falls

This 6-mile-long paved trail ends two miles east of Lake Alice Road with a view of Snoqualmie Falls. There is no way to make a loop, so it's an out-and-back ride. Access is off 308th Avenue in Preston.

Seward Park Loop
East end of Seward Park parking lot, Seattle

This short, 2.5-mile loop around the perimeter of Seward Park along Lake Washington is an ideal place for even the wobbliest rider to enjoy fabulous scenery and a flat, easy ride. The trail is a road that has been closed, so it is plenty wide. The views here are exceptional, with Mt. Rainier to the south and the city skyline to the northeast. Plan to swim at the lifeguarded beach at the end of your ride if it is a hot day.

Soos Creek Trail
13700 block of S.E. 208th St., to S.E. 264th St. and 150th Ave. S.E., Kent

This scenic, 4.5-mile-long paved trail stretches along Soos Creek, east of Kent. Parking is available at the trail's north end of Gary Grant Park, where families can take advantage of a picnic area. You can also access it at the central trailhead (148th Ave., S.E., between S.E. 240th and S.E. 256th) or the Meridian South trailhead (152nd Way S.E., 0.25 mile north of Kent–Kangley Road). The route is mostly flat, especially at the north end, and is divided for horse and bike traffic. It is not heavily traveled.

Tolt Pipeline Trail
Woodinville to Snoqualmie Valley

The 15-mile-long dirt and gravel trail, also popular with equestrians, is 100 feet wide and runs alongside a giant pipe. Best place to park is along the Sammamish River Trail on 145th Street, Woodinville. Parking is also available where the trail crosses Avondale Road at approximately the 14500 block. The trail will take you by houses and farms, and crosses some busy roads and a pedestrian bridge.

Horseback Riding

Does your child sleep with a hobbyhorse and wear cowboy boots to bed? Do you trip over little plastic horses whenever you enter your daughter's room? Horseback riding is a real thrill for young horse lovers, and all of the places listed below provide trail rides, and in some cases, riding classes, summer day camps, and overnight camps. Call for details on these classes and camps.

High Country Outfitters
315 W. Second St., Cle Elum
(888) 235-0111
www.highcountry-outfitters.com

This organization offers a variety of trail-ride packages in spring, summer, and fall, out of the Cle Elum area, varying in length and difficulty, from guided day rides to overnight trips. They also operate Camp Wahoo, an American Camp Association–accredited resident horse camp, and Red Gate Farm Day Camp in Issaquah, a summer day camp. Reservations are required.

Horse Country
8507 Hwy. 92, Granite Falls
(360) 691-7509 or (425) 335-4773
www.horsecountryfarm.com

Hours: Year-round, Tues.–Sun.

Rates: Begin at $20 for a half-hour ride

Horse Country features guided trail rides through forests and meadows and along the Pilchuck River. Rides are as short as one-half hour, and as long as two hours. Children must be at least 7 years old. No rider can weight more than 200 pounds. Reservations required. Other programs include lessons, summer day camps, and lead-around ponies for little ones.

....

Jorgenson Enterprises
P.O. Box 129, Duvall
(425) 478-2087
www.horserentals.com/jorgenson

Rates: Start at $50

Jorgenson Enterprises offers two- and three-hour trail rides in the Cascade foothills, extended pack rides, and a variety of other excursions, including wagon adventures and winter sleigh rides. Reservations are required. They'll also deliver ponies to your birthday party.

....

Little Bit Therapeutic Riding Center
19802 N.E. 148th Ave., Woodinville
(425) 882-1554

This nonprofit organization offers therapeutic horseback riding programs for differently abled persons, emphasizing their capabilities rather than their limitations. The center is always looking for volunteers to help riders, though volunteers must be at least 14 years old.

Tiger Mountain Outfitters
24508 S.E. 133rd St., Issaquah
(425) 392-5090

Hours: Year-round

Rates: $60/person for three-hour ride

Tiger Mountain Outfitters offers guided trail rides year-round for anyone over 10 years of age. Call ahead for reservations.

Pony Rides

If your child isn't ready to ride a horse, a pony might be just the solution. Pony rides and pony care opportunities are offered at the following locations.

- **Farrel-McWhirter Park**, 19545 Redmond Rd., Redmond, (425) 556-2300. Occasionally offers pony riding and care classes.

- **Forest Park Animal Farm**, 802 Mukilteo Blvd., Everett, (425) 257-8300. Free pony rides on some days, Memorial Day–Labor Day, weather permitting.

- **Kelsey Creek Farm**, 13204 S.E. Eighth Pl., Bellevue, (425) 452-7688. Horsemanship classes and programs for children ages 7 and up.

- **Lang's Horse and Pony Farm, Mt. Vernon**, (360) 424-7630. Offering trail rides, lessons, summer day camps, and birthday parties since 1975.

- **Pony Paradise Rides**, 8107 224th St. S.E., Woodinville, (800) 753-PONY. Brush a pony, ride on a pony trail, and feed treats! Riding lessons are also available. Their 4-Good Hooves program offers 20-minute pony rides, games, and a chance to feed the ponies for children with special needs. 10 A.M.–6 P.M. daily.

Mini-Golf

Dress your children in plaid pants and cardigans and teach them what the good life is all about in these outdoor mini-golf courses.

Green Lake Pitch 'n Putt
5701 W. Green Lake Way N., Seattle
(206) 632-2280

Hours: Mar.–Oct., 9 A.M.–dusk

Admission: $5/person

If you want to introduce your older child to the real game of golf, this is the place. Green Lake Pitch 'n Putt is not a true mini-golf course; it's a nine-hole, par 3 course on 8 acres of Green Lake's south shore. Holes range from 55 to 115 yards. You can bring your own clubs and balls or rent them.

Interbay Golf Center
2501 15th Ave. W., Seattle
(206) 285-2200

Hours: Year-round, 7 A.M.–9 P.M.

Interbay Golf Center, one of Seattle's newer facilities, features an 18-hole putt-putt course with a variety of layouts and challenges set among lush gardens, waterfalls, and ponds. The center also has a 9-hole golf course, driving range, putting green, and a cafe. Golf lessons and clinics are also offered.

Jazwieck's Golf
7828 Broadway, Everett
(425) 355-5646

Hours: Apr.–Oct., closed Sun.

This 18-hole course, built in 1961, was one of the first miniature golf courses in the Seattle area. It has traditional mini-golf obstacles and decorations.

Rainbow Run
10402 Willows Rd. N.E., Redmond
(425) 883-1200

Admission: $9/adults, $6/ages 14 and under; before noon, $8/adults, $5/ages 14 and under

Rainbow Run Putting Course is an 18-hole putting course that is part of the Willows Run Golf Center. The design of the course features special effects and journeys through four different climate zones.

Riverbend Mini Putt-Putt
2020 W. Meeker, Kent
(253) 859-4000

Hours: Mon.–Fri., 8 A.M.–9 P.M.; Sat.–Sun., 7 A.M.–9 P.M.

Run by the City of Kent, Riverbend is an outdoor 18-hole miniature golf course. Groups and birthday celebrations are welcome with advance reservations. There are also 18- and 9-hole golf courses here, as well as a driving range, three pro shops, and two restaurants.

Parent Tips

There's nothing that says summer night like watching a movie outdoors. The biggest challenge in the Northwest is that it becomes dark quite late—9:30–10 P.M.—making this a very late night for little ones. But if you have kids who don't want to go to sleep on those summer nights, this could be the perfect weekend outing.

Seattle

- Fremont Outdoor Cinema (3500 Phinney Ave. N.W., Seattle, *www.fremontoutdoormoviescinema.com*)
- Movies at the Mural (Seattle Center, 206-684-7200, *www.seattlecenter.com*)
- West Seattle Sidewalk Cinema (*www.sidewalkcinema.com*)

North

- Outdoor Nights (Edmonds, 425-771-0230, *www.ci.edmonds.wa.us/calendar.stm*)
- Cinema Under the Stars (Everett, 425-257-7107, *www.everettwa.org*)

South

- Outdoor Cinema at Liberty Park (Renton, 425-430-6700, *www.rentonwa.gov/living*)
- Zoo Cinemas, Pt. Defiance Zoo (253-591-5337, *www.pdza.org*)
- Metro Parks Tacoma Summer Sounds Cinema (253-305-1000, *www.metroparkstacoma.org*)

East

- Outdoor Films (Mercer Island, 206-236-3545)
- First Tech Movies@Marymoor, Redmond (206-296-4999, *www.metrokc.gov/parks/movies*)

Snow Fun

Seattle families are lucky to be able to jump into their car on a winter weekend and arrive at the mountains within a hour. There are plenty of opportunities for you and your kids to have some fun without enormous expense. Remember to dress kids well so they stay warm and dry, carry chains at all times in your vehicle, bring plenty of snacks, and check with the Washington State Department of Transportation Pass Report for road and weather conditions before you venture forth. Call 511 or go to *wsdot.wa.gov/traffic/road/mnts/mntbas.htm*.

Downhill Skiing/Snowboarding

Summit Central and Summit West at the Summit at Snoqualmie are two of the best areas for beginning skiers or snowboarders. They have several bunny hills and lifts that give novices a chance to master a few basic skills before facing steeper slopes. All of the following areas offer family-discount season passes that provide significant savings. Consider spending a day on the slopes during the week or in the evening, when lift tickets are generally cheaper.

All of the areas offer lessons and equipment rentals for the day. However, it's a good idea to look into renting equipment in the city, before heading for the slopes. Lines in rental facilities on the slopes can be long, especially on weekends. If you think this is something your kids will enjoy a number of times during the season, it's also possible to rent equipment for the entire season.

Crystal Mountain
Hwy. 410, 12 miles northeast of Mt. Rainier
(360) 663-2265 (general information); (888) 754-6199 (snow phone)
www.skicrystal.com

The terrain at the ski area is 13 percent beginner, 57 percent intermediate, and 30 percent advanced. There is a Kids Club program for ages 4–11. Children can participate in half- or all-day programs that include a lesson, lift ticket, and supervision while parents ski. Reservations are not accepted. Lessons are also available for older kids and adults.

A drop-off zone right in front of the ticket plaza allows one parent to unload the kids while the other parks the car.

Stevens Pass
U.S. Hwy. 2, 78 miles east of Seattle
(206) 812-4510
www.stevenspass.com

The terrain here is 11 percent beginner, 54 percent intermediate, and 35 percent advanced. The Kids Club, for ages 3–6, offers a supervised half or full day of skiing (reservations: 206-812-4510 ext. 245.) Lessons are also available for older kids and adults.

The Summit at Snoqualmie
I-90 at Snoqualmie Pass, about 50 miles east of Seattle
(206) 236-1600 (snow phone); (425) 434-7669 (general information)
www.summit-at-snoqualmie.com

The Summit at Snoqualmie comprises four ski areas: Alpental, Summit Central, Summit West, and Summit East. One ticket allows you to ride lifts at all four areas.

The terrain at Summit Central is 50 percent beginner, 20 percent intermediate, and 30 percent advanced. At Summit East, it's 42 percent beginner, 40 percent intermediate, and 18 percent advanced; Summit West, 35 percent beginner, 45 percent intermediate, 20 percent advanced; and Alpental, 10 percent beginner, 40 percent intermediate, 50 percent advanced.

Daily child care is offered at Summit West. Call (425) 434-7669 ext. 6520, for information and reservations. Lessons are available for ages 4 and up; call (425) 434-6700.

Cross-Country Skiing

Nordic centers at Snoqualmie's Summit East (I-90 at Snoqualmie Pass, 206-236-7277, *www.summit-at-snoqualmie.com*) and Stevens Pass (U.S. Hwy. 2, 78 miles east of Seattle, 206-812-4510, *www.stevenspass.com*) offer 50 kilometers and 28 kilometers of groomed trails, respectively, for cross-country skiers of all abilities. Trail fees range from $10–$14.

Skiers who prefer trails other than those at the ski resorts can purchase a Sno-Park permit that entitles them to park at designated lots at local passes. Permits are $108/day, $320/season; they are available at outdoor retail stores and ranger stations. (For a list of vendors, visit the Washington State Parks website at *www.parks.wa.gov/vendor1.htm*.) Good cross-country trails are also plentiful in the Leavenworth area.

Tubing

Snowflake Tubing Center
Snoqualmie Pass, southeast corner of Summit Central parking lot
(425) 434-6791
www.summit-at-snoqualmie.com

The Snowflake Tubing Center takes the work out of snow play by offering rope tows to carry sliders up the groomed hill. Ticket prices (per session: $12/ages 12 and under, $20/ages 13 and up) include a tube—and only the supplied tubes are allowed on the hill. Two-hour sessions begin at 9 A.M., with 15-minute breaks between sessions. Space for each session is limited, so come a bit early so you don't miss getting into the session you hoped for. There is a small lodge with limited food available.

Swimming/Wading

We are fortunate to have not only many outdoor swimming pools in our area but swimming beaches as well. With all the opportunities for water fun, be sure that all your children learn to swim and only enter the water at a beach or pool that has a lifeguard on duty. Check the city parks department websites to learn about the lifeguard schedules for the beach or pool you plan to visit.

Wading pools are a great way for little kids to splash around and enjoy a warm summer day. Seattle has an abundance of them—and encourages their use as part of a water conservation effort. It uses less water, the thinking goes, to fill up a wading pool for public use, than for many individuals to fill up kiddie pools or turn on backyard sprinklers.

The wading pools are emptied and refilled each day they're in use, as required by state law. The city opens its wading pools on sunny days when the temperatures are forecast to rise to at least 70 degrees. Usually, wading pools are only filled half-full, but the city pledges to fill them to the top on the busiest days.

Swimming Pools

The following outdoor pools are open only during the summer.

- **Colman Pool**, Lincoln Park, 8603 Fauntleroy Way, Seattle, (206) 684-7494
- **Cottage Lake Pool**, 18831 N.E. Woodinville–Duvall Rd., Woodinville, (206) 296-2999
- **Henry Moses Aquatic Center**, 1719 Maple Valley Hwy., Renton, (425) 430-6780
- **Lynnwood Recreation Center**, 18900 44th Ave. W., Lynnwood, (425) 771-4030
- **McCollum Pool**, 600 128th St. S.E., Everett, (425) 357-6036
- **"Pop" Mounger Pool**, 2535 32nd Ave. W., Seattle, (206) 864-4708
- **Peter Kirk Pool**, 380 Kirkland Ave., Kirkland, (425) 587-3335
- **Redmond Pool**, 17535 N.E. 104th, Redmond, (206) 296-2961
- **Vashon Pool**, 9625 S.W. 204th, Vashon Island, (206) 463-3787

Swimming Beaches

- **Bellevue:** Clyde Beach, Chism Beach, Enatai Beach, Chesterfield Beach, Meydenbauer Park, Newcastle Beach
- **Federal Way:** Five Mile Lake
- **Kirkland:** Houghton Beach Park, Juanita Beach Park, Waverly Park
- **Issaquah:** Lake Sammamish State Park
- **Maple Valley:** Lake Wilderness Park
- **Mercer Island:** Groveland Park, Luther Burbank Park
- **Mountlake Terrace:** Ballinger
- **Redmond:** Idlewood Beach Park
- **Renton:** Gene Coulon Memorial Park
- **Sammamish:** Pine Lake Park
- **Seattle:** Madison Park, Madrona Beach, Matthews Beach, Mount Baker Beach, Sand Point Magnuson Park, Seward Park

Wading Pools

The following Seattle wading pools are open most weekdays. For up-to-date information, call the Wading Pool Hotline at (206) 684-7796.

- **Beacon Hill**, 1820 13th Ave. S.
- **Bitter Lake**, 13035 Linden Ave. N.
- **Cal Anderson**, 1635 11th Ave.
- **Dahl**, 7700 25th Ave. N.E.
- **Delridge**, 4501 Delridge Way S.W.
- **East Queen Anne**, 160 Howe St.
- **E. C. Hughes**, 2805 S.W. Holden St.
- **Georgetown**, 750 S. Homer St.
- **Gilman**, 923 N.W. 54th St.
- **Green Lake**, N. 73rd and W. Green Lake Dr. N.
- **Hiawatha**, 2700 California Ave. S.W.
- **Highland Park**, 1100 S.W. Cloverdale St.
- **Judkins**, 2150 S. Norman St.
- **Lincoln Park**, 8011 Fauntleroy Way S.W.
- **North Acres**, 12800 First Ave. N.E.
- **Peppi's**, 3233 E. Spruce St.
- **Powell Barnett**, 352 Martin Luther King Jr. Way
- **Ravenna Park**, 5520 Ravenna Ave. N.E.
- **Sandel**, 9053 First Ave. N.W.
- **Sand Point Magnuson**, 7400 Sand Point Way N.E.
- **Soundview**, 1590 N.W. 90th St.
- **South Park**, 8319 Eighth Ave. S.
- **Van Asselt**, 2820 S. Myrtle St.
- **View Ridge**, 4408 N.E. 70th St.
- **Volunteer Park**, 1247 15th Ave. E.
- **Wallingford**, 4219 Wallingford Ave. N.

Water Sprays and Fountains

For kids, a fountain is an irresistible temptation. They quickly shed shoes and socks, and plunge in.

- **Downtown Park**, 100th Ave. N.E. and N.E. First St., Bellevue. A 12,000-foot canal, a 240-foot-wide waterfall, and a reflecting pond.
- **Harbor Steps Park**, Western St. and University Ave., Seattle. Cascading fountains and pools flow downhill to the waterfront.
- **International Fountain**, Seattle Center, Seattle. Water sprays in the fountain shoot up at irregular intervals.
- **Judkins Park**, 2150 S. Norman St., Seattle. Water spray area is next to the playground.
- **Pratt Park**, 1800 S. Main St., Seattle. A variety of water sprays.
- **Ron K. Bills Memorial Fountain**, Miller Park, 330 19th Ave. E., Seattle. Small fountain.
- **Waterfall Garden**, Pioneer Square, Second Ave. and S. Main St., Seattle. Water sculptures and fountains.
- **Water Fountain**, Waterfront Park, Pier 59, Seattle. Near the Seattle Aquarium.
- **Water Fountain**, Bell Street Pier, Pier 66, Seattle. Fish-shaped artwork with pool, spraying fountains, and a globe fountain.
- **Water Wall**, Westlake Park, Fourth Ave. and Pine St., Seattle. Huge fountain arch.

Boating

Seattle is surrounded by Puget Sound, Lake Washington, Lake Sammamish, and dozens of smaller lakes, so it's no wonder boating is so popular here. The state has one of the highest ratios of boats per capita in the country. Boating, like any water sport, can be dangerous, so take proper precautions before you push off. Check the weather conditions, and make sure everyone—even the best swimmer—is wearing a personal flotation device or life jacket.

When you are out on the water, protect your skin and eyes. Even if the sky is overcast, be sure that everybody uses sunscreen and wears hats and sunglasses.

Agua Verde Café and Paddle Club

303 N.E. Boat St., Seattle

(206) 545-8570

www.aguaverde.com

Hours: Mar.–Oct., times vary

Rent a kayak at this paddle club, located on Portage Bay between Lake Union and Lake Washington. Paddle past Seattle's unique floating homes, and if you're energetic, continue down to the waters around the arboretum and the University of Washington. When you return, you can stop in for a meal at the restaurant, which offers fresh and delicious Mexican fare. The restaurant is closed on Sundays, but during the summer, you'll find a take-out window open every day. It's a great way to spend a sunny summer day—as many Seattleites have discovered. Be prepared to wait for a kayak; just put your name on the list. A small park is nearby to make your wait easier. Hourly rentals are $15/single, $18/double.

Cascade Canoe and Kayak Centers

Enatai Beach, 3519 108th Ave. S.E., Bellevue

Cedar River Boathouse, 1060 Nishiwaki Ln., Renton

(425) 430-0111; (888) 4U-KAYAK

www.canoe-kayak.com

This outfitter rents canoes and kayaks at two popular locations. Rental are $12–$20/hour. From Enatai Beach, paddlers have easy access to the Mercer Slough, and can also enjoy the Lake Washington shoreline. The Cedar River Boathouse is near Renton's Coulon Park. You can paddle up the Cedar River or along Lake Washington's shoreline and get a different view of the Boeing plant.

Center for Wooden Boats
1010 Valley St., Seattle
(206) 382-2628
www.cwb.org

Hours: Year-round, daily in summer; closed Tues. rest of year

With interesting marine businesses, a variety of fancy and funky houseboats along its shores, and seaplanes from Lake Union Air taking off and landing frequently, Lake Union is a fun place to explore. The Center for Wooden Boats, located on the south end of Lake Union, offers rowboats and sailboats for rental year-round. Rentals are $12.50–$37.50/hour. If you want to rent a sailboat, you'll have to go through a skill check (cost $5). The center also offers sailing lessons and a number of programs for kids.

Gas Works Park, on the north side of Lake Union directly across from the Center for Wooden Boats, has a playground and is a good place to get out and let kids stretch their legs. East of Gas Works Park, just before University Bridge, is Ivar's Salmon House. Pull up to the dock and send someone up to the outside fish bar for tasty fish-and-chips.

Greenlake Boat Rentals
7351 E. Green Lake Dr. N., Seattle
(206) 527-0171

Hours: Apr.–Sept., daily, 11 A.M.–dusk

Located near the Green Lake Community Center, this small concession rents out rowboats, paddleboats, kayaks, canoes, and sailboards for $14–$20/hour. Kids love to navigate their way to Duck Island, though it's better not explored on foot—too wet and muddy. Boat reservations, though not necessary, are recommended during the summer months.

Green Lake Small Craft Center

5900 W. Green Lake Dr. N., Seattle
(206) 684-4074

This city-run facility offers rowing, canoeing, kayaking, and sailing lessons for children and adults, as well as youth summer camp. Located on the southwest "corner" of the lake.

Mercer Slough Nature Park

2102 Bellevue Way S.E., Bellevue
(425) 452-2752

Hours: Vary different seasons

Three-hour guided canoe trips ($6/Bellevue residents, $7/nonresidents) leave Enatai Beach Park on Lake Washington and paddle up the mouth of the Mercer Slough. No experience or equipment is necessary. However, kids who weigh 35 pounds or less must provide their own Coast Guard–approved life vest. Call to register.

Moss Bay Rowing Center

1001 Fairview N., Seattle
(206) 682-2031
www.mossbay.net

Hours: Open year-round, 8 A.M.–dusk

Conveniently located at the south end of Lake Union, Moss Bay has kayaks, rowing shells, and sailboats for rent. They also offer a boating camp for kids both here and at their San Juan Island location. Rental rates are $13/singles, $18/doubles for kayaking. Rowing shells, sailing boats, and dragon boats also available.

Mount Baker Rowing and Sailing Center

3800 Lake Washington Blvd. S., Seattle

(206) 386-1913

Another city-run facility, Mount Baker also does not offer rentals, but does have a wide variety of classes for kids and adults in rowing, sailing and sailboarding, beginning canoe, and kayaking.

Northwest Outdoor Center

2100 Westlake Ave. N., Seattle

(206) 281-9694 or (800) 683-0637

www.nwoc.com

Hours: Open year-round, hours vary seasonally

Rent a two-person double kayak from Northwest Outdoor Center and see Lake Union from a new perspective. Several different models are available for rental, seating one, two, or three people. Kids sit in front, adults in the rear steering position. Rentals are $13/hour for single kayak, $18/hour for double. The center also offers guided tours and classes.

University of Washington Waterfront Activity Center

Montlake Blvd. N.E., Seattle

(206) 543-9433

Hours: Feb.–Oct., daily, 11 A.M.–dusk

Enjoy a leisurely paddle through the arboretum in a canoe or rowboat rented ($7.50/hour) at the Canoe House, which is north of the Montlake Bridge and southeast of Husky Stadium. The Foster Island area is full of mysterious waterways and footbridges to navigate through and under, a multitude of interesting birds to observe, and an unlimited number of places to beach the boat for a picnic. Canoes seat up to three people; rowboats seat up to four. Life vests are available for children as small as 25 pounds. Boats are available on a first-come, first-served basis, so arrive early on sunny weekends.

....

Fishing

Kids 14 and under can fish during open season on any public dock in the area, without a license. Teens and adults must obtain licenses. For information on fishing licenses and regulations, call the Washington State Fish and Wildlife Department at (360) 902-2464. Many local sporting good stores sell licenses and offer booklets covering seasonal regulations.

In the city, you can fish at Green Lake and, of course, Lake Washington. Lake Washington is home to more than 40 species of fish, but most people who dangle a line are hoping to pull out rainbow and cutthroat trout, salmon, and steelhead.

You can also try to hook a saltwater fish in Puget Sound. A number of local docks offer access.

Green Lake Piers

- E. Green Lake Dr. and Latona N.E., at foot of 65th Ave. N.E., Seattle
- W. Green Lake Dr. and Stone N., at the south end of the Bathhouse Theater, Seattle
- W. Green Lake Way N., east of the Green Lake shell house, Seattle

Lake Washingon Piers

- Commodore Park, 3330 W. Commodore Way, Seattle
- East Madison Street Ferry Dock, end of E. Madison St., Seattle
- Lake Washington Blvd. S. and S. Jefferson St., Seattle
- Lake Washington Blvd. S., south of Madrona Park, Seattle
- Lake Washington Blvd. S., south of Mount Baker Park, Seattle
- Mt. Baker Park, 2521 Lake Park Dr. S., Seattle
- Reverend Murphy Fishing Pier, Lake Washington Blvd. S. and S. Juneau, Seattle
- Stan Sayres Memorial Park, Lake Washington Blvd. S. and 43rd Ave. S., Seattle

- Newcastle Beach, 4400 Lake Washington Blvd. S., Bellevue
- Longboom Park, 61st Ave. N.E. off Bothell Way, Kenmore
- David E. Brink Park, 555 Lake St. S., Kirkland
- Houghton Beach Park, 5811 Lake Washington Blvd., Kirkland
- Marina Park, 25 Lake Shore Plaza, at the foot of Central Way N.E., Kirkland
- Marsh Park, 6605 Lake Washington Blvd., Kirkland
- Settler's Landing, 1001 Lake St. S., Kirkland
- Waverly Park, 633 Waverly Park Way, Kirkland
- Luther Burbank Park, 2040 84th Ave. S.E., Mercer Island

Puget Sound Piers

Public fishing is popular at the Waterfront Park at Piers 57–61; the public seawall just north of Pier 70; and off Myrtle Edwards Park at Pier 86. Pier 86 is the most user-friendly spot, with covered areas and a bait-and-tackle shop. You can also fish at the Alki breakwater and from the pier at the south end of Golden Gardens Park. The pier at Mukilteo next to the ferry dock is an especially good spot.

Try a Trout Farm

Fishing at a trout farm may not paint the most realistic picture of what this sport is all about, but face it: Your child will have plenty of opportunities later in life to experience fishing and catching nothing. The ponds are so crammed, the trout seem to want to grab the hooks just to escape the conditions. The only downside of these ventures is that most proud fisherpersons will expect to eat their catch, and these warm-water fish aren't very tasty.

Some trout farms are seasonal; others are open year-round on a limited schedule. Visitors are charged only for the fish they catch (either by the inch or the pound). All gear, bait, and cleaning are included. No licenses are required. Groups are welcome by reservation.

Gold Creek Trout Farm, 15844 148th Ave. N.E., Woodinville, (425) 483-1415; year-round, Tues.–Sun., 10 A.M.–5 P.M.

Shellfish Harvesting

Kids typically like any activity that allows them to play in wet muck, and they quickly catch on to the fun of digging for butter clams and harvesting oysters and mussels off rocks. What's surprising, given the slippery texture of shellfish, is that most kids like eating them, too.

Here's what you'll need for your excursion: a bucket, boots (if you don't want wet feet), and a low tide. Seattle's public beaches are open for clamming year-round, unless pollution alerts are posted. Alki Beach is the most popular in-city spot, but digging is better in Edmonds and Mukilteo and on Whidbey Island. Children 14 and under don't need a shellfish license; for 15-year-olds, the license cost is $5.48. Adult licenses are $7.67. This covers shellfish, crab, and even seaweed. License information is available from the Department of Fish and Wildlife at (360) 902-2464, or by going to *www.wa.gov/wdfw*.

Harvesting mussels is remarkably simple; you just find a large mussel bed (Whidbey Island has many good spots) and pull them off the rocks. Oyster beds are a bit more scarce.

Clamming seasons are sometimes cancelled because of shortages; consult the Department of Fish and Wildlife for up-to-date information. There is also a danger of shellfish poisoning from a highly toxic microscopic organism that can turn the ocean water red (called "red tide"). Even cooking cannot eliminate it, so always call the Marine Biotoxin Hotline at (800) 562-5632 before you take the family out to gather shellfish.

Chapter 7

Parks

Seattle and the Eastside have an abundance of top-notch parks. King County alone manages **18,000 acres** of parkland and some 200 miles of **trails**. Seattle-area parks offer such diverse attractions as a salmon-shaped **slide**, a dragon-shaped spray gun, a human-powered trolley, sandy **beaches**, and giant wind chimes. So next time your children want to go to the park, make it a **new adventure** instead of a routine skip down the block. Unless otherwise indicated, parks are open daily year-round, from dawn to dusk.

Beach Fires

Alki and Golden Gardens are two Seattle beachfront parks that allow campfires. The parks department specifies, however, that fires are only allowed in designated fire pits, and are available on a first-come, first-served basis. Enjoy roasting those marshmallows, but be sure to douse your fire thoroughly before you leave. And remember that fires are not allowed during air pollution alerts.

Camping

Want to sleep outdoors without traveling far? Camp Long, Dash Point State Park, Saltwater State Park, and Tolt MacDonald Park all offer camping. See their listings elsewhere in this chapter for more information.

Environmental Learning Centers

Four Seattle parks—Camp Long, Carkeek, Discovery, and Seward—have environmental learning centers. This means that there is a building in each of the parks, staffed by park naturalists who are experts in wildlife habitat, forestry, and environmental practices, and eager to share their knowledge with park visitors.

Each center offers fun educational programs, many of which are extremely popular. There is sometimes a minimal charge for the programs, but often they are free. Many are geared to kids. Tot walks are particularly popular.

The idea behind the centers is to offer opportunities for citizens of all ages to be exposed to the natural wonders of the outdoors. See each park's website for a description of programs offered.

Picnicking

All of the parks in the region offer good picnic spots, but if you are planning a get-together with a large group and want to be sure you'll have enough tables, sheltered sites may be reserved year-round. In Seattle, picnic sites may be reserved at 21 parks, including Alki, Carkeek, Gas Works, Golden Gardens, Lincoln, Seward, and Lower Woodland. Fees vary. You can apply for a reservation early in the year; the most popular spots go fast. The parks department has a brochure that details the picnic shelter reservations process. For information on where to find a copy of the brochure, call (206) 684-4081; a PDF version of the brochure is available at *www.ci.seattle.wa.us/parks*.

Information

Most parks departments publish excellent guides that feature listings of parks and other recreation areas, maps, and details about various facilities. For more information, contact the following departments.

- **Issaquah**, (425) 837-3300, *www.ci.issaquah.wa.us*
- **Kirkland**, (425) 828-1100, *www.ci.kirkland.wa.us*
- **Mercer Island**, (206) 236-3545, *www.ci.mercer-island.wa.us*
- **Redmond**, (425) 556-2300, *www.ci.redmond.wa.us*
- **Seattle**, (206) 684-4075, *www.cityofseattle.net/parks*
- **King County**, (206) 296-8687, *www.metrokc.gov/parks*
- **State Park Department**, (360) 902-8844, (888) 226-7688 (campsite reservations), *www.parks.wa.gov*

....

Seattle and Mercer Island

....

Alki Beach
1702 Alki Ave. S.W., Seattle

When the first Seattle settlers landed on Alki, they were optimistic that eventually the area would become a bustling town. The name they gave their settlement was New York Alki ("Alki" meaning "by-the-by" in Chinook). No matter what those pioneers envisioned, one can be sure it wasn't the California-like beach scene that occurs here on hot summer days. The sandy, 25-mile-long strip skirting Puget Sound and an adjacent walkway are hugely popular with cyclists, sunbathers, in-line skaters, and pedestrians. Expansive views of downtown Seattle (with the Space Needle just peeking out) and the Olympic Mountains are added attractions.

However, the crush of humanity that flocks to the shore when the sun shines is not around most of the year. Year-round the beach offers families fine beachcombing and fresh salt air. Take along hot dogs and marshmallows if the weather is decent (small beach fires are allowed) and bring a kite to fly on the breezes. Restrooms are located at 57th Avenue and 60th Avenue.

If your kids get tired of sand or if the beach gets too windy, head over to Alki Playfield at 58th Avenue S.W. and S.W. Lander Street. There are two playgrounds; the one to the north, known as Whale Tale Park, is scheduled for renovation.

....

Powell Barnett Park
352 Martin Luther King Jr. Way, Seattle
Wading pool

The large, colorful, and creative playground structure is the centerpiece of this small (4.4-acre) park and on a sunny day you'll find it crawling with kids. It is cleverly designed to have an area for preschoolers as well as section where older kids can romp, and includes several slides, rope climbing features, and several bouncy and spinning toys you've never seen before. There is a tricycle maze and wading pool as well.

....

Camp Long
5200 35th Ave. S.W., Seattle
(206) 684-7434
www.ci.seattle.wa.us/parks/environment/camplong.htm

Hours: Lodge, Tues.–Sat., 10 A.M.–6 P.M.

One of Seattle's premier facilities, Camp Long is both a park and an environmental learning center with an extensive list of classes for all ages. With 68 acres of forest, nature trails, a 25-foot-high artificial climbing rock, and plenty of open areas, Camp Long is the ideal park to visit when the family wants to get away from it all without driving far. For many years, Seattle Parks and Recreation operated Camp Long exclusively for organized groups. Today, the cabins are open to the public as well, making it the only city park with overnight camping. You can rent one of the 10 rustic cabins, which come complete with double bunk beds and electricity, for $40/night. Bring your friends: The cabins sleep up to 12 people. Six cabins are wheelchair accessible. The wheelchair-friendly Rolling Hills Trail starts at the parking lot and provides access to these cabins.

At the beautiful old lodge next to the parking lot, you'll find an interesting historical and wildlife exhibit and an informative ranger who will give you the rundown at the park.

The Nature Trail, a one-half-mile loop through the woods, is perfect for young hikers who are long on enthusiasm but short on endurance. To get to the trail, follow the path down the hill from the lodge to the open field below. Take a left on the service road, passing Polliwog Pond on the right. At the north end of the pond, leave the road as it curves right and instead follow the path past the large, flat stone compass set in the ground to the sign marking the start of the trail. Start on the left fork. Longer trails loop around the eastern portion of the park.

Schurman Rock, an artificial climbing structure, is at the northern end of the park and was recently renovated and repaired through the efforts of the Seattle Parks Foundation. The climbing rock is open for everyone to use, during usual park hours. Children are welcome to climb—but should be supervised by adults. Nearby Glacier, a series of rock slopes built down a wooded hill, is used to train climbers in rappelling, but kids love the challenge of scrambling to the top (closely supervised by an adult).

The enormous open field in the middle of Camp Long is ideal for games that require plenty of space. A large campfire pit surrounded by benches lies at the south end of the field.

....

Carkeek Park

950 N.W. Carkeek Park Rd., Seattle
(206) 684-0877
www.ci.seattle.wa.us/parks/environment/carkeek.htm

Hours: Environmental Learning Center, Mon.–Fri., 10 A.M.–4 P.M.

The Environmental Learning Center at Carkeek Park is a center for environmental classes and lectures in the community. But the 216-acre park has a lot more to offer. You can see real salmon here in the fall, or your kid can slide down a salmon's mouth and come out its tail.

Carkeek Park is tucked away down a narrow road, but it's well worth finding. An imaginative playground features the aforementioned slide, a trail with a bridge and dry creek, riding toys in shapes of sea animals, and two rock-cave shelters.

A pedestrian bridge to the beach crosses over railroad tracks, offering a thrilling overhead view of passing trains. The long set of stairs is steep for little ones, so be prepared to carry them. More than six miles of trails wind through the park, including a paved trail along Piper Creek and a raised wooden walkway over wetlands.

The Environmental Learning Center is a great place to visit, even if you don't sign up for a class. You can give your kids a lesson in sustainable building. The structure was designed and built to be kind to the environment, and was the city's first building to receive a gold rating from the LEED rating system, which means that it was built with sustainable products and materials, and uses those in its operation. Among the building's features are a system that collects rainwater to be used for flushing toilets, solar electric panels to provide electricity, drought-tolerant landscaping, and the use of numerous recycled materials.

Deane's Children's Park
5500 Island Crest Way, Mercer Island

This pleasant little park was designed by the Mercer Island Preschool Association, especially for children ages 3–9. The play equipment is imaginative and fun, two tennis courts are nearby, and several short trails meander through the shady grounds.

Discovery Park
3801 W. Government Way, Seattle
(206) 386-4236
www.ci.seattle.wa.us/parks/environment/discovparkindex.htm

Hours: Visitor Center, Tues.–Sun., 8:30 A.M.–5 P.M.

Discovery Park is the largest and most diverse park in Seattle, boasting 500 acres of cliffs, beaches, self-guided interpretative loops, short trails, jogging trails, man-made ponds, and a thriving population of birds and animals.

In 1964, the Secretary of the Army announced that 85 percent of the land at Fort Lawton in Magnolia would become surplus. That set local and federal politicians in motion; they went to work on obtaining the land for public enjoyment. In 1972, the federal government gave the site to the City of Seattle, which aptly named the park Discovery (after Puget Sound explorer Captain George Vancouver's flagship, the H.M.S. *Discovery*). A handful of buildings and trucks are reminders of this park's military past. Also note the South Meadow, which was once maintained as an athletic field for military personnel. Today, it is an inviting open space with a majestic view of Puget Sound and the Olympics; spread a blanket and delve into a good book while the kids romp or fly a kite (there is always a stiff breeze off the Sound).

The park can be entered at the main gate at W. Government Way and 36th Avenue W., the south gate at W. Emerson near Magnolia Boulevard W., and the north gate at W. Commodore Way and 40th Avenue W. Unless you know where you are going, it is easiest to enter at the main gate on the east side, where you'll find a good map and a short history of the park, and the Visitor Center just ahead on the left. Restrooms are a good thing to scope out when taking little kids to this big park. You'll find them at the Visitor Center, South Meadow, North Bluff, and West Point. If you have children ages 5 and under, ask for a parking permit so you can drive to South Beach and thereby skip the three-mile round-trip hike.

Discovery Park rangers offer an exceptional variety of nature programs for adults and kids (some for as young as age 2). On the popular Night Walks, rangers lead families on a search for nocturnal life in the park—one example of the many activities offered. Naturalists arrange education programs for preschool and kindergarten classes, as well as nature day camps during the summer. The classes and workshops are low cost (or free) and invariably top-notch.

The Visitor Center features environmental interpretive exhibits. Numerous classes are available on a quarterly basis. Many offer children and their parents an opportunity to explore the natural wonders of the park. Several bald eagles live at the park, so ask the rangers at the Visitor Center where you can spot their nests. Bring binoculars!

The South Bluff, east of the park's meadow, offers a spectacular vista of the islands and mountains beyond, but the cliffs are steep and treacherous, so be careful to hold on tightly to your curious preschoolers. One of the most popular attractions at this bluff is a big pile of sand (fondly referred to by locals as "the dunes" despite its singularity), upon which such games as King of the Mountain and Bury the Feet can be played. At the higher point of the South Bluff are signs that point the way down to the South Beach and the West Point area, renowned for some of the best marine bird-watching and tidepooling in Seattle. The beach, like the park, is mixed terrain: There are sandy areas, rocky beds, mud-flats (when the tide is low), and the West Point Lighthouse, built in 1881.

The North Bluff was once site of military barracks and the noncommissioned officers' club. It offers another spectacular view and several picnic tables. On the area of land below the bluff, the Shihoh people lived until early in this century. To the left of the picnic area is a trail leading down to the North Beach, another ideal spot for exploring tidepools. Look for crabs, sea stars, sea anemones, and sea urchins. Remember to tell the kids to look but leave the sea life undisturbed. Luckily for the animals, the days of hauling sea creatures home in buckets have passed.

Just south of the Visitor Center are tennis courts, a basketball court, and a playground geared to younger children (none of this is visible from the parking lot).

One highlight of Discovery Park is not nature-made: the Daybreak Star Center (206-285-4425), a Native American cultural/educational center in the northwest corner of the park. The center is on 19 acres of property that have been leased to Daybreak. Twelve Native American artists were commissioned to create artworks for this beautiful building, and most of the pieces are large murals and carvings depicting legends and traditions, which children will find interesting. Daybreak Star's gallery features a variety of contemporary and traditional Native American art. There is no charge to visit the center. If you park in the north parking lot, it is a short walk to the center. Check the map in the southwestern corner of the north lot for directions.

Gas Works Park
2101 N. Northlake Way, Seattle

When park designers first presented the idea of incorporating the old gas works plant perched at the north end of Lake Union into a new park, critics complained noisily. But today, the grotesque remnants have become a familiar part of the cityscape, and the 20-acre park is a premier spot to enjoy a picnic and panoramic views of the downtown skyline.

This was a working gas refinery until 1955, and about one-third of the old machinery still stands. The old boiler house is now a picnic shelter with tables, fire grills, and an open area. The former exhauster-compressor building has become a brightly painted play barn. There is a small playground.

A grassy man-made knoll has become a favorite gathering spot for kite-flying enthusiasts. Look for a giant sundial, built in the ground near the top of the hill. The 28-foot-diameter dial is made of inlaid and cast bronze, shells, ceramic, and found objects that have been embedded in multicolored concrete.

To tell time, the viewer stands on a central oval and becomes the gnomon for the sundial, casting a shadow toward the mosaic hour markers at the perimeter. Children will delight in closely examining the dial to discover small figures, sealife, and other objects set in this beautiful piece of public art.

In case children ask, the six tall towers (kept behind cyclone fencing for safety) were oxygen gas-generator towers used to convert crude oil to heating oil.

Several years ago, a remediation project was completed at the park, involving the installing of pipes that gather gases and toxins from the soil and pipe them to an on-site incinerator for disposal. Because of this, the park today is much cleaner than in past years. But parents are still cautioned to make sure their children practice good hygiene here. Have children wash their hands after playing and before eating. Don't let them dig in dirt other than at the play area, and make sure they don't eat the dirt.

The Burke Gilman Trail runs by Gas Works Park, so it is a good place for walkers, runners, bikers, and skaters to have a picnic, enjoy the view, and take a restroom break. A spectacular fireworks display is held here each Fourth of July.

Golden Gardens
8498 Seaview Pl. N.W., Seattle

If you hanker for a beach fire and salt air, head to Golden Gardens on Shilshole Bay, at the west end of Ballard. The water will be chilly—or worse—even during the summer, but there is a warmer stream running into the Sound that is just right for water play. No lifeguards are on duty.

This is the place in Seattle to grab a beach blanket, marshmallows, and firewood for a beach fire and to watch the sunset. There's also a fishing pier. Two wetlands and the northern beach were restored several years ago, and a lovely, short loop trail was added.

A small play area features a climbing toy and swings. If your kids don't like dogs, avoid the upper part of the park where there is an off-leash area.

The recently renovated bathhouse—known as the Brick:House—offers community activities, summer concerts, and a snack bar during the summer.

For a fabulous beach walk, head out to Golden Gardens at a minus tide and walk north along a wide expanse of sand and rocks. If you walk far enough, you might run across geoduck diggers uncovering the grotesque mollusks. From out on the sand, you're likely to see a few trains pass by on the tracks above the beach, always a good diversion for young kids.

Green Lake
E. Green Lake Dr. N. and W. Green Lake Dr. N., Seattle
Swimming beach

Many Seattleites exercise religiously, and Green Lake has long been their mecca. Joggers, roller skaters, cyclists, and boaters (non-motorized craft only) of all shapes, sizes, and abilities make their pilgrimage to the lake whenever the weather permits (and often when it doesn't). Families, too, flock to Green Lake, because it offers plentiful picnic areas, as well as activities and amenities for all ages, including a playground (at the east entrance), lifeguarded beaches from mid-June through Labor Day, a big wading pool (northeast corner), a community center, boat rentals, an indoor swimming pool, and many nearby places to grab a tasty snack or meal. The parks department recommends the recently reconstructed 2.8-mile-long path around the lake for bikers, skaters, and walkers, and the 3.2-mile-long trail closer to the street for joggers.

The popularity of Green Lake threatens to ruin the pleasure, especially when families burdened by hauling kids and their assorted paraphernalia have difficulty finding a place to park on a hot day. It is best enjoyed with little kids when the weather is less than spectacular and the crowds have dwindled. The trails are often so crowded that they aren't always a good choice for wobbly young walkers, skaters, or bikers. See Chapter 5 for information on Evans indoor swimming pool and Chapter 6 for more information on outdoor activities.

In past years, Green Lake has been besieged by summer algae blooms, which have caused the city to close the lake for recreational use. However, the city has made extensive efforts to treat the problem, and it appears to be working well. Just to be safe, to avoid swimmer's itch you should wipe off with a towel after swimming and shower as soon as possible.

Boat rentals (canoe, paddle, and row boats) as well as windsurfing lessons are available at Green Lake Boat Rental (206-527-0171), a private company on the east side of the lake near the playground and the community center/indoor pool. Unfortunately, bike and skate rentals are no longer offered at Greg's Cycle across the street from Green Lake.

Occasionally, Green Lake—or portions of it—will freeze over in winter, tempting kids and adults to try to skate on the lake. It's unlikely the lake will ever freeze to the thickness needed to safely skate on it. Be sure to keep your kids off the ice!

Hamlin Park
16006 15th Ave. N.E., Shoreline

The 73-acre forested park offers a playfield, a playground, and a series of interlocking hiking trails through a natural area. It is also popular with mountain bikers.

Hiram M. Chittenden Government Locks
3015 N.W. 54th St., Seattle
(206) 783-7059
www.nws.usace.army.mil

Hours: Park, daily, 7 A.M.–9 P.M.
Visitors Center, Oct. 1–Apr. 30, Thurs.–Mon., 10 A.M.–4 P.M.; May 1–Sept. 30, daily, 10 A.M.–6 P.M. Free guided tours, Mar. 1–Nov. 30.

Most people, regardless of age, are fascinated by the remarkable sight of boats and water rising and dropping right before their eyes. The difference between the water level of Puget Sound and Lake Washington varies by anywhere from six to 26 feet. The locks protect the ecosystem of the lake by preventing saltwater from entering Lake Washington when boats go from Puget Sound into Lake Washington, and vice versa.

On a warm afternoon, bring a picnic to enjoy on the grassy knoll above the locks and watch the boat traffic parade past. Sundays are great for boat watching because many people are returning from a weekend in the San Juans. During the summer, free band concerts play every Sunday at 2 P.M.

Fish ladders next to the locks offer underwater viewing of salmon as they struggle to return to their spawning grounds. Salmon arrive from mid-June to late October; the best viewing is in July. Keep an eye out for seals and sea lions, especially from December to May.

The Visitors Center shows a 12-minute video tracing the history of the locks. A marble maze game allows children to pretend to be a salmon facing many obstacles to get home; they can also play lockmaster and move a boat through a model of the locks. A bookstore, open on weekends, sells videos, souvenirs, and posters. Weekend public tours begin at the Visitors Center, then proceed to the gardens, the locks, and the fish ladders.

Lakewood Park

11050 10th Ave. S.W., White Center
Swimming beach

Besides the usual ballfields, tennis courts, and trails, Lakewood—a King County park—has an 18-hole disc golf course. It also offers two play areas, a swimming beach on Lake Garrett, fishing, and three picnic shelters. A public boat launch is next to the park. See Chapter 6 for more details.

Lincoln Park

8011 Fauntleroy Way S.W., Seattle
Swimming pool (outdoors)

Spread out on 130 acres in West Seattle at one of the most scenic vantage points in the region, Lincoln Park offers breathtaking views of the Olympic Mountains and Puget Sound, as well as shady woods, wide-open playing fields, a fine stretch of beach (less crowded than nearby Alki), and Colman Pool. A short hike down a forest bluff takes you to the beach, which features plenty of sand and a long, paved path along the water. Trails wind through the park; a nice one meanders along the bluff over the beach. There are two play areas: The one on the north side, near the wading pool, has a toddler climbing structure plus a larger one with slides and riding toys. The playground was renovated in 1998.

Though Colman Pool started as a tide-fed swimming hole, it is now a beautiful, heated, outdoor saltwater pool. Situated right at the edge of the beach in Lincoln Park, Colman is maintained by the Seattle Department of Parks and Recreation and opens summers only. Kids will love the giant tube slide. Special events are planned each summer, such as a Kids Carnival, Monster Splash Day, and Wild 'n' Wacky Olympics. Call the pool for more information at (206) 684-7494.

The short, easy trek from Lincoln Park's parking lot, through deep woods down to the saltwater beach is likely to seem much longer and much steeper to the little ones when it's time to go home after a frolic on the beach. Be prepared to bribe and coax your short-legged hiking companions up the hill, or bring a carrier to tote them on your back.

The park is located right next to the Vashon–Southworth ferry dock; kids will enjoy watching the ferries come and go.

Madrona Beach

853 Lake Washington Blvd., Seattle
Swimming beach

Huge logs—arranged as if tossed onto the beach by a winter storm—and large rocks encourage climbing at this sandy beach along Lake Washington. Children enjoy spending hours playing with a child-sized spigot, which supplies water for a stream, where kids can make dams to control or footbridges to cross. There is a bathhouse and lifeguards on duty during the summer. Older children will enjoy swimming out to a floating dock and diving board. A large grassy area with picnic tables and a covered cooking spot is adjacent to the beach. During summer, a small take-out stand with delicious BBQ is open at the bathhouse. South of the beach is a fishing dock, which is a great spot for young anglers.

Matthews Beach

9300 51st Ave. N.E., Seattle
Swimming beach

Matthews Beach is popular with families during the summer. The lifeguarded beach is an exceptionally good swimming area, and easily accessible from the parking lot—a real plus for parents who are packing the usual assortment of beach and kid equipment. Located close to the Burke Gilman Trail, Matthews is also a good place to get off the bikes, and enjoy a quick swim and a picnic. A snazzy playground adds to the fun.

Myrtle Edwards Park

3130 Alaskan Way W., Seattle

Located just north of Pier 70 on the Seattle waterfront, Myrtle Edwards is a scenic strip along Elliott Bay with two paved, 1.25-mile-long paths: one for walking and one for cycling (see Chapter 6). The grassy areas are limited but the benches abundant. Look for a gigantic rock sculpture, *Adjacent, Against, Upon*, to climb and explore (near the south entrance). Cool sea breezes and a panoramic view are the finishing touches.

Myrtle Edwards is a good place to take a stroll at sunset, after a big meal at the nearby Old Spaghetti Factory. Just above Myrtle Edwards sits the Seattle Art Museum's wonderful Olympic Sculpture Park.

Pratt Park
1800 S. Main St., Seattle
Water-spray area

A fun water-spray play area, open in the summers only, is the main attraction of this park. It features giant water cannons shaped like animals, and a water maze with ground sensors that cause water to squirt up when they're stepped on.

Richmond Beach Saltwater Park
2021 N.W. 190th St., Shoreline
(206) 546-5041

This 40-acre park offers a sandy beach on Puget Sound, hiking trails, a playground, and picnic shelters and tables. It also offers a panoramic view of the Sound and mountains. Watch for special beach events offered throughout the year at low tide when naturalists are on hand to identify sea creatures. Watch (and listen) for sea lions.

To get there, take the N. 175th St. exit from I-5, and head west on N. 175th until you reach Highway 99. Turn right, go to N. 185th, and turn left. Follow N. 185th, which turns into Richmond Beach Road, for 2.5 miles. At 20th Avenue N.W., turn left. Follow 20th Avenue for three blocks to the park entrance. Park in the lower lot to go to the beach.

Sand Point Magnuson Park
7400 Sand Point Way N.E., Seattle
Swimming beach

Seattle's second-largest park, at 320 acres, is in the midst of a transformation from naval air station to a great mixed-use urban park. This park lies on the western shore of Lake Washington and has a mile-long stretch of shoreline. The recent addition of a huge playground—Seattle's largest—makes the park a major draw for families with children. Dubbed the "Air, Land, and Sea" playground by the Junior League, which provided funding, the playground was partly designed by children and built by volunteers at the site of the former naval air station's control tower. It features four separate play structures, seven slides, climbing walls, and a bouncy bridge. A sandbox is stocked with scooping and building toys, and there are pint-sized basketball courts. The best way to get to the playground is to enter the park at N.E. 74th Street from Sand Point Way N.E.

The park offers much more than a playground, however. You'll also find a swimming beach, a wading pool, sports fields, walking trails, and plenty of paved surfaces for bike riding.

Don't miss seeing some unique artwork when you visit Sand Point Magnuson Park. From Kite Hill and the beach, you can see *The Fin Project: From Swords to Plowshares*. The sculptural installation, made from decommissioned submarine fins, represents a pod of whales. It was created by John T. Young. Near the playground you'll see two red chairs atop two leaning blue poles. This installation, by Carol Bolt, is called *No Appointment Necessary*.

The north end of the park adjoins land owned by the National Oceanographic and Atmospheric Administration. NOAA developed its 114-acre site by integrating the shoreline walk with artworks that emphasize the relationship between man and nature.

A short distance past the gate separating the NOAA site from the park is a footbridge lined with passages from Herman Melville's *Moby Dick*. Just to the left of the bridge, a short path leads to *Sound Garden*, a sculpture of steel towers holding aluminum pipes that wail eerily when the wind blows. Listeners have to be very still and quiet to hear the soft and haunting sounds emanating from the sculpture.

Parent Tips

Thanks to the determined efforts of a group of parents, the Yellow Swing Campaign was launched in 2008 to put an accessible swing for kids with mobility limitations in all Seattle playgrounds. Contact Seattle Parks and Recreation Department at (206) 684-7328 for information about the swings.

Seattle Children's PlayGarden
1740 23rd Ave. S.
www.childrensplaygarden.org

The PlayGarden is a wonderful park-within-a-park, located just across from the new Northwest African American Museum. It is dedicated to providing children of all abilities full access to outdoor recreation space and offering inclusive programs that encourage every child's potential. The PlayGarden is a beautifully planned space with a playground, a garden, and in the future, indoor space for play programs. It is a safe and supportive place where families with children with special needs can bring all their children to play and learn.

Seward Park
Lake Washington Blvd. S. and S. Juneau St., Seattle
www.cityofseattle.net/parks/parkspaces/sewardpark.htm
Swimming beach

Situated at the end of a long scenic drive along Lake Washington Boulevard, this 277-acre park covers an entire peninsula. A paved 2.5-mile loop around the perimeter is very popular with walkers, joggers, and cyclists (see Chapter 6). The status of the fish hatchery on the east side of the park was unclear at publication, but kids will still have fun playing in the small creek and waterfall off the path. The park also holds six picnic shelters. There are places to play in the sand along the northern edge of the park, and there is a lifeguarded swimming beach in the summer.

Though the part of the park next to the lake jumps with action on hot summer days, the old-growth forest above remains cool and tranquil. Several broad trails penetrate the woods in the park; the closed road that leads to the top of the park, past the preschool playground and amphitheater, is perhaps most inviting for strolling.

The Seward Park Art Studio (206-722-6342, *www.sewardparkart.org*), located in the brick bathhouse next to the beach, offers pottery classes for both children and adults.

Audubon Washington and Seattle Parks and Recreation are partners in the creation of the Seward Park Environmental & Audubon Center (5902 Lake Washington Blvd. S., 206-652-2444, *sewardpark.audubon.org/*), located in the Tudor-style building at the park entrance. The Center is part of the national Audubon vision to establish neighborhood nature education centers in urban areas of high ethnic diversity. The 277-acre park is the outdoor classroom for school programs and classes for children and adults, as well as special events. Check the website for information about programs at the Center. Also on the website, look under The Park and The Center for an excellent history of the park's ecosystem.

....

Volunteer Park
1247 15th Ave. E., Seattle
Wading pool
Hours: Conservatory, Labor Day–Memorial Day, daily, 10 A.M.–4 P.M.; Memorial Day–Labor Day, daily, 10 A.M.–7 P.M.

This elegant old park on Capitol Hill, designed by the Olmsted Brothers, is home to the Seattle Asian Art Museum; a 75-foot-tall brick water tower with stairs to climb; a conservatory; and *Black Sun*, a sculpture by Isamu Noguchi, which overlooks the reservoir and frames a spectacular view of the city and the Olympic Mountains beyond. The circular, black granite sculpture is irresistible to children, who like to crawl through the slippery, big opening in its center.

Volunteer Park's conservatory, located at the north end of the park, envelops its visitors in lush greenery, sweet heavy fragrance, and humid air. It has five "houses" with different specialty plants. All except one are heated to 72 degrees with 60 percent humidity—making the conservatory a very nice place on a cold, rainy winter day. This splendid glass structure contains monstrous cacti, breathtaking orchids, and other flora that will capture most children's attention.

Just east of the conservatory is a large wading pool, a popular playground with slides, climbing toys, and an interesting sculpture kids can climb on.

Woodland Park
Aurora Ave. N. and N. 59th St., Seattle

Just east of the Woodland Park Zoo, Woodland Park offers one of the most popular spots in town for big picnics. With plenty of covered shelters, lots of open space, and close proximity to Green Lake, it is a good place to settle for a lazy summer afternoon of barbecuing and Frisbee tossing. Soccer, baseball, and softball fields and a running track are located at the bottom of the east slope of the park; tennis courts are at the south side and down near the soccer fields. The softball fields recently received major improvements, and the baseball field is also undergoing renovation, thanks in part to a $1 million Major League grant, a thank-you to the city for having hosted the All-Star game in 2002. A 2.5-acre rose garden by the south entrance to the zoo has delighted noses and eyes since 1922. To get to Green Lake, take a footbridge over Aurora Avenue and walk across Lower Woodland Park.

Eastside

Beaver Lake Park
25005 S.E. 24th St., Sammamish

Older folks might remember Beaver Lake Park as Camp Cabrini, a wilderness summer camp run by the Catholic Youth Organization for 28 years. Now it is an 82-acre county park with ball fields, picnic tables, a shelter with barbecue pits and fireplace, a fishing spot, trails, a playground, and some fine examples of Native American art. Story poles and totem poles stand near the shelter, on the lakeshore, and near the park entrance.

Interpretive nature programs are offered periodically at the renovated Issaquah Lodge. The lodge is also available for rent.

Blyth Park
16950 W. Riverside Dr., Bothell

Sand diggers, a long slide, and a tower of tires make this play area special. There is equipment for toddlers, as well as for older children. A covered picnic area and a grassy space are great spots to eat lunch before walking on trails that cut through woods around the park or lead to the Sammamish River Slough.

Bothell Landing Park
9919 N.E. 180th St., Bothell

Bothell Landing Park, which sits across the river from the Sammamish River Trail, features a small playground, an interpretive trail through wetlands, lots of waterfowl, and an amphitheater and plaza. The Bothell Historical Museum (open Sunday afternoons) is housed in one of the area's original homes and is decorated with authentic furnishings. A couple of other historic buildings are also at the park.

Downtown Park
N.E. Fourth St. and 100th Ave. N.E., Bellevue

This 20-acre island of green space located just south of Bellevue Square is a pleasant place to unwind after a shopping spree at nearby Bellevue Square. You can walk along a one-half-mile circular promenade with a canal on one side and shade trees on the other. Or let the kids run through wide grassy areas. Other features include a cascading, 240-foot-wide waterfall and a preschool play area with a bright castle toy. The park is a great place to fly a kite, and a popular spot for public concerts and special activities during the year.

Farrel-McWhirter Park
19545 Redmond Rd., Redmond

Farrel-McWhirter covers 68 acres with a children's animal farm, covered picnic shelters with electricity, multi-use trails, an orienteering course, swings, and a nature trail.

Grass Lawn Park
7031 148th Ave. N.E., Redmond

Located where Redmond, Bellevue, and Kirkland intersect, Grass Lawn Park offers plenty of space and activities for all ages. A large portion of the park is devoted to playing fields, but there is also a play area, featuring climbing apparatus and swings, set in a woodsy, nicely shaded spot. Children, both preschool-age and older, will enjoy riding their bikes and trikes along the paved pathways.

Juanita Beach Park
9703 Juanita Dr. N.E., Kirkland
Swimming beach

During the summer, this 35-acre county park, with its large, sandy beach and enclosed swimming area, is very popular with families with small children. A long dock circles the swimming area. Other amenities include ball fields, a picnic shelter, a small playground, and a large grassy area.

Kelsey Creek Community Park/Farm
13204 S.E. Eighth Pl., Bellevue
(425) 452-7688

Kelsey Creek Park covers 150 acres of wetland, forest, and pastures located just east of downtown Bellevue. Kelsey Creek Farm, with a barn full of farm animals, is at the center of the park and offers classes for children. There are also hiking trails, a playground, and picnic tables.

Lake Sammamish State Park

20606 S.E. 56th St., Issaquah
(425) 455-7010
Swimming beach

A large, sandy swimming beach is the main draw of this huge park at the south end of Lake Sammamish. It's also a popular boating area, with a large boat launch. If you didn't bring your own Jet Ski, you can get out on the water by renting a kayak. There are two children's play areas with structures. A great wheelchair-accessible playground has a triple slide, a mini-climbing wall, and a tire swing. The park offers food concessions and dozens of picnic and barbecue areas. Bring your own net for volleyball or horseshoes to throw in the sandpit. Reserve your picnic tables if you are bringing a big group. Fishing is allowed in the lake but not in Issaquah Creek, which runs through the park. There are also trails for hiking and biking. If you tire of the beach, Gilman Village, on the south side of I-90, offers good browsing and numerous snack places.

Lake Wilderness Park

23601 S.E. 248th St., Maple Valley
Swimming beach

This forested, 108-acre park has a swimming beach, a boat launch, a fishing pier, a playground, walking trails, an arboretum, barbecues and picnic areas, playfields, and tennis courts. At the Lake Wilderness Center, notice the three-story totem pole surrounded by a spiral staircase. The building, which can be rented, has meeting rooms, a dance/fitness studio, an arts and crafts room, a large patio, and a catering kitchen.

Luther Burbank Park

2040 84th Ave. S.E., Mercer Island
(206) 296-4438
Swimming beach

Until recently a county park, Luther Burbank is now owned by the City of Mercer Island. It covers 77 acres on the eastern shore and is a favorite among local families. The clean, sandy beach, with its shallow swimming areas and ideal sandcastle spots, is a paradise for young children. And if that's not enough to keep the kiddos occupied, a wooded trail along the water's edge will take them to a playground full of slides, tunnels, swings, balance beams, and crawling nets.

The north parking lot provides access to the playground; go to the south parking lot if you are headed to the beach. Try not to pack too much, as it's still a good walk from the parking lot to the beach. If you plan to bring food, keep in mind that the picnic area by the beach (which has barbecue grills) gets crowded on summer weekends. Call ahead for reservations if you are taking a big group.

The park has an outdoor amphitheater, which is frequently used for summer concerts and is available for rental. There's also a fishing pier and boat dock. Large areas of the park are undeveloped, and there are two small wetlands—and a lot of wildlife. A couple of brick buildings in the park are all that remains of the park's original function as a school for boys.

Marina Park

25 Lake Shore Plaza, Kirkland
Swimming beach

With a beach surrounded by a concrete bench, a long dock, and close proximity to downtown Kirkland's ice cream shops and restaurants, Marina Park is a great place to watch boats, dip your feet, and throw pebbles in the water.

South of downtown Kirkland, scattered along Lake Washington Boulevard, are several other easy-to-spot waterfront parks, with sandy beaches, docks, grassy areas, and playground equipment. Houghton Beach (5811 Lake Washington Blvd.) is especially nice. North of downtown is secluded Waverly Beach (633 Waverly Park Way).

Marymoor Park

6064 W. Lake Sammamish Pkwy. N.E., Redmond
(206) 205-3661
www.metrokc.gov/Parks/Marymoor

If you only visit one park on the Eastside make it Marymoor, which gets the prize for the most-used park in the King County system. Its 638 acres encompass a huge range of activities with room enough for all. In addition to the numerous athletic fields that make the park a popular center for soccer and softball games, Marymoor includes two playgrounds, a velodrome for bicyclists, a climbing rock, the largest off-leash dog park in the area, a large field dedicated to flying remote-controlled airplanes, a pea patch, miles of walking and bicycle trails, and lots of wide-open space perfect for kite flying or Frisbee tossing. Near the entrance you'll see two buildings: a charming windmill and a large house—Clise Mansion. Both were part of the original Willowmoor Farm, where the park is located.

Just how can you enjoy yourself today at Marymoor? If you're at the park on a clear evening, drive past all the sports fields to the dedicated remote-controlled airplane area, where most kids will be thrilled to watch the model aircraft buzzing around. For guaranteed action, show up on a Tuesday night between May and September, when the airplane club holds training sessions. The spiky 45-foot-tall climbing rock on the edge of the park has some low rock holds to challenge older children, who might also enjoy watching climbers in harnesses and ropes crawling up and then belaying down the high pinnacles. It is open daily during regular park hours, until dusk. If you and the kids like to walk the dog together, head over to the park's southern portion where you'll find a 40-acre off-leash site. Outside the off-leash area there is the Marymoor Park Pet Garden, the first of its kind in the region. The 1.25-acre area is an oasis where families may celebrate a living, lost, or deceased pet. This serene area seeks to honor the bond so many people have with their animals. For more information, call (206) 296-4232.

There's also outdoor movie nights and outdoor concerts held throughout the summer months—check the website for event dates both if you wish to attend or if you are trying to avoid the traffic jams that accompany the larger concerts.

The 10.9-mile Sammamish River Trail begins at Marymoor and ends in Bothell so a walk, skate, or bike ride from here on the trail will take you to Woodinville and its wineries (see Chapter 6 for more details on hiking and biking). The trail offers extraordinary views of the river, the broad Sammamish River Valley, the Cascade foothills, and Mt. Rainier. Also, folks who want to spend some lazy hours drifting upon the Sammamish Slough in inner tubes or rafts often start at Marymoor. For obvious reasons, the park is usually jammed on hot summer days. There are fireworks at the park on the Fourth of July. Go early on the 4th and expect backed-up traffic.

Meydenbauer Park
419 98th Ave. N.E., Bellevue
Swimming beach

Located on the shores of Lake Washington's Meydenbauer Bay in Bellevue, this park is nestled—almost hidden—among tall trees and residential areas. It's very popular with neighborhood residents. A small playground with swings and climbing equipment is above the beach. There is also a dock. There are plenty of shady picnic areas, but try to pack light as the walk from the car is a long one if you're loaded down with gear.

Newcastle Beach
4400 Lake Washington Blvd. S., Bellevue
Swimming beach

This 28-acre park, located on Lake Washington between Bellevue and Renton just south of Newport Shores Marina, is wonderful for kids. It's flat and wide open, with a nice, shallow swimming area and a sandy beach. Near the beach is a first-rate playground with swings, slides, and climbing equipment. The park, which has its own wildlife reserve, also features nature trails and a fishing dock. It's also a popular place for sailboarders to launch.

Peter Kirk Park
202 Third St., Kirkland
Swimming beach, wading pool

This 12-acre park in downtown Kirkland is the city's recreational centerpiece, with ball fields, a nice playground, tennis courts, a skateboard park, paved pathways, and outdoor swimming and wading pools. The Kirkland Library and Senior Center adjoin the park as well, and a parking garage serves them all. Be sure to check out several pieces of public art scattered around the park including a horse, a bronzed couple sitting on a bench, and a group of "gossips" in a circle on the lawn.

The ball field at this park is one of the area's premier facilities. A semi-professional team holds games there during spring and summer.

Pine Lake Park

228th Ave. S.E. and S.E. 24th St., Sammamish
Swimming beach

You can fish from a pier, launch a boat, or swim at the beach at this 16-acre wooded park. It features two new play areas, tennis courts, a baseball field, and picnic facilities.

Robinswood Park

2432 148th Ave. S.E., Bellevue

A wonderful children's play area is enough to attract kids to this park, but it offers a number of other features, as well. There's a duck pond, walking trails, a horse arena, playing fields, and a tennis center with four indoor courts.

St. Edward State Park

1445 Juanita Dr. N.E., Kenmore
(425) 823-2992
Swimming pool (outdoors)

When the Catholic diocese closed the seminary that had occupied this 316-acre forested property since 1931, the state snapped it up. It was a wise purchase, considering that the area has 3,000 feet of waterfront, the largest remaining undeveloped shoreline on Lake Washington.

Also included in the deal were a gymnasium, tennis courts, outdoor handball courts, baseball fields, an indoor swimming pool, soccer fields, picnic areas, and about 7 miles of trails. The trails follow along ravines and are quite steep—not a good bet for very young children. Bikes used to be allowed on the trail, but recently have been restricted. Many of the trails lead to the lake, but swimming is not advised, as there are no lifeguards and the shoreline drops away abruptly about 30 feet out. Expect at least a 0.6-mile downhill walk to get to shore.

A fantastic playground, conceived and built by community volunteers, is a major attraction of the park. Wooden towers, a bouncy bridge, a tree house with slide, a submarine and periscope, rings, a tot climbing net, an animal-print maze, and a rock climb are but a few of the features of this fanciful and fun playground.

The 25-yard-long Carole Ann Wald Memorial Pool at St. Edward is open for public swims; for information, call (425) 823-6983.

....

Tolt MacDonald Park & Campground
31020 N.E. 40th St., Carnation
(206) 205-7532

This 450-acre rural park is the only county park with a campground. The park is located on both sides of the Snoqualmie River. It has space for recreational vehicles (but no hookups), car camping, and walk-in sites. Campsites are $15 a night. Several ball fields and a playground are also on-site, and there's a playground and large, grassy meadows. If you explore the park's hiking trails, keep an eye out for such wildlife as bears, deer, coyotes, bald eagles, and red-tailed hawks. If you don't mind heights, you can walk over a 500-foot-long suspension bridge swaying 28 feet above the Snoqualmie River.

A historic Dutch Colonial barn was renovated in 1995 to serve as a picnic shelter. The rest of the park was built in 1976 by more than 20,000 Boy Scouts, who cleared debris, leveled areas, and built campsites and picnic shelters.

....

Wilburton Hill Park
12001 Main St., Bellevue

This 105-acre community park has a charming children's play area with playhouses, a boat, climbing structures, and a spiderweb. More than three miles of trails wind through the park, which also offers ball fields, tennis and basketball courts, and group picnic facilities.

The park is home to the Bellevue Botanical Garden (12001 Main St., 425-688-8551), which features 35 acres of gardens, including an alpine garden with a zigzagging path, a Japanese garden, and lush perennial borders. Kids will immediately be drawn to the fountain located near the visitor center, which gurgles out and runs down a path to a small pond. Trees and an arbor are lit up during December in the Garden D'Lights display.

North

Edmonds Waterfront Parks

The beaches on Puget Sound in Edmonds are very popular with families. Underwater Park at Brackett's Landing is popular with divers as well as beach walkers. It has creature-filled tidepools at low tide. Olympic Beach (Dayton St. and Railroad Ave.) is a small park with a picnic area, trails, and fun public art that kids will enjoy climbing on or posing next to for photos. Marina Beach Park on Admiralty Way S. offers a basketball court, a playground, a picnic area, and a little hill for flying kites.

Forest Park
802 E. Mulkiteo Blvd., Everett
(425) 257-8300
Water spray area, swimming pool (indoors)

Forest Park is a 197-acred wooded park that hosts an animal farm (see Chapter 2), an indoor swim center, and a playground with separate areas for toddlers and older children. During the summer, a new water spray park keeps kids cool. The Music in the Park series is held in the summer.

Heron Park
2701 155th St. S.E., Mill Creek

Swings, climbers, and sculptures will entertain kids before you can entice them for a walk along a winding nature trail with small ponds. There's also a demonstration garden located here. A large, covered picnic area provides a pleasant place to eat lunch.

Lynnwood Heritage Park
19921 Poplar Way, Lynnwood

This new park highlights the 1919 Wickers Building, housing a heritage museum and information center. The park also includes an interurban trolley and a reproduction of 196th Street S.W., as it appeared in the early 1900s. Play equipment, historic displays, heritage landscaping, picnic areas, and demonstration gardens are also part of the park.

Thornton A. Sullivan Park at Silver Lake
11405 Silver Lake Rd., Everett
Swimming beach

This 27-acre city park offers a sandy beach with a roped-off swimming area that is watched by lifeguards in the summer, as well as canoe and paddleboat rentals, boating classes for ages 7 and up, and a large playground. Movies are shown after dark in the summer.

Yost Memorial Park
96th Ave. W. and Bowdoin Way, Edmonds
Swimming pool (outdoors)

The serene, forested park is delightful on hot summer days, when the trees keep it deliciously cool. The 48 acres hold a tennis court, playground, picnic area, and trails. It's also the site of an outdoor swimming pool, open during the summer.

Parent Tips
If you stretched out Puget Sound's 2,000 miles of shoreline, it would reach from Seattle to Disneyland. The area also has 16,000 miles of rivers and streams. More than 10,000 species inhabit Puget Sound.

South

Dash Point State Park
5700 S.W. Dash Point Rd., Federal Way
(253) 661-4955
Swimming beach

Dash Point is a 392-acre camping park with 3,301 feet of saltwater shoreline.
The beach provides spectacular views of the Sound and great opportunities for
studying marine life. If you want to camp close to home, this is a great place to
go. Dash Point features 138 campsites, including 30 hookup sites for RVs. There
is camping year-round, although the upper camp loop closes in October and
reopens in late April. For cost and reservations, call (888) 226-7688, or go to
www.parks.wa.gov/reserve.asp to reserve online.

    Dash Point's day-use area includes a playground, picnic tables, and the
beautiful beach. About 11 miles of trails traverse the woodsy, 398-acre park.
Mountain bikes are permitted.

Five Mile Lake
36429 44th Ave. S., Federal Way
Swimming pool (outdoors)

Swim in the lake, take a walk on a trail, fish off the pier, enjoy a children's play
area, or play tennis or basketball at this 26-acre King County park. Two large
meadows are perfect for playing catch or throwing a Frisbee around. Bring a
picnic. The park boasts 135 tables and 19 barbecues.

Parent Tips
The following parks offer some of the best birding and wildlife viewing in
the area: Camp Long, Carkeek Park, Cougar Mountain Regional Wildlife
Park, Discovery Park, Juanita Bay Park, Lincoln Park, Mercer Slough Nature
Park, Richmond Beach Saltwater Park, Seward Park, Tolt MacDonald Park.

Flaming Geyser State Park

23700 S.E. Flaming Geyser Rd., Auburn

(253) 931-3930

Don't go to this lovely park expecting to see an Old Faithful sort of display from its namesake. The geyser lets out natural gas that is lit on summer weekends to create a small flame. The flame flicker hardly seems worth naming a park after, but there are plenty of other attractions to make a visit worthwhile, including a nice playground. There are 56 sheltered and 172 unsheltered picnic tables.

Trails follow a creek through lush lowland forest; another goes along the river. The park is a very popular launching site for people who want to float down the river on inner tubes or rafts. The park has 3 miles of freshwater shoreline. The water moves pretty quickly, so it's more for wading than swimming. A separate area serves as a remote-controlled airplane site. The park is located 2.5 miles south of Black Diamond.

Gene Coulon Memorial Park

1201 Lake Washington Blvd. N., Renton

Pets and in-line skates not allowed

Swimming beach

Located at the southeasternmost tip of Lake Washington, next to Boeing's Renton plant, 55-acre Coulon Park is the city's pride and a youngster's delight. The major attraction is the large, sandy swimming beach. The kids will quickly target the play area, which sits near the beach and is equipped with slides, swings, climbing toys, and a big sandbox. A footbridge crosses to a small island, which is kept as a nature preserve. Other attractions include a 1.5-mile-long paved trail, plus volleyball and tennis courts. There are also several picnic shelters.

Food concessions are a rarity at public parks, but you'll find them here, where you can choose between an Ivar's Fish Bar and Kidd Valley Restaurant. You can eat inside, while watching the action on the water, or take your meal outside and have a picnic. A large, covered pavilion with tables and benches is a perfect spot for a picnic—even on a rainy day.

If you do want to picnic on the grass, be sure to bring a blanket. As is the case with many waterfront parks, geese—and what they leave behind—can be abundant. There's usually plenty of nearby parking, even on the sunniest days.

....

Saltwater State Park
25205 Eighth Pl. S., Des Moines
(888) 226-7688 (reservations) or (360) 902-8844 (information)

This 88-acre forested park, on the edge of Puget Sound, is one of the few overnight camping sites in the Seattle-Tacoma region. There's also boating, hiking, scuba diving, and water play—all of which help to make this one of the most used state parks in the area. Many of the overnight campsites lie next to McSourley Creek, which winds down the park's ravine; the steep, wooded hillside absorbs the noise of the nearby bridge traffic to give campers and hikers some unexpected quiet. However, the park is in the flight path of Sea-Tac, so expect noise from jets.

The park offers 50 tent sites for $15/night from April through September. Some sites accommodate RVs, but there are no hookups. The campground is filled seven days a week in July and August, so come early to find a spot. No reservations are taken. Because the park can be crowded, it is not a good place to let kids wander alone, especially on trails.

You don't have to be a camper to enjoy this park, but you'll likely wait in line at the gate on sunny summer weekends (no fee for day use). Try going after Labor Day to avoid the crowds, and be sure to seek out the sandy beach—it's one of the best on the Sound. You'll find 1,445 feet of shoreline and plenty of picnic tables, many along the beach.

Chapter 8

Spectator Sports

For many parents, sharing the thrill of an exciting sports event is one of the first opportunities for establishing common ground with their children. Although it is tempting to get cynical about the corrupting influence of money and politics on professional sports, lessons in **fair play**, team cooperation, the agony of **losing**, and the glory of **winning** still abound at all levels of sports competitions. The cost of a family outing to a professional sporting event can be prohibitive, especially when you add parking and food expenses to the price of the tickets. Keep in mind that **professional teams** don't always provide the best entertainment. Don't forget smaller arenas, such as **local high school** and **college events**. You'll spend less, often see thrilling games, get better seats, and usually avoid the traffic hassles of the bigger events.

Emerald Downs

2300 Emerald Downs Dr., Auburn

(253) 288-7000

www.emdowns.com

Sport: Horse racing

Season: Apr.–Sept.

Admission: $5/person, free/kids ages 17 and under

Though some people might not find gambling at the racetrack an appropriate outing for the kids, fans disagree. Of course, you don't have to bet; you can go just to give the kids the thrill of watching a thoroughbred horse race. Kids 13 and under must be accompanied by a parent or guardian. You must be 18 or over to wager.

The 166-acre facility features a six-level stadium and special events throughout the summer catering to families, including Sunday Family Days with special activities for kids. Free Saturday morning stable tours are available by appointment. Call (253) 288-7711 for reservations.

Everett Aquasox

Everett Memorial Stadium, 38th and Broadway, Everett

(425) 258-3673

Sport: Baseball

Season: Mid-June–Labor Day

Admission: $7/person

The Aquasox are the Class A farm team of the Seattle Mariners. Everett Memorial Stadium is a wonderful place to watch a ball game—there's even a playfield where kids can play catch or wait for a foul ball. Homer Porch allows fans to stroll behind the right-field fence to wait for a home-run ball. Players enter and exit the field through public areas, making it easy to get autographs before or after the game. Many games have special events for kids.

Seattle Mariners
Safeco Field, 1250 First Ave. S., Seattle
(206) 346-4000
www.seattlemariners.com

Sport: Baseball

Season: Apr.–Sept.

Admission: Starts at $8/person; $22–$30/person for family reserved section; free/children 2 and under (must sit on adult's lap)

The Mariners have made a big effort to keep America's favorite pastime affordable and fun for families. Many promotional events are offered throughout the season. Check out the Mariners website for upcoming game and community events.

The spectacular Safeco Field, opened in 1999, is reason enough to attend a game. If you get lucky, the rain will either stop or start during a game and you and your child will get to watch the roof close or open—an architectural and engineering marvel to behold. The roof structure covers nearly 9 acres, weighs 22 million pounds, and contains enough steel to build a skyscraper 55 stories tall. The three movable panels glide on 128 steel wheels powered by 96 ten-horsepower electric motors. A push of a button closes or opens the roof in an average of 10 to 20 minutes.

Special alcohol-free family sections are available for all Mariners games. The Outside Corner Picnic Patio, directly above the Home Plate Gate entrance, is a another good place for families; it has views of Puget Sound, and tables and benches for picnic lunches.

Children's Hospital Playfield, located on the Main Concourse behind center field, lets kids work off excess energy on fun, baseball-themed playground equipment. It features a state-of-the-art playground, Moose's Munchies Concessions (with a counter at "kid height"), and the Kid's Clubhouse Store. Televisions are also conveniently placed so parents won't miss any exciting baseball action.

The Knothole Gang is the Mariners' fan rewards program geared just for kids. Members receive points for each home game attended, at participating concession stands, and at the Mariners Team Store. They can also earn gifts, receive free coupons, and are eligible for special prize drawings and random rewards.

Seattle Seahawks

Qwest Field, Seattle
(888) 635-4295
www.seahawks.com

Sport: Football

Season: Aug.–Dec.

Admission: $28–$79/person

Games usually sell out for the Seahawks, especially since the team's 2005–06 run to the Super Bowl, so you'd better buy your tickets very early or count on an invitation from a friend if you want to attend. At the new Qwest Field, there is a family section where consumption and possession of alcoholic beverages are not allowed. Consider taking a child interested in football to a Husky game or a high school game. All in all, it will likely be a more relaxed experience, and if the game gets slow and/or Junior gets restless, you might not feel so bad about leaving early.

Seattle Sounders FC

Qwest Field, Seattle
(800) MLS-GOAL
www.soundersFC.com

Sport: Men's soccer

Season: Mid-Apr.–mid-Oct.

Admission: $16–$35/person

Seattle Sounders FC became a professional soccer team in 2008 and began playing in Seattle in 2009. Even if you don't have a soccer player in your house, the Sounders provide a great spectator sport experience for families. A Youth Pass, at $50 for 14 home games, is a good deal for avid fans ages 18 and younger. The Sounders also have a summer camp, the Youth Development Academy.

Seattle Storm
KeyArena, Seattle Center, Seattle
(206) 217-WNBA
www.storm.wnba.com

Sport: Women's basketball

Season: May–Sept.

Admission: $14–$55/person

The Storm launched their first WNBA season in Seattle in 2000. Since then, they have grown to become one of the best spectator sports teams for families. Tickets are reasonable, and the level of play is top-notch. If you want to show your daughter some awesome sports role models, this is the place to find them. The Storm partners with local businesses, individuals, and organizations to provide tickets for youth who otherwise might not have an opportunity to attend a women's professional game. To purchase, call (206) 217-WNBA.

Seattle Thunderbirds
KeyArena, Seattle
(206) 448-7825
www.seattlethunderbirds.com

Sport: Ice hockey

Season: Sept.–Mar.

Admission: $12–$20/person

Since Old Man Winter doesn't freeze the ponds around Seattle very often, it's easy to forget about hockey and other ice sports, but locals are lucky to have a Western Hockey League team, the Thunderbirds.

Hockey is a fast-paced and easy-to-understand sport that many kids enjoy watching. Given the intensity of the play and frequent fights on the ice, it's best to warn a young spectator that the raucous atmosphere is "all part of the fun." The family section does not allow alcohol and offers a calmer viewing environment.

Tacoma Rainiers
Cheney Stadium, 2502 S. Tyler St., Tacoma
(253) 752-7700, (800) 281-3834
www.tacomarainiers.com

Sport: Baseball

Season: Early Apr.–Sept.

Admission: $6–$14/person

Come watch the Mariners' Triple-A farm club with Mt. Rainier as a backdrop on a clear day.

University of Washington Huskies
(206) 543-2200, tickets@u.washington.edu
gohuskies.cstv.com/tickets/oly-ticket-info.html

Sports: Football, baseball, men's and women's basketball, men's and women's soccer, track and field

Admission: Varies by sport

At UW sporting events, for a fraction of the price you would pay at a professional event, you can watch highly talented athletes compete. The women's basketball team has become a very popular family event in town, with nail-biting games and reasonable ticket prices.

Baseball is played outdoors in a new stadium on real grass. Both the men's and women's soccer games play on a new soccer field near the baseball stadium and provide great learning by example for young soccer players.

Some years a family sports pass is available, which provides tickets to four family members to all events except men's basketball and football at a fraction of the cost. The Papa Junior Husky Club offers membership to all kids ages 12 and under, but is limited to the first 1,000 applications received. For an annual membership fee of $15, kids receive a T-shirt; a Harry the Husky basketball bobblehead doll; special Junior Husky Club events; a birthday card autographed by one of the Husky sports teams; a quarterly newsletter; a special $5 general-admission ticket to a designated Husky football game; 2-for-1 admission to all home, regular-season nonconference men's basketball games; free admission to all home, regular-season women's basketball games; and free admission to all home, regularly scheduled Olympic Sports events.

....

Velodrome
Marymoor Park, 2400 Sammamish Way, Redmond
(206) 675-1424
www.marymoor.velodrome.org

Sport: Bike racing

Season: Mid-May–Aug.

Admission: $3/adults, free/children under 12

The 400-meter velodrome at Marymoor Park is home to a full season of bicycle racing and events. Each year, some of the country's best racers compete here. Friday evenings from May to August, families bring picnics and enjoy the races, weather permitting.

The Marymoor Junior Program introduces kids 5–18 years old to track cycling. Participants are instructed in the basics of track riding and racing by experienced coaches and national- and international-level bicycle racers.

Various sessions are held throughout the summer with classes meeting twice a week for three weeks. At the end of each three-week session, participants are eligible to compete with their age group in Friday Night Racing under the lights.

Chapter 9

Eating Out with the Kids

Seattle abounds with **good eating opportunities** for families. This selection is just a small sample. To compile our list of recommended restaurants, we used the following criteria:

1. Good food. Without this, what's the point?

2. Kid friendly. Even if your kids don't always act like short British diplomats, the whole family should feel welcome. Your server should help clean up the spills, not glower as the behavior at your table begins the inevitable slide downward.

3. Fair prices. A typical kid goes through numerous eating stages, ranging from nibbling two bites per meal to inhaling everything in sight and still feeling "starved." Both phases are costly when you eat out. Even if the parents choose to splurge on their entrée, prices for kid meals should be reasonable.

4. Fast service. Most young kids sitting in a restaurant are time bombs waiting to go off. In everyone's interest, your server must aim for top efficiency, recognizing you are here to refuel, not linger over meaningful conversation.

5. Entertainment. A floor show is not required, but it sure helps to have a cup of crayons or, better yet, a real play area.

Pricing Guide
(adult meals, per person)

Inexpensive:	$	Less than $8
Moderate:	$$	$8–$15
Expensive:	$$$	More than $15

Agua Verde Restaurant and Paddle Club
1303 Boat St., Seattle
(206) 545-8570
www.aguaverde.com
$$

Between the Montlake and Fremont Bridges, on the north shore of Portage Bay, sits Agua Verde Restaurant and Paddle Club. Perched above a dock of kayaks (available for rental), it is a colorful place to enjoy a delicious meal of Mexican fare at very reasonable prices.

In the gray days of winter the small inside dining room is cozy, but in summer sit on the large outside deck to enjoy a front-seat view of the busy lake activity. Or, if you worry that the kids will be too restless in the crowded indoor space, order your food at the take-out window and eat at the picnic tables on the waterfront. Unless you go early or late there is usually a wait, but given the setting, time usually passes painlessly.

The menu has lots of yummy vegetarian options. The tacos are little and come three to a plate—just right for sharing. Several of the delicious side dishes are well suited to kids' palates: cranberry slaw, pineapple-jicama salsa, whole pinto beans with cotija cheese. Chances are good you'll be too full and content after you dine at Agua Verde to want to rent a kayak, so if that is part of your plan, paddle first and then eat.

Alki Homestead

2717 61st Ave. S.W., Seattle

(206) 935-5678

$$

Inside this log house, built in 1904 and sitting just a half block off Alki Beach, you'll find old-fashioned fancy—cut-crystal candleholders and lace table-cloths—just the place for a child who wants a special birthday dinner with food they will really like. Doris Nelson was the Alki Homestead for 44 years. When she died in 2004, the restaurant faced an uncertain future, but in 2007 a new chef was hired and it has kept the old favorites (best pan-fried chicken in town and melt-in-mouth biscuits) while making some positive changes, including upgrading the veggies from canned to fresh. The good old Alki has accumulated a huge fan club over time, so be sure to make reservations.

Nearby fun: Alki Beach

All-Purpose Pizza

2901 S. Jackson St., Seattle

(206) 324-TOGO

www.allpurposepizza.com

$

You'll find creative toppings and yummy sourdough crusts at this comfy Leschi neighborhood pizza joint. More surprising, you might even manage to have a real conversation with your partner. Most kids will gravitate to the great play area set up to be a restaurant—with rolling pins, a toy cash register, and a phone—plus anybody who wants one gets a small ball of pizza dough to make their own creation. In addition to the pizza it has pasta dishes, including a kiddie-only pasta with butter and parmesan.

Anthony's Beach Café

456 Admiral Way, Edmonds

(425) 771-4400

www.anthonys.com

$

A stroll through downtown Edmonds, a beach walk, and then lunch at Anthony's Beach Café, located near the Edmonds Marina, is a good outing. There's an outdoor deck for dining in good weather and a little sandbox for the tots to play in when they get tired of sitting at the table. Inside it is rather noisy, so you won't have to worry too much about your child making a racket, and there are windows all around so it is easy to get a good view of the Edmonds–Kingston ferry coming and going. The menu is the delicious seafood that you find at all Anthony's: fish tacos with mango salsa are highly recommended. The highlight on the children's menu is the $1.25 hot fudge sundae. There are more Anthony's restaurants in the greater Seattle area, including Anthony's Home Port, a nicer restaurant above the Beach Café in Edmonds; the Anthony's/Bell Street Diner/Pier 66 on the Seattle waterfront; Chinook's (described below); and also at Point Defiance State Park in Tacoma. All warmly welcome families.

Nearby fun: Walk on the Edmonds–Kingston ferry and enjoy the 60-minute round-trip across Puget Sound.

....

Anthony's Bell Street Diner/Pier 66/Fish Bar
2201 Alaskan Way, Pier 66, Seattle
(206) 448-6688
www.anthonys.com
$ (Fish Bar), $$ (Bell Street Diner), $$$ (Pier 66)

You have three different options at this location. Starting at the top, location and price-wise, Pier 66 is the most elegant and has the more sophisticated (expensive) food choices. It is a good place to take an older child for a fancy birthday celebration. Downstairs at the Bell Street Diner, the atmosphere is more casual and noisy kids will fit in well. There's an outdoor deck that offers a sensational view of Elliott Bay. You can still find delicious salmon and other fish plates here, plus the famous crab cakes that are also served upstairs, but at the Diner there's also more casual items such as mahi mahi fish tacos and burgers. Or if you want to let the kids run around outside, get takeout at the fish bar. This option gives you the best view, at the lowest price. There is a little fountain to play in, picnic tables and most days during the summer, an enormous cruise ship is moored right at the pier—a sight that will impress and entertain.

Nearby fun: Odyssey Maritime Discovery Center, Seattle Aquarium, Olympic Sculpture Park, Myrtle Edwards Park, Seattle Water Taxi to West Seattle

Blue C Sushi

Village at Alderwood Mall, Lynnwood, (425) 329-3596
3601 Fremont Ave. N., Seattle, (206) 633-3411
University Village, Seattle, (206) 525-4601
Westfield Southcenter, (206) 27-SUSHI
www.bluecsushi.com
$$

The flash and fun of the sushi-delivery system is enough to make this place a hit with the kids: A conveyer belt circles the tables with pretty little plates of food that you grab as they go by. The plates are color-coded for price—lime green $1.50 on up to dark blue $4—so you can steer away from the expensive items. Best of all, it is good sushi. There's several not-raw fish options plus delicious cream puffs or mochi ice cream balls for dessert, so even squeamish eaters will be happy.

Buca di Beppo

701 Ninth Ave. N., Seattle
(206) 244-2288
4301 Alderwood Mall Blvd., Seattle
(425) 744-7272
www.bucadibeppo.com
$$

The atmosphere is always festive and the servings are always gigantic at this Italian restaurant that sits between South Lake Union and the Seattle Center, as well as in a new location in Alderwood Mall. The seating arrangements vary from long tables to comfy booths, including a table that sits right in the middle of the action in the kitchen, and everything about the place suits a big family gathering or post-soccer tournament celebration dinner. But even a twosome can make it work—they offer three different portions—Buca Mio (single portions), Buca Small (serves two or more), and Buca Large (serves four or more), but given the size of these portions you can double the number of eaters they will serve. Baked pasta specialties—chicken sausage cannelloni, nine-layer lasagna, and penne campofiore—are among the most popular items on the extensive menu.

If you are coming from downtown you can leave your car behind and take the South Lake Union Streetcar (*www.seattlestreetcar.org*)—the restaurant is two blocks west of South Lake Union Park at the corner of Broad and Ninth Avenue N.

Nearby fun: Pacific Science Center, Seattle Children's Museum and Experience Music Project at the Seattle Center, the Center for Wooden Boats at South Lake Union

....

Central Cinema
1411 21st Ave., Seattle
(206) 686-MOVIE
www.central-cinema.com
$$

If the Central Cinema is playing a movie that the family can enjoy together, head on down to this cinema/restaurant just off Union Street in the Central Area. You can sit at comfortable banquettes or single seats with fold-down tables and eat tasty thin-crusted pizza (or a salmon burger, lasagna, and other tasty dishes) while you drink a beer and watch a movie on the big screen. The youngsters will be happy chowing down on the Kid's Special—pigs in a blanket.

There's also a small cafe if you just want to eat. Central Cinema is available for birthday rentals.

....

The Cheesecake Factory
700 Pike St., Seattle
(206) 652-5400
401 Bellevue Way, east end of Bellevue Square, Bellevue
(425) 450-6000
www.cheesecakefactory.com
$$

This popular chain restaurant serves gargantuan portions and, at least in Seattle, there is often a wait to get seated on weekend nights. However, it's an easy and festive place to take kids for a brunch, lunch, or dinner "out on the town." The 30-page menu is so extensive that it is impossible not to find something to suit everybody's tastes, and you can easily feed an entire T-ball team from one entrée—the portions are huge. Kids favor the mini "slider" cheeseburgers, quesadillas, nachos, and pizza bread, as well as the frozen smoothies. Leave room for the 35 kinds of cheesecake and other desserts.

Chinook's at Salmon Bay

1900 W. Nickerson St., Seattle

(206) 283-4665

www.anthonys.com

$$

Part of the Anthony's chain of restaurants, Chinook's is the place you take the out-of-town guests to appreciate good Northwest seafood without the downtown prices. It is located on the working Fishermen's Terminal just south of the Ballard Bridge so you can walk along the dock or sit at a table by the window and watch the commercial fishing boats come and go. Any of the crab dishes or the fresh-caught fish from Chinook's daily galley sheet are highly recommended. The children's menu is basic and very reasonably priced, including the Anthony's signature kids' hot fudge sundae for $1.25. But don't be tempted by the ice cream on the dessert menu—the berry cobbler is too good to miss. It also serves breakfast on the weekends, which is crowded, but is well worth the wait. If you prefer a fast alternative to the inside dining, there is a fish-and-chips bar outside—"Little Chinooks."

Nearby fun: Discovery Park

Cocina Esperanza

3127 N.W. 85th St., Seattle

(206) 783-7020

www.cocinaesperanza.com

$$

After a day in the Ballard neighborhood, treat your family to some authentic regional Mexican cuisine. This little gem serves some of Seattle's best Mexican food. The menu items reflect a desire to create healthy and flavorful meals from all fresh ingredients. There are always other families dining here, and the brightly colored walls, large windows, and high ceilings create an atmosphere that is warm, inviting, and casual.

Nearby fun: Golden Gardens Park

Cupcake Royale/Vérité Coffee

1101 34th Ave. (Madrona), Seattle, (206) 709-4497
4556 California Ave. S.W. (West Seattle), Seattle, (206) 932-2971
2052 N.W. Market St. (Ballard), Seattle, (206) 782-9557
www.cupcakeroyale.com
$

This coffeehouse and cupcake bakery serves the best darn cupcakes this side of the Mississippi. Chocolate or vanilla cupcakes with pastel-colored buttercream frosting laden with sprinkles, coconut, or sugared flowers, they are $2.50 each. These cupcakes taste just like something out of Grandma's kitchen—a very hip kitchen, that is. Kids love to pick their own cupcake toppers: little clown faces or special trinkets to customize their cake, and there's the baby cakes for $1.50 each, if a regular cupcake is too much of a good thing.

Elliott Bay Brewery and Pub

4720 California Ave. S.W., Seattle
(206) 932-8695
www.elliottbaybrewing.com
$$

Conveniently located right in the center of the junction in West Seattle (where California Avenue meets Alaska Street) this brewpub/restaurant prides itself on making sure that its littlest of customers are happy. The Kidd Chow menu is extensive and very reasonable. Elliott Bay's fries are a must—thick and perfectly seasoned. Pita bread, oyster crackers, apple juice, and mandarin oranges are all extras that you can request to keep small dinner companions happy before the meal arrives. Tell the kiddos that if they give the parents five minutes of uninterrupted conversation they'll earn a cone from across the street at Husky Deli—a local institution famous for delicious homemade ice cream.

Nearby fun: Lincoln Park

Endolyne Joe's
9261 45th Ave. S.W., Seattle
(206) 937-JOES
www.chowfoods.com
$$

This is the perfect stop in West Seattle's Fauntleroy neighborhood for a family breakfast, lunch, or dinner after exploring nearby Lincoln Park or after getting off the Vashon ferry. Endolyne Joe's is bright, loud, and full of families, and serves creative and delicious comfort food. There are plenty of booster seats and high chairs, along with crayons and placemats for the kids to color. The restaurant staff takes pride in good customer service. Kids love the "Mickey cakes"—shaped exactly like you-know-who—for breakfast, the cheeseburger at lunch and dinner, and the mini hot fudge sundaes for dessert. The kids' menu is quite extensive and well rounded. Adults enjoy the calamari salad (not fried), fresh fish plate, and hot turkey sandwich with mashed potatoes and plenty of gravy. Endolyne Joe's is owned by the same folks who run Atlas Foods at University Village, Mio Posta Pizzeria in Mt. Baker, The 5 Spot in Queen Anne, and Coastal Kitchen on Capitol Hill—all are family-friendly restaurants with consistently good food.

Nearby fun: Lincoln Park and Coleman Pool

Hale's Ales Pub
4301 Leary Way N.W., Seattle
(206) 782-0737
www.halesales.com
$$

Hale's is a favorite of Ballard/Phinney Ridge families, due to simple fare, a casual atmosphere, kid-friendliness, and the somewhat forbidden fun of taking the kids to the local pub. It is also conveniently close to the Burke Gilman Trail, in case you want to justify the meal by exercising to get there.

This is an actual brewery, so you can watch them brew their many varieties of excellent beer and then sample some with your meal. It has the usual highchairs and crayons, and a pretty standard kids' menu consisting of five meal choices, each served with fruit, veggie sticks, and beverage. Young kids will likely enjoy the friendly servers and the double-decker bus parked out front. Adults will appreciate the good food that won't break the bank and the impressive beer selection.

Nearby fun: Ballard Locks

Il Fornaio's Resotteria

600 Pine St., Seattle (street-level at Pacific Place)
(206) 264-0994
www.ilfornaio.com
$$

If you want to drop in for quick Italian food while shopping downtown or before a movie upstairs in Pacific Place, here's your restaurant—a more casual version of the fancier dining room upstairs. There is nothing extraordinary about the menu—just the usual Italian standards that kids (and most adults) uniformly adore—pizza and pasta (plus wonderful risottos), all well prepared. Service is fast and kind-to-kids.

Nearby fun: Seattle Art Museum, Pike Place Market

Ivar's Fish Bar

401 N.E. Northlake Way, Seattle
(206) 632-0767
www.ivars.net
$

The Fish Bar is located on the west side of the Salmon House restaurant, a beautiful cedar replica of a Northwest Indian longhouse, complete with an open-pit Native American—style barbecue for preparing fish. Children will enjoy the masks and photographs on the walls, but the food at the restaurant is nothing special so just go to the Fish Bar, grab fish-and-chips, chowder, or alder-smoked salmon with cornbread and coleslaw and take your food to the large floating deck that sits in front of the restaurant. The entertainment on the deck is outstanding—a constant parade of boats going by, seagulls and ducks begging for scraps, and best of all, the University Bridge that spans the waterway connecting Lake Union and Portage Bay opens regularly for tall-masted boats—a wondrous sight that will impress even the most fidgety young diner.

Nearby fun: Gas Works Park

Madrona Eatery and Alehouse
1138 34th Ave., Seattle
(206) 323-7807
$$

Be prepared—between the hours of 5 and 8 P.M. there is a baby and/or toddler at every single table. We brought friends who were contemplating starting a family, and a meal here set them back a few centuries. The atmosphere is perfect, though: Big tables can easily be pushed together for large, multifamily gatherings. Terrific waitstaff is used to, and seems to thrive on, kids. It offers crayons, toys, puzzles, coloring pages, and a small but fine kids' menu consisting of mac 'n' cheese, hot dogs, and grilled cheese. The focaccia chicken sandwich and homemade soups are excellent choices for the grown-ups; there's also a daily special pasta dish or pizza. Get there early to snag a coveted booth.

Nearby fun: Madrona Park and Playground

Meskel
2605 E. Cherry St., Seattle
(206) 860-1724
www.meskelrestaurant.com
$$

An Ethiopian meal is always a kid-friendly experience—no parents telling them not to use their fingers to eat and flavors that appeal to all ages. The Ethiopian style of piling a variety of vegetables, stews, and legumes on a "plate" of injera bread, then eating the meal by tearing off a piece of injera and scooping up the food, comes easily to the younger diners. There are many Ethiopian restaurants around Seattle, but this is one of the best. It is a pleasant and welcoming place, always humming with the sounds of interesting conversation enjoyed over a good meal.

Nearby fun: Powell Barnett Park and Playground

Old Spaghetti Factory
2801 Elliott Ave., Seattle
(206) 239-9556
www.osf.com
$$

The food is very reasonably priced (dinner for family of four under $25), but food reviews are mixed. We include it because of the location and because you can get something other than the seafood offered at most waterfront restaurants. The atmosphere is kitschy and friendly, if somewhat dusty. You can eat in a trolley car booth, and the kids' menu is good. Best of all, it is located right across from the beautiful Olympic Sculpture Park. The Old Spaghetti Factory sits at the north end of the downtown waterfront and you used to be able to ride the George Washington Waterfront Streetcar to get here, but that service was suspended in 2005 due to heavy construction. Check the website (*transit. metrokc.gov/tops/wfsc/waterfront_streetcar.html*) to see if it has been restored.

Nearby fun: Myrtle Edwards Park, Olympic Sculpture Park

Pho Than Brothers
516 Broadway E. (Capitol Hill), Seattle
7714 Aurora Ave. N. (Greenlake), Seattle
2021 N.W. Market St. (Ballard), Seattle
4207 University Way N.E. (U District), Seattle
4822 California Ave. S.W. (West Seattle), Seattle
7844 Leary Way N.E. (Redmond), Seattle
(206) 527-5973
www.thanbrothers.com
$

Pho is a Vietnamese rice noodle soup, sometimes served with meat and chicken. You are given veggies (sprouts, cilantro) and other goodies to add. It is a parent's healthy alternative to fast-food burgers—fast service, inexpensive, and ideal for kids because kids love noodles and each serving can be seasoned to taste. These Pho Than Brothers restaurants are small and nothing fancy but they are very speedy and best of all, the meal ends with a free cream puff for everybody.

Red Mill Burgers

312 N. 67th St., Seattle, (206) 783-6362
1612 W. Dravus St., Seattle, (206) 284-6363
www.redmillburgers.com
$

Don't let the long lines deter you! These burgers are the real deal. Red Mill is hands down one of the best burger joints in Seattle. It's super-popular with families because of the great prices for yummy, juicy cheeseburgers, huge, tasty onion rings, and thick, creamy milk shakes/malts. Each burger is made to order with a variety of toppings, including lots of different cheeses, including American, green chiles, and the "Mill" sauce.

Nearby fun: The Dravus location is close to Discovery Park; the Phinney location is five blocks north of the Woodland Park Zoo.

Rusty Pelican Café

1924 N. 45th St., Seattle
(206) 545-9090
www.rustypelicancafe.net
$

The Rusty Pelican is a great example of basic fare done well. It offers pizza, pasta, sandwiches, burgers, and excellent salads. It also serves a great breakfast all day long, which is always popular with the younger set. The children's menu boasts more than 10 items (each of which includes a beverage and ice cream), and there are always free lollipops at the counter. The restaurant is large and roomy, meaning you rarely have to wait for a table and your kids' voices probably won't disturb your neighbors. There is free parking in the back and great people-watching out the front, as the restaurant is in the heart of ever-popular Wallingford. Prices are reasonable, and service is always friendly. The Rusty Pelican is a "Steady Eddie" that never disappoints.

Serendipity Café

3222 W. McGraw St. (Magnolia), Seattle
(206) 282-9866
www.serendipityseattle.com
$$

Self-described as a family friendly restaurant, run by two families, this attractive restaurant became a neighborhood institution within weeks of its opening in 2008. There is a tasty, reasonably priced kids' menu, a toy-stocked play area and delicious sandwiches, soup, and salads for the bigger people. Open daily for breakfast at 6 A.M.—plus lunch and dinner every day except Sunday, when it closes at 3 P.M.—this is the kind of cozy place where you can seek the company of fellow parents when at the crack of dawn an early waking baby sends one parent out the door so the other parent can sleep.

Nearby fun: "Pop" Mounger Outdoor Pool (summer only), Discovery Park

Shanghai Garden

524 Sixth Ave. S., Seattle
(206) 625-1688
$$

Located across the street and just north of Uwajimaya Village in the International District, Shanghai Garden is a favorite for many Seattle families. The food is excellent and service is super fast. Don't miss the hand-shaved noodle dishes and bean curd sheets and the stir-fried pea vines.

Nearby fun: Uwajimaya Village, Elliott Bay Books in Pioneer Square

Snappy Dragon

8917 Roosevelt Way N.E., Seattle
(206) 528-5575
www.snappydragon.com
$$

If you are a fan of authentic Chinese food, then you really should try lunch or dinner at Snappy Dragon. This is excellent fare at reasonable prices. There is no children's menu, but all of the meals can be cooked to order at whatever level of spiciness you desire. And there's always rice and pot stickers for the less adventurous appetites. Kids are welcome at the restaurant, and there are usually many local families dining here. However, delivery and takeout are options to consider, since this isn't a large place and it is often crowded, so small fries may get impatient for dinner. Snappy is famous for "Judy's homemade noodles," and if you order the chow mein, then definitely go for these noodles. It's most fun if you dine with a crowd and can sample lots of different dishes together, plus the kids can entertain each other—there isn't a whole lot to keep the little ones amused beyond really yummy Chinese food.

St. Clouds

1131 34th Ave., Seattle
(206) 726-1522
www.stclouds.com
$$

It is hard to know where to start when recommending St. Clouds. The food is always good and sometimes dazzling, but the open-arms feel of the place is just as extraordinary. The menu covers comfort food such as "Home for Dinner" (herb roasted chicken, slow roasted ribs, burgers) to seasonal offerings on the "Out to Dinner" menu (curried roasted yam and sweet potato sauté and chickpea cakes, parmigiano-crusted roast pork tenderloin). Kids are 100 percent welcome and the kids' menu is exceptional. There is live music, usually jazz, starting around 8:30 P.M. on Mondays, Thursdays, Fridays, and Saturdays so if you linger enough over your meal the kids can dance while you savor the last crumbs on the plate. St. Clouds' two owners, John Platt and Paul "Pablo" Butler, take seriously their responsibility to feed the community. Anyone who is willing to help out—including kids—can participate in their monthly (and holiday) Homeless Cooking Project, when volunteers meet at the restaurant or a nearby church to prepare "homemade" food for six area homeless shelters.

In the summer of 2008 it opened another restaurant, St. Clouds' Café (2300 S. Massachusetts St., 206-518-5258), in the Central Area's new African American Museum.

Nearby fun: Madrona Park and Playground, or a short drive away, Powell Barnett Park with a playground that got an "extreme makeover" in 2005 and is one of the best in town.

....

Tutta Bella

4918 Rainier Ave. S. (Columbia City), Seattle
(206) 721-3501
2200 Westlake, Suite 112 (South Lake Union), Seattle
(206) 624-4422
4411 Stoneway N. (Wallingford), Seattle
(206) 633-3800
www.tuttabellapizza.com
$$

We have searched far and near for good Italian-style pizza in the Seattle area, and found pizza mecca at Tutta Bella. This is the only pizza in the area that has been sanctioned by the Italian government as a provider of true Neapolitan pizza. We're not sure exactly what that means, but we do know that the pizza is scrumptious: just the right amount of sauce and cheese, and a crust that's light but chewy. Kids love the kids' cheese pizza ($4.95 for a pizza that easily serves two), and the house special with Italian sausage, onions, and fresh mozzarella is nice as well. The ambience at Tutta Bella is perfect for families: 10 high chairs get plenty of use, and the service is quick and attentive. Don't miss the large salads to share, and save room for the homemade gelato! Your server will go out of his or her way to make dining at Tutta Bella a pleasure for all ages in your group. Counter service is only available at lunch.

Nearby fun: Columbia City location is close to Seward Park. South Lake Union location is located above Whole Foods Grocery, close to the South Lake Union Trolley. Wallingford location is close to Fremont Troll, Woodland Park Zoo, Greenlake Park and Playground.

Twede's Café
137 N.W. Bend Way, North Bend
(425) 831-5511
$$

If you are looking for a great spot to eat before or after shopping at the North Bend Factory Mall (good outlet shopping), or before or after a hike or skiing at Snoqualmie, this is the place to try. Twede's Café is a gem in the heart of North Bend. It has more than 40 types of burgers, and some very impressive breakfast items, which are served until noon. The portions are huge and the atmosphere is casual, with big booths and waitresses who call you "honey." This is the cafe made famous by the *Twin Peaks* TV show, so you have to try the homemade cherry pie with your "damn fine cup of coffee." The kids' menu has lots of choices, all for under $4; and the regular menu has many American standards at very reasonable prices. You really can't go wrong here. Be sure to try the truly Big Breakfasts.

Nearby fun: All kinds of Snoqualmie Pass outdoor fun is found about 30 minutes further east on I-90.

Vios Café and Marketplace
903 19th Ave. E., Seattle
(206) 329-3236
www.vioscafe.com
$$

After taking the kids to the lovely Volunteer Park, you will thoroughly enjoy stopping for breakfast, lunch, dinner, or a gelato at Vios. It offers delicious salads and sandwiches, traditional Greek appetizers, and inexpensive bottles of wine. The food is wonderful and the atmosphere warm and convivial. Little ones will have a blast playing in the exceptional children's play area. Be sure to ask for the special kids' sandwich (a delicious grilled cheese) if it's not on the board—the staff is happy to comply. Reservations required for the prix-fixe family-style dinner.

Nearby fun: Volunteer Park, which includes the Seattle Asian Art Museum and the Conservatory

Chapter 10

Out-of-Town Excursions

When you hanker for more than a **jaunt** across town, but less than an overnight trip, head out of the city for a **day trip**. You'll return to the comfort of home **refreshed** and having **learned** something new.

Point Defiance Park

5400 N. Pearl St., Tacoma
(253) 305-1000, info@tacomaparks.com
www.metroparkstacoma.org

Hours: Daily, year-round; hours vary by area within park

Admission: Free; fees for some attractions

Directions: From I-5 take Exit 132 and follow signs to Highway 16. Turn left at the Sixth Avenue exit from Highway 16, turn right onto Pearl Street, and follow signs to Point Defiance Park.

Don't go to Point Defiance Park expecting to see and do everything in one visit: you can't possibly experience all it has to offer in one day. Owned and operated by Metropolitan Park District of Tacoma, Point Defiance is among the 20 largest parks in the country.

About a 45-minute drive south of Seattle, the park covers 702 acres and includes the Point Defiance Zoo and Aquarium (see Chapter 2), Never Never Land, Fort Nisqually, the Camp 6 Logging Museum, and Boathouse Marina. The park grounds consist of scenic floral gardens, an old-growth forest, playgrounds, tennis courts, and first-rate picnic areas featuring grills, water, electric outlets, and covered shelters. There are also two beaches, where you can rent boats, fish, and swim. Five Mile Drive winds through the park's beautiful old-growth forest, with spectacular views of Puget Sound, the Tacoma Narrows Bridge, the Olympic and Cascade mountain ranges, and Vashon. The drive is closed to cars every Saturday until 1 P.M.—a wonderful place to take a bike ride, skate, or walk. In 2008 the car-free hours were extended to include Sundays until 1 P.M. during July and August—check before going to see if this is continued the following summer. Here are some other highlights of the park:

Boathouse Marina

(253) 591-5325

The marina revolves around fishing activities. Rentals of small motorboats are available year-round. In the fall, fishing classes are offered by Salmon University. Fishing poles and crab pots are available for rental. Salmon, bottom fishing, crabbing, and squid jigging are popular here. Call for details. Next door is the popular Anthony's at Point Defiance, with an outdoor eating area in warm weather.

Camp 6 Logging Museum

(253) 752-0047
www.camp-6-museum.org

Located on a 14-acre forested site and established in 1964 by logging engineers, Camp 6 looks and feels like a logging operation with a replica of an operating railroad connecting the working sites with the bunkhouses and bunk cars of the camp.

The P.D.Q. & K. Railroad operates Logging Train Rides on weekends, April through September, with departures starting at noon. The train departs every 30 minutes, and rides last about 15 minutes. Fares are $4/ages 13–54, $2.50/ages 3–12. The Camp 6 Santa Train operates the first three weekends of December.

Fort Nisqually

(253) 591-5339
www.fortnisqually.org

Admission: Summer, $4/adults, $2/children ages 5–12; free rest of the year

This is a restored Hudson's Bay Company fort, complete with a working blacksmith shop and several restored buildings, as well as a gift shop. The best time to visit is Wednesday to Sunday, Memorial Day through Labor Day, when the historic buildings are open for viewing and staffed by costumed workers. Although admission is free the rest of the year, buildings are often not staffed—call ahead to confirm hours of operation.

Special events include the Brigade Encampment in August with a reenactment of the 1855 arrival of a brigade at the fort; the Candlelight Tour the first weekend in October when costumed volunteers carry out typical tasks of the 1850s while discussing events of their time; and the 19th-century Christmas the first weekend in December. Fees vary for these events.

Other Tours and Sights

Boeing Tour/Future of Flight Aviation Center
Everett
(800) 464-1476, everett.tourcenter@boeing.com
www.futureofflight.org

Hours: Daily, 8:30 A.M.–5 P.M., except Thanksgiving, Christmas Day, and New Year's Day

Admission: $15/adults, $8/children under 15; advance ticket convenience charge of $2.50

Directions: From I-5 north or south take Exit 189 to Highway 526 west. Drive about 3½ miles and then follow signs to the Tour Center at the west end of the assembly building.

The Boeing Everett factory manufactures the 747, 767, 777, and 787 commercial airplanes in the largest building in the world by volume (472,000,000 cubic feet). On the tour, visitors will see airplanes in various stages of flight test and manufacture.

Reservations may be made in advance (there is a $2.50 convenience charge). Children must be 4 feet or taller to go on the tour. Children under 15 who meet the height requirement must be accompanied by an adult.

Unreserved tickets are sold on-site for same-day tours, beginning at 8:30 A.M. until all tickets for the day are gone. Visitors may pick up tickets for any tour during the day. Tickets are available on a first-come, first-served basis and tend to go rapidly June through September.

Capitol Tours

State Capitol, Olympia
(360) 902-8880
www.ga.wa.gov/visitor/guide.htm

Hours: Tours, daily, year-round, on the hour 10 A.M.–3 P.M. Special tours available by reservation.

Admission: Free

Directions: Take I-5 south to Exit 105A (105A bears left to Capitol Campus; Exit 105B bears right to City Center). Travel west on 14th. Cross Jefferson Street and through the tunnel to Capitol Way. To get to the Visitor Center parking lot, continue on 14th past the light on Capitol and take your first left. The entrance to the parking lot will be on your left.

The workings of democracy are not easy for a parent to understand, let alone explain to their children. It's hard to describe the nuts and bolts, checks and balances, without getting too far into elephants and donkeys. A tour of the Capitol will refresh your understanding and make the learning process more fun for all.

Public tours are led by docents year-round and last about 45 minutes. Meet at the foot of the rotunda steps on the north side of the building, just inside the main entrance. The most interesting time to visit is during the legislative session, when tours include a visit to the Senate and House galleries for an up-close view of Washington's elected officials in action. Tours when the legislature is in session are often crowded; reservations are recommended. Bring a picnic lunch and enjoy the beautiful Capitol grounds if the weather is good.

Specialty tours of the legislature, judicial, and executive branches, the State Capitol Museum, and historical landmarks can be arranged. These tours often run two to four hours and can be tailored to any visitors, from preschoolers to seniors, physically and mentally challenged, school groups and individuals. Reservations are required.

Tours of the Governor's Mansion are available Wednesday afternoons by reservation only; children's groups for this tour must be sixth-grade level or higher.

The State Capitol Visitor Center can help make your visit more enjoyable. For information on the state campus and the legislature, call (360) 586-3460. For special accommodations for the disabled, call TDD (360) 664-3799.

Enchanted Village and Wild Waves Park

36201 Enchanted Pkwy. S., Federal Way

(253) 661-8001

www.wildwaves.com

Hours: Late May–early Sept.; seasonal events in Oct. and Dec. Call for exact dates and park hours.

Admission: $34.99/adults, $29.99/persons under 48 inches tall, free/children ages 2 and under. Buy and print tickets online or purchase at Safeway stores for $28.99. Season passes, $74.99/person.

Directions: From I-5 south, take Exit 142B. Follow exit to right, get in left lane, and turn left at first stoplight onto Enchanted Parkway South. Go approximately one mile. Turn right at first light after crossing the freeway overpass. Continue to main parking lot.

Located about 40 minutes south of Seattle, Wild Waves offers both the best amusement-park rides and waterslides in western Washington. A small, wooded area in Enchanted Village that is home to some very gentle rides is ideal for preschoolers. The rest of the rides are geared to grade-schoolers and teens. Most of the water park rides have a minimum height requirement of 42 inches, or 36 inches if accompanied by an adult. Outside food and beverages are not allowed into the park; food concessions are available in Enchanted Village. No metal or zippers on swimwear allowed on water attractions.

There is a large wading pool in the rides area, but the other water attractions are in a separate section of the park. For obvious reasons, hot weekends are the busiest.

The steep price of admission most likely makes this an infrequent treat, so make the most of it by giving your family plenty of time at the park. Leaving one-half hour before closing time, or being the very last people out of the park, will let you avoid the traffic jam in the parking lot right at closing time.

Although the thought of visiting an amusement park might sound stressful, the fact that you pay one price, which allows everybody to ride as many times as their heart desires, cuts down on the negotiating and badgering that usually happens when parents are paying for each ride. Just bring something to read in case somebody opts to ride the merry-go-round 20 times.

In October the park transforms into Wild Waves SCREAM Park.

Pioneer Farm Museum and Ohop Indian Village

7716 Ohop Valley Rd. E., Eatonville
(360) 832-6300
www.pioneerfarmmuseum.org

Hours: Farm tours Sat. and Sun, Mar. 15–June 15 and Sept. 1–Nov. 23; daily from Father's Day–Labor Day, 11:15 A.M.–4 P.M., Village tours: Father's Day–Labor Day, Fri., Sat., and Sun., 1 P.M. and 2:30 P.M.

Admission: $7.50/adults, $6.50/children ages 3–18. Group rates available.

Directions: From Seattle, take I-5 south to Highway 512 east to Highway 7 south. Turn left on Ohop Valley Road and look for signs for Pioneer Farm. From the Eastside: Take Highway 167 south to Highway 161 (Meridian) south. Turn right on Ohop Valley Road.

Although at first glance the lack of glitz and glamour might disappoint your children, by the end of the visit you will likely have to pull them out of here.

The 1.5-hour tour of the Pioneer Farm includes a visit to the homestead cabin built in the 1880s and learning about the families who lived in it. In the activity cabin, children do the chores that pioneer children did, such as grinding grains, churning butter, scrubbing laundry, and carding wool. They may also dress up as pioneers, get their hair coiffed with a curling iron, and get a shave with a dulled straight razor. There are also barn chores, such as milking and finding eggs, and blacksmith work to be done.

During the 1.5-hour tour of the Ohop Indian Village, your group will do the work that the Ohop did seasonally. These include target shooting with a bow and arrow, shaping an arrowhead, chipping out a canoe, weaving on a Salish loom, grinding food in a stone bowl, and making a bracelet you get to take home.

Pioneer Farm offers an extensive assortment of programs for school and other groups, including overnight adventures with cooking over an open fire and sleeping in the hayloft.

Snoqualmie Falls Park
Located 25 miles east of Seattle; take Exit 27 from I-90

Hours: Open year-round

Admission: Free

Just outside the town of Snoqualmie, the Snoqualmie River plunges 270 feet over a rock gorge. Go in late spring or early summer, when the snow is melting, for the most dramatic cascade. This scenic two-acre park, located in the foothills of the Cascade Mountains, is owned and operated by Puget Power. There is an observation deck, picnic areas, a gift shop, and a cafe. A half-mile trail leads down to the river's edge for an even better view of the falls. The trail is steep however, so be prepared to help the youngsters on the way back up.

Parent Tips
The stunning Chihuly Bridge of Glass is a footbridge connecting the Glass Museum to the Washington History Museum and the Tacoma Art Museum. All three museums have teamed up to offer a midweek special on Wednesdays that provides admission to the three museums at a reduced rate: $18/adults, $14/children ages 6–18, free/under age 6.

Tacoma Glass Museum
1801 E. Dock St., Tacoma
(253) 396-1768
www.museumofglass.org

Hours: Summer, Mon.–Sat., 10 A.M.–5 P.M.; Sun., noon–5 P.M. Fall–spring, Wed.–Sat., 10 A.M.–5 P.M.; Sun., noon–5 P.M. Year-round, every third Thurs., 10 A.M.–8 P.M.

Admission: $10/adults, $4/children ages 6–12, free/under age 6

Given the fragility of the objects, a glass museum might seem an odd choice for an outing with kids. However this remarkable collection of glass and ceramics is so dazzling that all ages will be impressed. The stunning building includes several outdoor plazas with reflecting pools and views of the Tacoma waterfront, so kids have a fine place to run off excess energy. An amphitheater lets you watch the magical art of glassblowing.

Family Day programs happen several times a year and include workshops for all ages. Kids Design classes are also offered. The Museum Café is a good place to take a rest and get a delicious snack or lunch.

....

Victoria B.C. on the Victoria Clipper
Pier 69
(206) 448-5000
www.victoriaclipper.com

Hours: Operates year-round; call or visit website for schedule

Tickets: Fares vary widely according to season and destination. Children ages 1–11 are half-price. A variety of packages, including hotel stays, are available.

Victoria is a popular destination for families, and a great place to visit with a school-age child, either for a day or overnight. The trip takes two to three hours each way, and there is plenty to see and do in Victoria within easy walking distance of the Inner Harbour, where the *Clipper* docks.

It is worth going to Victoria for a day just to visit the outstanding Royal British Columbia Museum (675 Belleville St., 250-356-7226 or 888-447-7977, *rbcm.gov.bc.ca*), located one-half block away from the Clipper terminal. It is one of the finest natural and historical museums in the world. On the second floor, you can walk through the spectacular dioramas with authentic sounds and smells of such places as the seashore and a coastal rain forest. The history section features full-scale working models of a sawmill, coal mine, and gold-sluicing operation, as well as a full-scale Victorian town. The reconstructed hull of Captain George Vancouver's H.M.S. *Discovery* is astonishing in its realism. In an outstanding exhibit on native Canadian history and culture, visitors can sit in a longhouse and hear the sounds of the village. If kids are at all claustrophobic, skip the underwater simulation. The museum is open daily, 9 A.M.–5 P.M. Admission is $13/adults, $10/ages 6–18, free/ages 5 and under (all prices in Canadian dollars).

The Royal London Wax Museum (470 Belleville St., 205-388-4461) is also located near the harbor; watch out for the truly gruesome Chamber of Horrors.

Washington State History Museum

1911 Pacific Ave., Tacoma

(888) BE-THERE; (253) 272-9518

www.wshs.org

Hours: Call for hours or check website

Admission: $7/adults, $5/children ages 6–12, free/children under 6, $20/family. Free Thurs., 5–8 P.M.

Directions: From I-5 north or south, take Exit 133. Follow the I-705/City Center signs to 21st Street, where you'll turn left, and then turn right onto Pacific Avenue. The museum parking lot is located on Pacific Avenue and behind the museum near the Group Entrance.

The Great Hall of Washington History inside this beautiful massive building allows visitors to not only walk through the history of our state, but to listen in on personal experiences. In the traditional Southern Coast Salish plank house, you can hear a conversation between a blanket maker and her granddaughter; in a Seattle Hooverville shack, two residents, Mac and Leon, discuss the Depression. History becomes something you can experience, as you sit on the seat of a covered wagon and explore a coal mine or dress up in pioneer clothing. The 49 interactive exhibits in the enormous museum put you right in historical situations.

Anyone who loves model railroads will delight in the still-in-progress, 1,800-square-foot permanent exhibit, which displays a model railroad depicting the rail lines that ran from Point Defiance Park to Stampede Pass. Both indoor and outdoor theaters offer life presentations, reenactments, and films.

Train Rides

Amtrak
Third Ave. at S. Jackson St., Seattle
(800) 872-7245
www.amtrak.com

If you want to take a day trip to either Edmonds or Tacoma and really go in style, consider hopping on Amtrak for the ride. For around $32, an adult and one child can take the half-hour ride round-trip to Edmonds, and for close to $45 you can take the train to Tacoma and back. Reservations are essential. Public transportation from the train station in Tacoma out to Point Defiance Zoo and Aquarium is available.

Lake Whatcom Railway
Hwy. 9, Wickersham
(360) 595-2218
www.lakewhatcomrailway.com

Hours: July–Aug., Sat. and Tues., noon

Tickets: $18/adults; $9/children, free/under age 2 (rates vary for special events)

Most years, the Lake Whatcom starts regular operation—one 1.5-hour ride a day at noon—the first weekend in July and operates until the end of August. It is important to arrive a half hour before departure and to call or check the website to check the schedule before you go.

The vintage steam train runs through a tunnel (always a highlight) and stops for a 20-minute break near a lake. They usually have holiday (Valentine's Day, Easter, and Christmas) trains, with entertainment and refreshments. Reservations are required. The depot is 10 miles north of Sedro-Woolley, about two hours from Seattle near Bellingham.

Mt. Rainier Scenic Railroad
Hwy. 7, Elbe
(888) STEAM-11 (reservations); (360) 492-5588
www.mrsr.com

Hours: Memorial Day and late Sept., Sat., 10:30 A.M. and 2:30 P.M., Sun., 2 P.M. Also Thurs., 2 P.M., depending on group reservations.

Tickets: $20/adults, $15/ages 4–12, free/children 3 and under

Enjoy the 1.5-hour excursions from Elbe to Mineral Lake on a train pulled by a vintage steam engine with tourist and open cars. There's also a BBQ train in the summer, an Easter Bunny Express, Mother's Day Express, Father's Day BBQ Express, Fall Leaves Express, the Great Pumpkin Express and Halloween Logger's Revenge in October, and the Snowball Express in December. Special event trains run on different schedules and have different rates; check the website. The railroad station is 40 miles southeast of Tacoma.

Puget Sound and Snoqualmie Valley Railway
38625 S.E. King St., Snoqualmie
(425) 888-3030
www.trainmuseum.org

Hours: Apr.–Oct., Sat.–Sun.; call or check website for departure times and special event schedules

Tickets: $10/adults, $7/children ages 2–12, free/children under 2

Directions: The train can be boarded at either the Snoqualmie or North Bend depot.

To Snoqualmie, take Exit 27 off I-90, turn left at the stop sign, and pass under the freeway to North Bend Way. Proceed for approximately 0.75 mile. Turn left on Meadowbrook Way. Proceed for approximately one-half mile, crossing over the railroad tracks. Turn left on Railroad Avenue (SR 202). Proceed approximately one-half mile into downtown Snoqualmie. The depot is on the left at the intersection of King Street. There is diagonal parking on Railroad Avenue and parallel parking on side streets. There is an additional railroad parking lot off of Fir Street, one block north of the depot. To North Bend, take Exit 31. Turn left at the stop sign and pass under the freeway to SR 202 (Bendigo Street). Follow Bendigo Street for approximately one mile into downtown North Bend. Turn right on North Bend Way. Proceed two blocks and find street parking. The depot is located behind the North Bend Bar and Grill and the Texaco station.

Travel aboard the historic Puget Sound and Snoqualmie Valley steam train for a one-hour ride aboard antique railroad coaches through the Upper Snoqualmie Valley, between the towns of Snoqualmie and North Bend. The tracks run along the South Fork of the Snoqualmie River, over trestles, and through rural areas in the shadow of Mt. Si.

The train can be boarded at either depot. There is a one-hour stopover at both depots, so you have time for a picnic in nearby parks or a walk around town. Round-trip or one-way trips are offered.

The popular Santa Train sells out every year, so make reservations early. There are also rides on Mother's Day, Father's Day, Grandparent's Weekend, and other special events; check the website for details. In July, Thomas the Tank Engine makes a special appearance—another very popular event that requires early reservations.

The Northwest Railway Museum offers a School Train program in May of each year. The program is designed for students in grade 4 and targets the study of Washington State history but is adaptable to other age groups. It includes a railroad safety presentation and a tour of the 1890 Snoqualmie Depot, the oldest continuously operating train station in the state. Students learn about local history and the railway's impact on area development. The highlight of the program is an excursion aboard the museum's interpretive railroad, where participants experience firsthand what it was like to travel by train in an era before interstate highways and jet aircraft. School Train can accommodate a maximum of 100 people for each two-hour session. There is also a Preschool Train program in May for preschoolers and toddlers that includes a 25-minute scenic train ride and activities.

The Snoqualmie Railway Museum, located at the depot, features railroad artifacts and photographs. Admission is free.

Information Resources

Health & Safety

For emergencies, always call 911. For non-emergency questions about health and development check out:

Children's Hospital Resource Line and Website
(206) 987-2500
www.seattlechildrens.org

Newspapers & Websites

The following two monthly free magazines offer information about community events, relevant issues, local services, and businesses serving families. Free copies are available at libraries, community centers, and businesses serving families. Both publications also maintain useful websites that include calendars of events for families.

ParentMap
(206) 709-9026
www.parentmap.com

Seattle's Child
(206) 441-0191
www.seattleschild.com

A web-only calendar of events and other things to do with kids in the greater Seattle region:

GoCityKids
www.gocitykids.com

Quick Index

🎁 Birthday parties

🅰 Classes and/or workshops for kids

🚐 Educational field trips

Playgrounds

Restaurants nearby

Wheelchair/stroller accessible

Index

A

Aarstad Blueberry Farm, 114
Agate Design, 25
Agua Verde Café and Paddle Club, 183, 233
Airplanes, 70–72, 168, 214, 221, 253
Alki Avenue, 38, 167
Alki Beach, 167, 189, 193, 194–95
Alki Homestead, 234
Alki Playfield, 195
All-Purpose Pizza, 234
Amtrak, 260
Amusement parks, 137–38, 255
    See also Family entertainment centers
Animals. *See* Aquariums; Farm visits;
    Wildlife viewing; Zoos
Anthony's Beach Café, 234–35
Anthony's Bell Street Diner, 235
Aquariums, 19, 43–45, 47–48, 50
Arcades, 18, 137–38
Arena Sports Fun Zones, The, 142–43
Argosy Cruises, 13–14, 88
Art, public. *See* Public art
Art galleries, 22–23, 34, 199
Art museums
    Bellevue, 61
    Seattle, 67, 68, 79–81
    Tacoma, 257–58
Arts and crafts
    art studios, 125–26, 127, 132
    ceramics/pottery, 128–29, 208
    museum programs, 61, 65
Asahel Curtis Nature Trail, 164
Auburn Ave. Theater, 91
"Ave.", The, 37

B

Bainbridge Performing Arts, 92
Ballard Locks, 51
Ballet, 102, 103, 104
Ballinger, 180
Baseball collectibles, 7, 8
Baseball teams, 27, 225, 226, 229
Basketball teams, 228, 229–30
Batting cages and ranges, 129, 137, 138

Beaches
    Alki Beach, 167, 189, 193, 194–95
    Beach Naturalists, 189
    beaches allowing campfires, 193, 194, 200
    Discovery Park, 159, 197–99
    Edmonds Waterfront Parks, 218
    fishing piers, 188, 200, 203, 204
    Lincoln Park, 189, 203
    Pacific Science Center, 78
    Richmond Beach Saltwater Park, 189,
        205, 220
    shellfish harvesting, 189
    See also Swimming beaches
Bead Zone, The, 6
Beaver Lake Park, 209
Beecher's Handmade Cheese, 9
Bellevue Art Museum, 61
Bellevue Botanical Garden, 162, 217
Bellevue Civic Theatre, 92
Bellevue Eastside Youth Symphonies, 83
Bellevue Philharmonic Orchestra, 83–84
Bellevue Skate Park, 151
Berry picking, 109, 110, 111, 113–14
Bike racing, 230
Biking, 166–71
    Eastside, 167, 169, 170, 171, 211, 214, 230
    North, 202
    Seattle (Greater), 167, 168, 170, 200, 204,
        206, 207
    Seattle Waterfront, 21, 168, 204
    South, 168, 169, 170, 220, 251
Biringer Farm, 109, 114, 118
Black Sun, 208
Blue C Sushi, 236
Blue Dog Farm, 114
Blue Highway, 125
Blyth Park, 210
Boat museums and attractions
    festivals, 36, 64
    fireboats, 16
    locks, 13, 51, 202
    museums, 20, 63–64, 73, 75–76, 258
Boat rides/tours, 13–15, 16, 37, 63, 235, 258
Boathouse Marina, 252
Boating, 182–87
    Eastside, 183, 185, 212, 213, 216
    North, 219
    Seattle, 36, 64, 163, 183, 184–87, 201
    South, 203, 222, 251–52